W9-ABY-501

Interruptions

PS3562
I785
I5

Interruptions

David Littlejohn

Grossman Publishers

New York

1970

NO LONGER THE PROPERTY
OF THE
UNIVERSITY OF R. I. LIBRARY

Copyright © 1970 by David Littlejohn
All rights reserved
Published simultaneously in Canada by Fitzhenry and Whiteside
Library of Congress Catalogue Card Number: 72–94087
Manufactured in the United Sates of America
First Printing

Certain of these essays were first published in other books or periodicals: "On Reading Black Authors" is the first chapter of David Littlejohn's BLACK ON WHITE: *A Critical Survey of Writing by American Negroes* (Grossman, 1966); "The Anti-Realists" appeared in *Daedalus;* "The Tropics of Miller" in *The New Republic;* "Henry Miller and Lawrence Durrell," "Everybody's Shakespeare," "Pottle's Boswell," "Troyat's Tolstoy," and "Turnbull's Thomas Wolfe" in *The Reporter;* "The Permanence of Durrell" in *The Colorado Quarterly;* "Robinson Jeffers," "George Steiner," and "Three Glimpses of Scott Fitzgerald" in *Commonweal;* and "The Grader Replies" in *The Harvard Crimson.* The author would like to express his thanks to all the editors involved.

For Ben Lehman

Foreword

I have no excuse for the effrontery this collection implies, except that I think its materials good. Its existence is to be explained by the fact that I have in Dick Grossman a friend and publisher willing to indulge my need for an audience and a certain self-display. For some reason, it seemed important to me to sum up and declare myself now, as the decade changes, and he has allowed me to do so, for which I thank him here.

If one is so bold as to choose to reprint his earlier work, he ought not to apologize for it; no one is forcing his hand. Let me only state the probably obvious, and then let the materials I have chosen defend themselves as best they can: that one moves and changes in ten years, even in one year, that the opinions and evaluations and interpretations of 1962 *ought* not to be those of 1969. My essay on *The Rosy Crucifixion* (1967) specifically takes issue with that on the *Tropics* (1962). The American race war has moved in directions I never dreamed of in 1966. The shapeless and very personal affection out of which I wrote the three short pieces on Fitzgerald has since been expanded, with the help of certain students, into a sounder, more complex, more critical respect, and I should probably be more scrupulous today in anything I wrote about him. But this is not to disown the materials here. What are tacitly disowned are the materials *not* included.

A statement of the critical principles that underlie this collection, if one is wanted, can be gleaned, I hope, from the pages "From an American Notebook" with which it concludes.

If the name and shadow of André Gide seem to appear with tiresome frequency throughout these pages, this is in part because it was a book or books on him, now too many years in progress, of which most of these efforts were indeed "interruptions." The impatient young journeyman of letters keeps telling himself, keeps trying to persuade himself that he *is*, really, going to write that Great Work—of verse, of fiction, of criticism, of scholarship; that all the little essays and reviews by which his time is seduced are just diversions and distractions: that he *will*, directly, get back to work. Until one day he gives in, half-way, and admits that he has neither the patience nor the humility nor the right kind of energy to sustain the Great Work, and that it is of precisely such "interruptions" as these that his life's work is going to be made. There are worse vocations than that of the literary journalist.

I thank many people, places, and institutions, especially, here, the excellent man to whom this collection is dedicated.

Contents

4 *Portraits*

5

6 *Looking Back*

I

On Reading
Black Authors [1966]

The Pains

It may one day be different, but a white American today will find it an exhausting and depressing enterprise to immerse himself for long in the recent literature of the American Negro—for a number of reasons. Much of the writing, like much of the writing of any race, is simply poor, the product of small minds that happen to be Negro. But aesthetic pain is a minor pain; more dispiriting is the simple experience of dwelling in the dull dark prison yard that is so often the Negro writer's world. A white reader is saddened, then burdened, then numbed by the deadly sameness, the bleak wooden round of ugly emotions and ugly situations; the same small frustrated dreams, the same issues and charges and formulas and events repeated over and over, in book after book. Economic oppression, dehumanization, ignominious role playing, the constant dealings with the very bottom of the human heap—the responding spirit is dulled, finally, bored by the iteration of hopelessness, the sordid limitation of the soul in the tight closet of the black imagination.

Not all of the poems and plays and novels of the American Negro, of course, are miserably bleak—only most of them; but even the few positive works still convey heavily to a white reader the sense of the "prison," of the debasing life sentence that being a Negro can mean in America. Taken all together, the works of recent American Negro authors evoke a closed, colorless, nonextensive world that the most despairing white existentialist will never know.

There is also a moral exhaustion involved in reading these works, which is more painful than even stylistic abrasion or imaginative claustrophobia. The occasion and the substance of most Negro writing in America is still the undeclared race war in which all Americans are, by definition, involved. This writing often becomes a weapon in the race war, and from the point of view of white readers, an enemy weapon. Some of it is meant to give pain, to disconcert and unbalance. Now, a great deal of literature will give pain, will disconcert and unbalance —momentarily. But as the product of integrated imaginations, more or less at peace, it will provide the reader with a means of digesting the pain, of attaining a new and better balance. "The excellence of every art is its intensity, capable of making all disagreeables evaporate . . ." The pain in most Negro literature of the American race war, however, remains solid and undigestable. It juts up, it rankles, it rubs raw like an ulcer. As it is meant to.

Sometimes the design is quite conscious: writing is one way of getting back at the enemy. The Negro's satisfaction will be doubled, of course, if his foolish white reader can be made to pay for and to praise the materials of his own discomfort. Such a conscious intent to give pain is clearly present, for example, in the plays of LeRoi Jones, the colored writer in America most notoriously possessed by the race-war concept of literature. Richard Wright's fiction, from the very start, was designed not simply to describe violence, to represent it, but to be an act of violence itself. Even James Baldwin, who tries so hard to stay balanced and upright, will at times leap into the field of battle and flail away with belligerent unreason.

> White Americans seem to feel that happy songs are *happy* and sad songs are *sad*, and that, God help us, is exactly the way most white Americans sing them—sounding, in both cases, so helplessly, defensively fatuous that one dare not speculate on the temperature of the deep freeze from which issue their brave and sexless little voices.
>
> (James Baldwin, *The Fire Next Time*)

Rufus Scott and his sister Ida talk like this often in *Another Country*. Surely the insult, the anti-white affront is not entirely an accident of the creative unconscious.

Such works are designed, with more or less open intent (more in the case of Jones, less in the cases of Wright and Baldwin), to assert the moral superiority of the oppressed, and to force the unoppressed to grovel in guilt and fear. The "white liberal" reader—the term is one of scorn in some Negro circles —if he is not conscious of active guilt, is at least conscious of his exemption from suffering, which can be made to seem every bit as shameful. If he is not an oppressor, he is still one of the unfairly unoppressed.

From his supposedly comfortable position, the white reader, however pure of heart, may find it absurdly difficult to ward off the blow, to say no to the Joneses and Baldwins. He is forced, in a marvelous turnabout of traditional roles, to assume ridiculous poses and postures. Typically (as in Irving Howe's "Black Boys and Native Sons") he relinquishes moral and critical clarity in the anxious effort to jump on some pro-Negro bandwagon he has made. He may even (as in Norman Mailer's "The White Negro") plead that he is really, at heart, a Negro himself. The contemplation of such moral contortions must provide Negro observers with at least partial revenge.

But even those Negro writers who are driven by no great urge to wound or revenge—and such generosity is not often to be expected—can produce in white readers the same uneasiness, even pain. Why is this?

In the first place, many of the works, especially the lesser novels of the Richard Wright tradition, depend very considerably on sadism or brutality. Unquestionably sadism and brutality form, continue to form, thanks to the American Negro's fellow citizens, a major aspect of his heritage. Such episodes will, probably should, be continually redramatized. But readers of all races will continue to respond with the imaginative equivalent of nausea.

Behind the sadism and brutality, secondly, are the sadists and brutes, the legions of bitches and boors, of near subhuman moral monsters who throng the pages of Negro writing. Detached from its specific national/racial setting, the literature of American Negroes may be read as one giant case against man at his worst. Even the white reader philosophic enough not to identify himself in guilt with these disgusting (white) human specimens, not to read them as personal indictments, will see in the genuineness of their portraits a dispiriting, Swiftian reminder that man, at his low point, is incredibly vicious and foul. It is not a pleasant reminder, and Negro literature hammers it in.

Thirdly, there is the pain of comparative class consciousness excited in sensitive, leisured readers by the experience of proletarian literature—and American Negroes, certainly, compose this country's proletariat, "the lowest social or economic class of a community" in Webster's definition. A leisured white reader will feel not only the existential comfort of being white, but also the relative comfort of being sufficiently educated, wealthy, and at ease to be sitting reading a book about the suffering poor. The contrast between his position and theirs induces reflection so depressing, so empty, and so generally fruitless that it may well be called pain.

Fourthly, there will always be a strain in the attempt to respond to works that engage deep and bewildering emotions. Just what the emotions are in this case, the dark passions beneath the race war, is still something of a mystery, hedged round with a lot of preconscious taboos. The whole idea of race, of blood, has something about it primevally disturbing. The mythic force of color, of Blackness and Whiteness, resonates deep in the American spirit. Inwrought here too, somewhere, is the Western myth of Africa, of the awesome Heart of Darkness, kept constantly alive to the sensitive and superstitious imaginations of white Americans by the skins and facial structures of their Negro neighbors. And beneath it all run the underground currents of sex—sexual envy, sexual fear, sexual desire: the root, no doubt, of America's racial dilemma.

> . . . there is probably no greater (or more misleading) body of sexual myths in the world today than those which have proliferated around the figure of the American Negro. This means that he is penalized for the guilty imagination of the white people who invest him with their hates and longings, and is the principal target of their sexual paranoia.
>
> (James Baldwin, *Nobody Knows My Name*)

The imaginative literature of American Negroes stirs up all these radical emotions, brings the psychic foundations of race hatred very close to conscious surface. It is no wonder that even less belligerent examples can be profoundly disturbing.

Fifthly, for a number of reasons—the lives Negro writers have led, their motivations for writing, the pressures on them to be "race men"—the substantial content of Negro writing often seems to be nothing more than a catalogue of white oppression. Richard Wright's *Black Boy* (1945), and the communist lawyer's speech in his *Native Son* (1940) fixed the pattern; Wright's own later novels, and those of Chester Himes, Julian Mayfield, Carl Offord, John O. Killens, W. G. Smith, and others repeat the design. Poems like Margaret Walker's "For My People," Robert Hayden's "Middle Passage," Wright's "Between the World and Me" continue the technique—the unrolling of the white man's abuse of the Negro in America, from the inhuman slave ships and plantations of ante-bellum days through the lynchings and beatings and brutalization and the stunting economic imprisonment of yesterday and today. Negro literature often appears to be nothing more than a recital of this litany of abuse. And though the white reader may never before have felt any particular race kinship with other whites, though he may himself be the most benevolent of humanists, in the face of this harrowing creative evidence he will frequently allow the responsibility for all white cruelty to Negroes to devolve, somehow, on himself.

Why this assumption of guilt? Why should beneficent, intelligent white readers take to themselves (or pretend to take to themselves) moral responsibility for all the bestial Southern peasants and Chicago policemen who happen to share their color? For the same reason, perhaps, that Negro readers felt ashamed of black Bigger Thomas, the immoralist hero of Wright's *Native Son*. A race war (even a literary race war), like any other war, intensifies one's sense of identification with the Side, the Team. The literature of the race war polarizes Americans; it forces them to take sides they would rarely take in life.

Moreover, many of the black heroes of these books assert the shared responsibility of all white men. They draw no distinction between the just and the unjust; they, the poor characters (or their creators), blame or hate *all* white men.

> Though thou hast sworn the sin is theirs alone,
> Their guilt is no whit greater than thy own.
> (George Allen, "Pilate in Modern
> America," in *Negro Caravan*)

Or as Ida Scott puts it in Baldwin's *Another Country*, "All you white bastards are the same." This assertion may be detailed and absolute, like that of Bigger Thomas' lawyer or Baldwin's (Negro) self-projections. Or it may simply take the form of figures of speech, quiet and assured: Ofay, The Man, Mr. White Man, Mister Charlie, Whitefolks, the White Devil, "White is Right." Or even the simple, damning question of a fictional Negro child: "Mama, what makes white folks so mean?"

This polarization, with the implicit assumption of all the suffering by one side and all the guilt by the other, is enforced by the frequent and usually unnoticed use of We-They rhetoric in Negro writing, a usage that presumes the myth and fosters the fact of racial war: of We versus They. James Baldwin (who has, or once had, the power to become an American National Conscience) depends to an unhappy degree on this device. He mixes the two pronouns with flagrant imprecision, adopting all positions to himself by turns, until even the emotional truth of his rhetoric is corrupted. In any case, the dogmatic use by Negro writers of the warring-camp pronouns helps to enforce in white readers the disturbingly irrational sensation that their hands are on every whip and every torch. (The habit is not confined to Negroes: Police Chief Parker of Los Angeles declared, when victory over the 1965 Watts rioters seemed to be near, "We're on the top now and they're on the bottom.")

A number of Negro authors—Richard Wright is again the classic case, but Chester Himes, LeRoi Jones, and others have followed—intensify the white reader's moral dilemma by positing "immoralist" black heroes, all but defying the white reader to object. This may be a simple act of war, designed to entrap the white reader, to make him squirm; it may be intended to demonstrate the brutalizing effect of oppression (as in *Native Son*); it may simply be a nonracial assertion of Immoralism. But whatever their purpose, such creations thwart the white reader's need to make moral discriminations in fiction. There is no doubt of the "Power of Blackness" to intimidate the judge and to blunt the judgment. This is not to say that all white Americans may not, in some metaphysical way, be responsible for the plight of all Negro Americans—as all Germans, in some people's thinking, are responsible for the Jewish pogroms, or all sinners responsible for the death of Christ. Such speculations, however, I find singularly impractical. They are unlikely ever to ease the discomforts of either Negro or white. Let us confine ourselves, so far as possible, to more useful ground.

The Escapes

Several responses to these discomforts are possible, other than abject groveling, or slapping a book closed, stomping out of the theater.

The wounded white reader/auditor may choose to regard such books and plays as documentary accounts, and then dismiss them as inaccurate (the Southern philistine's answer to Faulkner). People aren't really like that, he can prove; things aren't that bad. Or he may claim that writers are by nature extremists; that they are abnormal, sick, shrill, paranoiac, hypersensitive, atypical; and Negro writers especially. Their attacks, therefore, may be dismissed or discounted. Lynchings are now more common in fiction than they are in fact; not one Negro in ten thousand suffers the spiritual anguish of James Baldwin; the only Negroes who write are those who hate exceptionally.

He may go further and elude the intended lash by the armor of pride, by moral smugness: how *good* of me to be reading these ranting Negro works!

> Americans, unhappily, have the most remarkable ability to alchemize all bitter truths into an innocuous but piquant confection and to transform their moral contradictions, or public discussion of such contradictions, into a proud decoration . . . The "protest" novel, so far from being disturbing, is an ac-

cepted and comforting aspect of the American scene . . . we receive a very definite thrill of virtue from the fact that we are reading such a book at all.

(James Baldwin, *Notes of a Native Son*)

The wounded white reader may even try to reduce out the color content, and claim that these are simply the histories of any oppressed minority, regardless of race. (And then confront that accusation as he will.)

Even the painful, raceless reminder of the vileness of man may be used by the sophistical reader to elude the *intended*, the less philosophical pain of racist antagonism; to pretend away the specific, the current, the very American nastiness of race-war writing. One can bemoan, on his bald mountaintop, the human debasement symbolized by an Alabama lynch mob, forgetting that, to a Negro, the mob is not only symbolic.

Such attempts to deflect the pain of Negro writing are like the evasion-interpretations, the "explainings-away" of Book IV of *Gulliver's Travels*. Horses really aren't Houyhnhnms, you know; people really aren't Yahoos. Gulliver has obviously gone mad; Swift was psychotically misanthropic, and so on.

The last, the most sophisticated escape, in such cases, is through "literary" judgment: It's poorly done. Amen. End of problem. One tends to fall back on this last evasion (if it is an evasion) quite frequently in the case of the more militant Negro literature: It isn't literature. Propaganda with a plot (or in rhyme, or in acts). Unconvincing; lifeless; unearned; unfelt; uncrafted. Such criticisms *are* often only illicit self-defenses against pain; a reader slips on the rubber gloves of criticism to avoid the sting. But has he, the white reader, then, no right to make literary judgments—in wartime, as it were? Many of these critiques, interior or in print, are of the nature of moral evasions; but many of the wounds being evaded are illicit and unfair. Is the white reader simply to sit there, turning pages and squirming?

Before answering this question of critical evaluation, let us consider first *why* a white reader might want to bother with all this painful reading in the first place; and then how he ought to treat it.

The Reasons

One reason white audiences may devote themselves to Negro literature is the customary dim sense of obligation concerning racial affairs. Another, probably more common, is the popular vogue at present (though nothing like the "Harlem Renaissance" craze of the twenties) for several authors—James Baldwin and LeRoi Jones in particular.

A more honorable reason for interesting oneself in Negro writing, if one is white, is the constant, nagging white American's urge to know "what Negroes are like." The white American of good will is disturbed by his culpable ignorance. He is likely never, unfortunately, to have met a Negro on intimate terms; or, if he has, to have felt capable, for all his good intentions, of penetrating beyond the forbidding brownish integument.

"I could not help wondering," James Baldwin wrote of a white man, "if he had ever really *looked* at a Negro and wondered about the life, the aspirations, the universal humanity hidden behind the dark skin." Many, of course, have not; but many have, and have turned away bewildered. A white clergyman, last year, trying to conciliate between policemen and demonstrators in Washington, D.C., asked a young Negro why he was lying down in the middle of the street. "Because I'm black. You wouldn't understand." In a sense, half the race war will be over the day white Americans come truly to "know" Negroes as human beings, to understand the experience of being a Negro. William Faulkner, who of all people might at least have had an idea, "could not imagine himself a Negro for two minutes."

At present, when an American white man tries to imagine himself black, the resultant sensation is likely to be a shudder of gratitude that he is not, the whole idea is so compact with pity and fear. All the white man knows is the outside reactions he would encounter if he *were* colored, because these reactions have been his own: curiosity, the patronizing stare, the glazed sad eyes; he would be treated always, he knows, for better or worse, as the exception, be looked at like a pair of mysterious hard-boiled eggs in a mahogany mask. What he does *not* know are the inner resources he might muster—he would still be human, after all—to meet such ignorance. He does not know the quality of the life within, or the life outside when no white men are present. Ralph Ellison (in *Shadow and Act*, 1965) has tried very hard to convince white Americans that Negroes *do* lead rich, varied, complicated lives; that the worlds Negroes make and find, inside and out, are not just the bleak torture chambers sympathetic white men have imagined, driven by Richard Wright and their prickly consciences.

It is this ignorance, this lamentable failure of imagination that the reading of Negro literature can help to correct. The creative writing of American Negroes *can* begin to lead outsiders to an understanding of "what Negroes are like." It will never make a Negro of one born white. However vivid the experience of reading, a white reader will always retreat into his profitable whiteness when the reading is done. Still, the good book, the powerful poem *will* change the reader somehow; he will carry away in himself some portion of Negro experience, now made a part of his own.

And the truths will not be simply learned, as from interviews or sociological texts, but coexperienced, borne "alive into the heart with passion." Here is reason enough for reading this disturbing collection. If it turns out as well to be good, if purely literary, extraracial benefits accrue in the meantime, of course so much the better.

Discriminations

This brings us back, though, to the question of whether there is any useful distinction to be made between better and worse. As much can be learned, one might claim, from the failures of Negro art, the fixations, the authorial neuroses, as from the fully achieved creations of integrated minds. By the author's standards, moreover, it may well be the degree of unalleviated pain caused that matters, the dynamic, unidirectional intensity of the reader's reaction: not some high and harmonious reconstruction of the spirit, or whatever the effect of fine art is taken to be. These books may be meant as high explosives, racial textbooks, and not *objets d'art*. Some few, in addition, may be written specifically for other Negroes.

The pain, the moral oppression—the "war" element—is too evidently a fact of the reading to be ignored. It severely conditions any white critical response, it blocks most attempts at imaginative participation. Robert Bone, in *The Negro Novel in America* (1958, revised 1965), attempted to confine his discussion to "formal" literary criticism, to structure, symbolic patterns, prose style, and the like. The result was somehow fidgety, uncomfortably precious. Some very large thing seemed to be missing.

It is wrong to try to ignore or deny the pain caused by strong protest literature. But no one white reader can tell another that (or how) he should suffer. Literary criticism is subjective enough, without becoming confessional. Let us grant that the white American reader ought to let himself be tested by these works, by the writings of people men of his color have tormented. But let us also grant that this testing is very much a private affair. The only conclusions he can draw from the test will apply to his own attitudes and behavior; they cannot be extended into monitions or standards or valuations for anyone else. Reading for self-examination and reading for objective evaluation are two different undertakings: not everything that can be said about a work should always be said out loud.

There may even be an absolute difference, for critical purposes, between dynamic or "protest" literature—the book as missile—and literature that is self-contained and harmonious, between literature that hates and literature that loves, between *Dutchman*, say, and *Go Tell It on the Mountain*. If this is the case, then quite different sets of standards will apply to the two, and it would be idiotic to ask a work of one sort to be a work of the other. Henry James should not be asked to review Dostoevsky, nor a Jamesian to review Jean Genet. As it turns out, since very few Negro works are pure anything, pure protest or pure "art," this distinction is simply another way of asserting that the *dynamic* element, the element of pain, should not be ignored—even by the professional white critic. He, too, after hours, is a moral agent.

But aesthetic judgment, *total* judgment of American Negro literature, even without this distinction, is not just an irrelevant luxury to be indulged in, "after the war is over." Even on our standard of information, the education of the white imagination to the truths of Negro experience, it is the achieved, the balanced, the self-contained works that will embrace the widest domains of truth. Not all teaching is done by facts—even "true" facts. The protest novels, the pain-causing works can tell only part of the story. The greater art is to contain, to hold together more, the suffering *and* the joy, the hate and the love. This is the fine point of Ralph Ellison's answer to Irving Howe, who insisted (in "Black Boys and Native Sons") that *all* Negro writers should be producing hate novels in the Richard Wright tradition.

> . . . Evidently Howe feels that unrelieved suffering is the only "real" Negro experience, and that the true Negro writer must be ferocious. But there is also an American Negro tradition which teaches one to deflect racial provocation and to master and contain pain. . . . even as life toughens the Negro, even as it brutalizes him, sensitizes him, dulls him, goads him to anger, moves him to irony, sometimes fracturing and sometimes affirming his hopes; even as it shapes his attitudes towards family, sex, love, religion; even as it modulates his humor, tempers his joy—it *conditions* him to deal with his life and with himself.
>
> (Ralph Ellison, *Shadow and Act*)

Wright's novels, and others like them, can tell the reader about their authors, show him something of the shape the war myth can take in Negro imaginations. But, as Ralph Ellison points out (with all respect), Richard Wright is, among Negroes, an extraordinary freak. *His* Negro world exists only in his books and in his angry unconscious mind. It is, unlike the "real" Negro world, entirely devoid of tenderness, love, communality, loyalty, music, religious faith and hope, all of the solace and all of the joy. It is still *true*, since it is true for Wright, and full of salutary pain; but its educational value is negative or small. One can, with care, learn something of "what it is like to be a Negro" from the single-minded activist; but he can learn far, far more from calmer, more careful writers who try harder to tell the whole truth. It is for this reason that the artists and works of art among Negro letters are especially to be treasured by white readers—the humbler, the more careful: Langston Hughes, Ann Petry, Gwendolyn Brooks, the James Baldwin of *Go Tell It on the Mountain*. Incorporated into Ellison's *Invisible Man* is more of what matters of the Negro's experience of America than in a dozen burning novels of protest—if we only knew how to find it, if we only had the patience and the skill to extract it.

Even by the standard of "salutary pain," the works of true art have a case. We should distinguish between varieties of mental anguish—some are more useful than others.

The greatest discomfort involved in reading the works of the enemy (and also the most valuable) was not included in my catalogue of pains at the start of this essay. It is not aesthetic distaste, or imaginative claustrophobia, or the revulsion from horror, or the view of human depravity, or the arousal of uncomfortable passions. It is not even the moral intimidation—exacerbated class consciousness, impotence in the face of insult, the heavy weight of shared white guilt, the paralysis of one's moral sensibility. The greatest, the most salutary discomfort may rather be the proper *resisting* of all these, insofar as they ought to be resisted. A proper reading, an honest evaluation, will be the hardest task of all—and the most liberating. It may be superhumanly difficult for a Negro writer to keep straight his moral bearings in the face of his white tormentor, but the "white tormentor," as reader, has his obligations too. It is all too morally easy to grovel, to cringe beneath the lash. Not all the history of racial oppression in America should be allowed to paralyze the moral sensibility, the critical faculty, the ability even of white men to "discriminate," or the war has indeed been lost. To read with a sharp, Gidean conscience ever awake, monitoring, regulating, correcting; to resist the unfair imposition, the bullying intimidation; but to acknowledge, too, to accept and heed the insults that are deserved: this is the way to read the literature of war.

And it is the better works, one finds, that require the most total self-examinations, the most radical self-surgery.

> Heavenly Hurt, it gives us—
> We can find no scar,
> But internal difference,
> Where the Meanings are.

I found the sheer effort of discrimination involved, for example, in reading James Baldwin's two collections of essays so internally exhausting, the expense of spirit in honest evaluation so arduous and so demanding, that it proved impossible to read more than a few essays a day. (And *not*, necessarily, because Baldwin is always telling the truth; no one tells half-truths so eloquently.) It is hard to keep one's wits about one while being beaten—especially if one envies the flagellator's style. The real pain of reading the Negro literature of the race war is as oppressive as it is beneficial. If a new truth does not really hurt—not "literarily," but really—it is probably no truth.

The Anti-realists [1963]

The anti-realistic novel—the novel of fantasy, illogicality, and absurdity—represents a dark and powerful underground current in the stream of modern fiction: "underground" not only in the sense that such novels go so often unread and unregarded, even by those whose business is fiction, but also in that the best of them can present, with a sometimes compelling force, the dream-life of a civilization, the nightmares and visions of an age. If the realistic novelists represent man awake, man active and thinking, the anti-realists are attempting to recreate, in their troubled and often difficult fictions, the no less revealing life of the dreaming, subconscious self.

Unlike the French anti-novelists or even the Southern Romantics, the anti-realists are members of no national school, no coherent and continuous system of influences and imitations. Classics of the genre have been written in Prague, Trieste, Montevideo, and even Hollywood; and many of its living masters have doubtless never heard of one another. Nor does the title signify only an historical reaction, a war against "realism," however defined, though doubtless just such a conscious reaction afforded a source of propulsive energy for many of its authors. The anti-realists, as we shall see, share many characteristics, but essentially they may be recognized by one—a radical and willful distortion of the nature of real experience, a distortion commonly made in the manner of dreams or other manifestations of subconscious experience. These novels may be regarded as the fictional counterpart of abstract painting, of the surrealist film, or, most recent, of "The Theater of the Absurd"—of all modern movements, in fact, that take as their basis an extreme manipulation, even a total elimination, of the expected, everyday forms. As their brother-artists have rejected conventions of the theater or mechanical perspective, the serious novelists of anti-realism have found themselves compelled to abandon many of the expected elements of realistic fiction—structures of cause and effect, a coherent plot (or any plot), setting, motivation, or characters in any recognizable sense, even syntax and logic altogether—in order most vividly to express and to dramatize their central concerns.

Although the origins of modern anti-realism may be traced back to any number of nineteenth-century works, its real first generation is represented by James Joyce, Franz Kafka, and the French Surrealists. Their masterpieces—the Nighttown sequence of *Ulysses*, Molly's dream, parts of *Finnegans Wake*; *The Castle*, "Metamorphosis" and several other Kafka tales—are still among the most vivid dramatizations of subconscious experience ever penned.

The second generation, only slightly less distinguished, may be represented by such writers as Djuna Barnes, Malcolm Lowry, Nathaniel West, and Henry Miller; and to some degree William Faulkner. The third generation, those practicing today, would include among the "pure" anti-realists Samuel Beckett, Jorge Luis Borges, John Hawkes, and Joseph Heller; and, among the "marginal" anti-realists, in whose work willful distortion and subjective fantasy also play a major role, writers like Lawrence Durrell, William Golding, J. P. Donleavy, and Vladimir Nabokov. It is in particular to this third generation, to the major contemporary writers in the "mainstream" of anti-realism, that I wish to devote my attention.

Samuel Beckett, a Paris-based Irishman now writing in French (which he then translates into English), has perhaps the most valid claim to classic stature among the anti-realists writing today. Although best known as one of the three leading figures, with Ionesco and Genet, in "The Theater of the Absurd,"

Beckett has also written six novels and several shorter works of fiction.

Those familiar with Beckett's plays, notably *Waiting for Godot* and *Endgame*, will be aware of the single subject of his concern: the existential predicament of man. The Essential Man, man stripped and alone, has been from the start his only character and concern, in the plays and novels alike. The plays, simpler and more accessible than the novels, stress the dramatic *image* of desolation. They attempt to elicit a profound and immediate response of emotional conviction, through a gripping if unexplainable sequence of dreamlike events onstage: bums on a road, waiting for they know not what, trying desperately to fill up the day with meaningless music-hall chatter; sadistic masters unable to stand, idiot servants unable to sit, stumps of parents mouldering in ashcans—all closed up in a room with nothing outside. It is with images such as these that Beckett, as a playwright, makes his dreams—and tries to make them ours.

There is a limit, however, to the value of purely emotional communication. Beckett has more to say than the dramatic form allows. What his plays can only present as stark, immediate experience, the novels can both dramatize *and* discuss, discuss with a more rigorous honesty and a more painstaking thoroughness.

His first novel, *Murphy*, was written in English in 1938. The richness of the novel for the reader today is almost entirely that of its language and its humor. It is full of splendid high-comic nonsense, Marx-Brothers dialogues, and ludicrously rhetorical clichés. But even in this "juvenile" work, one can find the pattern of things to come. Murphy's longing for the will-less, silent dark, his serious wishing for the "little world" of the lunatics, the madhouse setting itself: all suggest the more thoroughgoing rejections ahead.

By his second novel, *Watt* (written in 1941, but not published until much later), Beckett had abandoned even the vestigial plot, setting, and characters of *Murphy*. His novels from now on were to be simply investigations of a state, rather than narratives of action. Each of his title-men henceforth was to find himself lost in a dreamlike nowhere, "without memory of morning or hope of night," performing a few pointless, repetitive gestures and talking endlessly to himself.

Watt, although the first of these more "serious" novels, is not worthy of general attention. It is a literary experiment almost devoid of content, an elaboration of meaninglessness into two hundred and seventy pages, and represents a stage in Beckett's technical development rather than an achievement of any consequence in its own right.

Had he stopped after *Murphy* and *Watt*, Beckett might still be only a footnote in the biographies of Joyce. But in five years of astounding productivity upon his return to Paris after the war, he went on to write not only *Waiting for Godot* and *Endgame*, but also all three novels of his trilogy (*Molloy, Malone Dies*, and *The Unnamable*, 1951–1953), and the prose pieces (largely untranslated) included in *Nouvelles et Textes pour Rien*—all the work, in fact, on which his reputation rests today, as well as another novel and play as yet unpublished.

The three novels of the trilogy are all first-person monologues—continuous, compulsive monologues by voices endlessly questioning themselves about the problems of being. This is not, be assured, empty drawing-room philosophizing: it is simply, as Beckett has arranged matters, the only subject left them to talk about. Beckett has reduced his characters to a state that is little more than mere existence in the case of the first two novels, mere "being" in the last. All they can do—these three characters who are, he admits, really all the same, really all Beckett—is to keep trying either to invent stories out of nothing, to fill up the day with nonsense, or to find out (a hopeless task) just who, why, and where they are. The implication, of course, is that we ourselves, however thickly we may have built the wall of civilized distractions over our own Beckett-like innermost selves, can do little more.

Beckett's trilogy is virtually barren of "events" in the customary sense. The few there are—and the hungry reader grasps for them—are either too dreamlike, or too sordid, or too foolish to afford much satisfaction. The narrators' strangely captivating, highly personal tones of voice may help in some way to make up for this paucity of events, as may the rich incantatory rhythms, the occasional touches of humor, the dirty words. But for works so difficult, often so tiresome, so ostensibly barren and distasteful, this may scarcely seem enough for the average reader.

The real reward of Beckett's major novels is something deeper and more durable than the usual satisfactions of story or style. By reducing man to this minimal, essential self, he is able to dramatize quite vividly a metaphysical anxiety he feels to be universal. No one, he hopes, can quite escape *some* feeling of kinship with his decaying, basket-case philosophers: stripped of our own inessential accretions, he is saying, we might be much the same. It is the paradox of Beckett's dreamlike, difficult narratives that they may gradually hypnotize the reader into a sense of ice-clear awareness—awareness of a "reality" more profound by leagues than our objective, everyday fact.

Beckett is a twentieth-century "philosophical Poet," dramatizing, through his plays and novels, a deeply-reasoned and deeply-felt Existentialism, as writers like Dante and Goethe and Hardy have dramatized the philosophies of their times. In the novels, as in the plays, he makes constant use of inspired physical metaphors for metaphysical states; but in the novels he is also able, in the voices of his oppressed, universal title-figures, to define more explicitly his sense of this total human desolation.

A second "philosophic" anti-realist, though of a different order entirely from Beckett, is Jorge Luis Borges, the Argentine writer with whom he shared the Prix International des Editeurs in 1961. Following the award, two English translations of his enigmatic little *ficciones* have appeared, and he has finally gained, at sixty-three, serious international attention. One of his American publishers, at least, is now suggesting him for the Nobel Prize.

Borges is vastly more accessible than Beckett, far easier to read. His standard format is a simple, densely-packed narrative of from five to ten pages in which, almost unfailingly, he manages to present a fully-imagined new world, an order of reality radically different from our own. Beckett's anti-realism is achieved through a reduction and intensification of reality; Borges' through a radical and systematic distortion. Beckett's philosophic statement is made directly through the commentary of his suffering narrators, or by means of some vivid dramatic image of an existential state. Borges, instead, works through "parables," elaborately strange and other-worldly. Although a serious, even an Olympian insight into things, an evaluating and questioning is certainly present in Borges' works; and although his remarkable imaginings must violently extend the reader's own imagination, I cannot, in the last analysis, think him as serious a writer as Beckett or as expressive of the same sort of contemporary significance. Too often his rare imaginings seem only brilliant, philosophic little games.

Unlike most anti-realists, the essence of Borges' meanings can be communicated in the "plot"—there is, after all, little else. The writing is explicit and pure; the dreams or imaginings are recorded with an almost pathological insistence on factual documentation. In order to establish the veracity of his fantasies, Borges often devotes half or more of his scant space to an elaborate, straight-faced structure of footnotes and scholarly authorities—the manner recently adopted by Vladimir Nabokov in *Pale Fire*. At the start such pretenses may help to beguile the reader into a suspension of disbelief, but they eventually appear only as another element in the elaborate game-system that Borges apparently needs. The insistently authentic, reportorial tone is, like other of Borges' qualities, strongly reminiscent of Kafka: Gregor's metamorphosis is related with the same strangely uncolored detachment.

The primary element of anti-realism in Borges' fictions is this creation of new orders of reality. Borges details his worlds with such meticulous albeit economical care that, often before we have finished a page, they are quite unquestionably "there." The mere fact of their existence on the printed page becomes evidence for their conceivable existence beyond—which is, in point of fact, one of Borges' major themes, the evolution of the imagined ideal into the real. In "Tlön, Uqbar, Orbis Tertius," the most elaborately imagined of his fictions, Borges builds with great care and consistency a thoroughly documented universe of pure ideality, where "time" is a non-existent fancy, and nouns no more than metaphors, where ideas nudge themselves into existence and spontaneously create their opposites. Although the whole complex of documents from which Tlön was deduced, the reporter adds in a postscript, may be only part of an elaborate, centuries-old hoax, many of its invented details have already "intruded" into reality, been gradually discovered to exist in fact. A world anxious for order at any cost has yielded to the fantasy of Tlön, and the mysterious artifacts now being discovered are only the portent of a more universal yielding to come.

This manner of willing fantasies into being is particularly successful when Borges elects to incarnate more commonplace daydreams. The fancy that we may all be only characters in someone else's dream (immortally argued by the Tweedle-twins to Alice) must have occurred at one time or another to almost everyone. In "The Circular Ruins," Borges attempts to electrify it anew into fact. In "The Library of Babylon," one of the more oppressive and Kafkaesque of his parables, the author plays with the old speculation of the monkeys at their typewriters, eventually hitting out by accident all of Shakespeare's plays. The universe is conceived as a virtually infinite hive of cells, each filled with books, no two alike. Every possible combination of the letters of the alphabet has been printed and bound, and somewhere shelved. Somewhere, therefore, in this labyrinth of cells, one could find not only all the greatest (and poorest) books written and unwritten, but accurate predictions of every man's future, keys to the understanding of the universe, and directories, most valuable of all, to the Library itself. The task of course is hopeless: no one has so far found, to the narrator's knowledge, anything more than a word or two of sense in mountains of gibberish.

Borges appears to me the creative writer today most sympathetically attuned to the thinking of modern science. Many of his fables could almost be skillful dramatizations of the anti-materialism (anti-realism?) implicit in so much of contemporary experimental science. Posited particles lapse into reality and create their anti-material opposites, indeterminacy becomes a principle, and the universe a finite but unbounded continuum of many dimensions. It is hard to say whose reality is the more fantastic, Borges' or the physicist's, or whose demands the greater leap of imagination.

The most important element in Borges' work may be best represented by contrasting "the Lottery of Babylon," his chilling allegory of the existing world of chance, with "Tlön, Uqbar, Orbis Tertius," his vision of an ideal world of order. But even in these, ingenuity has as high a place as moral vision, and though troubling, the visions are forgettable. Ultimately, the greatest value of Borges' *ficciones* may be the exercise they require of a reader's own stiff, half-atrophied imaginative muscles, forcing them to stretch so far beyond the demands of a closed and traditional scheme.

The writer, since Kafka, who most purely offers a "distortion of real experience in the manner of dreams"—our basic definition of anti-realism—is the young American John Hawkes. He has written five short nightmare-novels: *The Cannibal* (1949), *The Beetle Leg* (1951), *The Owl* and *The Goose on the Grave* (1954), and *The Lime Twig* (1961). The first, which appeared when Hawkes was only twenty-four, I still find the freest, the most hallucinatory, the most intense, and in many respects the best. The next three seem to me an unfortunate decline. In *The Lime Twig*, Hawkes returns with full force to the nightmare-tone of *The Cannibal*, increasing the content of sheer personal torment, omitting the mytho-historical basis, and consciously using, for the first time, the shadow of a crafted, realistic plot.

The novels of John Hawkes not only defy any neat pattern of literary development, they have a way of defying criticism and evaluation altogether. Of the power and intensity of *The Cannibal* and *The Lime Twig*, there can be no question. Hawkes has no equal for the communication of revolting, inescapable terror. He is also skilled at the writing of a highly sensuous realism, shot here and there with gleamings from some kind of evil beneath. He has at times, particularly in *The Cannibal*, written with a language rich and incandescent, suggesting some of the wonder of *Nightwood*, Djuna Barnes's poetic masterpiece of the 1930's

But much of the horror seems only willed, unnatural sadism; and Hawkes's hypersensitivity to ugliness, deformity, and decay may prove, I fear, an insurmountable block to otherwise willing and appreciative readers. The novels, on the whole—particularly *The Lime Twig*—are compounded of grotesquely unpleasant experiences, with little of Beckett's redeeming philosophic vision. With a few important exceptions (to which I shall turn directly), much of Hawkes's high literary skill would seem to be expended in vain, unless there is value for the reader in undergoing an intense new realm of experience for experience's sake alone.

In *The Cannibal*, Hawkes had the wisdom to base his personal nightmare on a genuine historical nightmare, the abandoned decay of Nazi Germany after the collapse of her war. The novel progresses in a series of Joycean collages, simultaneous vignettes of a ruined and starving German town on a single day, interspersed with telling historical memories of its citizens now dying away. Although most of the sudden visions of terror and ugliness are not directly "translatable" as specific commentary on the war, together they do express and communicate a total and surely valid reaction. Nazi Germany in dissolution served Hawkes as a fine crystallizing point for his own images of horror—corpses rotting in swamps, talking monkeys frozen upright in the courtyard of an asylum in riot, starving wild dogs that chase and overtake a train, a cripple who projects the same film every night to a theater of empty seats, an old woman and an idiot mumbling together in the cellar of a mouldering house, an aged Duke—The Cannibal—relentlessly chasing a terror-stricken boy through the night. Even here, one may feel an unnecessary surfeit of diseased sexuality and "ashcan school" realism; but for the most part, such images are justified by the monumental horror of the chosen locale. The unpleasantness of the reading-experience may no more need defending than that of Chapter 27 of Shirer's *The Rise and Fall of the Third Reich*.

The Lime Twig cannot be so readily defended by an historical analogue since its nightmare is primarily a personal one. But Hawkes has again found a quasi-surrogate for his strange imaginings, this time in the person of Margaret Banks, the pathetic English housewife who finds her tormented daydreams turning into unspeakable fact. He first establishes her as a simple *femme moyenne sensuelle* in a sordid London flat, then drags her gradually into a tragicomic hell of vague, unexplainable terror, fully in the manner of a dream. Once again, I feel, he goes too far; but up to the point where an excess of sadism detaches our sympathies with a jolt, Margaret's case is made poignant and painfully human.

In addition to such justifications as these, Hawkes's uncomfortable fictions may perhaps be defended by their mastery of anti-realistic techniques, if not for the general reader, at least for the novelist and student of fiction. I can think of no better case-book in the re-creation of vivid and effective nightmare. Hawkes seems to know precisely what overlay of disease and sexuality, what strange dislocations of structure, what vague omissions, what tiny twists in the otherwise real, what imagery, what language, what tone can most effectively engage the root terrors of the deeper unconscious. More judiciously, sparingly used, and used to more thoughtful and consistent purpose, these elements may yet combine to make a novel not only of force but of lasting consequence.

Were one to base the entire case for anti-realism on a single novel, he could do no better than to choose Joseph Heller's *Catch-22*, an extraordinary first novel published in America in 1961. Heller's fantasy is nowhere so extreme as that of the three novelists preceding. It is, in fact, his very closeness to the truth that makes this extravagant novel at once so ludicrous, so painful, and so important. Heller's method is one of a grotesque and elaborate comic exaggeration of a "reality" bitterly tragic; but one forgets, one almost refuses to admit that any "exaggeration," any absurdity or anti-realism is being used, so undeniably just is the total effect.

Catch-22 uses for its universe a U.S. bomber squadron on a non-existent Mediterranean island in World War II. It is not a "war novel," except insofar as the war and army life accentuate so grotesquely certain basic human characteristics. Heller's island in war serves the same microcosmic purpose as Hawkes' asylum in riot, or Borges' lottery in Babylon—or, for that matter, as Thomas Mann's magic mountain or Katherine Anne Porter's ship of fools. In each setting, the condition of isolation and intensification helps to dramatize with clarity and conviction the author's bleak vision of human nature.

Heller's mad army-life setting proliferates as if naturally into bureaucratic nightmares and labyrinths of impossible nonsense. A living man is officially declared dead when the plane he pretended to be flying crashed; his pay is stopped, no one will feed him or talk to him, and his "widow" mourns in the luxury of pensions and insurance, disregarding the pleading letters some ghoul is sending in his name. A mess clerk takes over the war, and virtually the world, working for either side at cost-plus-six per cent, in what is at once fantasy so incredible and satire so true that it achieves the stature of myth. He bombs his own base under contract to the Germans, kills his own men (each at a bounty), and defends himself on the sacred texts of the American business ethic.

Heller is obviously blessed with an imagination for incident and character of near-Dickensian dimensions, a profusion of exuberant fancy, and what appears at first to be a rich kind of Max Shulman, Goon-Show nonsense. It rapidly transmutes into something much more serious, but even the nonsense has its point. In a manner comparable to the foolishness of Ionesco's plays, it can be seen as a reflection of the breakdown of language, the inability of men to communicate, and a pervading sense of a deeper *absurdité*. Without this façade of nonsense, Heller would most likely have been unable to express, and we unable to bear, his bitter, Swiftian anguish.

As it is, even with its veneer of brittle idiot-comedy, the book becomes increasingly painful to read. His fantasy and surreal exaggeration cannot hide for long the acid, anti-human depths of Heller's tragic vision. Anti-humanity, the quenching of one human soul by another, the refusal of each imprisoned ego to acknowledge even the identity of another, is Heller's major theme. Yossarian, his Alice-in-Wonderland hero, trying hopelessly to stay sane in an insane world, goes even further, and attacks the malicious, non-existent God he holds responsible for this moral chaos. But Heller has his hands full with man: inherent in every range of his absurd exaggerations, from the most trivial to the most dark, is this vision of inhuman, unloving man.

The great anti-realistic novels of the last generation, works surely no less distinguished or powerful than those just discussed, have never risen in popularity far beyond their limited coterie (excepting the always-exceptional case of Henry Miller, who is probably not being read entirely for his anti-realistic genius). Faulkner, of course, is only occasionally a novelist-of-the-subconscious, and generally a great deal more. *As I Lay Dying* (1930) and the "Benjy" sequence of *The Sound and the Fury* (1929) are the closest he has come to pure anti-realism, presenting as they do so graphically the hallucinatory or primitive points of view of the simple or the mentally deranged. As for the others, all three of the great anti-realistic novels of the 30's—Djuna Barnes's *Nightwood* (1936), Nathaniel West's *The Day of the Locust* (1939), and Malcolm Lowry's *Under the Volcano* (written in the late 30's, published in 1947)—have settled into a strong underground level of acceptance and admiration, which is probably the most that can be hoped for any anti-realist smaller than a Kafka or Joyce.

Djuna Barnes's *Nightwood* is more poetry than fiction, one of the richest and most evocative works of poetry of our time. Few modern writers, of poetry *or* fiction, have manipulated the English language with such stunning and total effect. With works such as this, the old distinctions between poetry and prose have ceased to have meaning: selections from *Nightwood*, as well as from Joyce's *Finnegans Wake*, are contained in a leading anthology of modern verse. At core, the book, like so many anti-realistic works, is perversely and unpleasantly odd. It is a motionless case-study of the "Night People," the haunted, hallucinated world of the sexual invert. But the distasteful (although very real) Lesbian relationship about which the narrative plays is primarily a mechanism of release, a trigger for the lush Jacobean monologues of Djuna Barnes's deputy-spokesman, the un-shut-uppable, near-Shakespearean Doctor Matthew Mighty-Grain-of-Salt Dante O'Connor. *Nightwood*, admittedly, may seem decadent, degenerate, often sick and distasteful, a little too consciously *fin de siècle*. But most often it is poetry of the highest order and well worth the *malaise* that surrounds it.

Under the Volcano is another book wrung out of the author's own anguish, an alcoholic nightmare spun out over three hundred and seventy pages. It is a tortured, difficult tale of personal disintegration, which traces, through the fragmented nervous visions of the last day of a dipsomaniac British consul, the decline and fall of a social ideal. Though the reference is specifically to the Spanish Civil War, the implication is insistently universal. The non-existent but closely, hypnotically detailed Mexican city in which the consul's decay is set, affords the overpowering force to the book; and its primitive, hot bleakness becomes the setting for our own shattered and shifting nightmare. *Under the Volcano*, in a way, is a remarkable *tour de force*. Lowry has used, it would seem, every device in the novelist's handbag, has incorporated the styles and tics and gestures of any number of his colleagues and antecedents (notably Conrad and Joyce), and has studded his novel with phrases and allusions, in the Eliot-manner, from eight different languages and literatures. But the book is no mere derivative pastiche, any more than is *The Wasteland:* Lowry's socio-alcoholic vision has made it uniquely his own. The kaleido-scopic horror of the drunken consul set loose at a Mexican car-nival, the macabre nightmares in which the consul and his wife both meet their deaths at the end, are among the most extraor-dinary scenes in all of anti-realism.

Nathaniel West is still the most popular of the three, but, like Joseph Heller—who so very much resembles him in man-ner—his popularity will always be limited by the sour black-ness of his satire. If Lowry and Beckett and Barnes may be traced, at least in some degree, to the impressive influence of Joyce, and Borges perhaps to Kafka, Nathaniel West can claim kin to the all-but-forgotten French Surrealists of the 1920's. His first novel, *The Dream Life of Balso Snell* (1927), was the purest surrealistic fantasy, an account of the travels of his dreaming hero inside the belly of a horse. His second, *Miss Lonelyhearts* (1934), remains to this day an almost perfect lit-tle piece of acid-etched grotesquerie. *The Day of the Locust,* his most ambitious work, is blessed with a setting ready-made for sardonic anti-realism: Hollywood, where the book was written. West makes of this already other-worldly setting something strangely misshapen, a little left-of-real, and then peoples it with minor monsters who are, like Heller's amateur hangmen, all too recognizably alive. Hollywood, like Heller's Pianosa, becomes through selection, confusion, and hyperdefi-nition "in the manner of a dream," West's microcosm of American society. A sequence of episodes, feverish and vaguely connected, carved in the most painfully careful prose, climaxes in a sort of modern Last Judgment, the screaming in-sanity of a Hollywood premiere.

Altogether, the experimental, anti-realistic fiction of our own time and the decades preceding represents a collection of high distinction. In the content and quality of its imaginative energy, of sheer original invention (if not in stylistic or structural control), it may be unequalled for a collection of novels of such size. And yet while anti-realism in the other arts (in painting, in the drama, in the film) has been accepted for so long it is now almost taken for granted, in the novel it has not been much more accepted than the Dadaist cults of the 20's. The man who professes to admire a surrealist or abstract painting, who can enjoy a Beckett or Ionesco play, a Bergmann or Cocteau film, will still balk at a reordering of reality surely no more radical in such novels as *Nightwood* or *The Lime Twig* or *The Unnamable*. Even serious critics often refuse to pay them regard.

The reasons are not hard to find. For one thing, as we have seen, the works of this tradition are, almost to a novel, perverse and ugly visions of human animals being skinned alive: they hurt. The hurt may be salutary, reinforming, truth-giving, but it is unlikely ever to win for its perpetrators a wide appeal. There is secondly, as I have mentioned, a tradition of realism in the novel which seems by now to have incorporated itself into the common definition: the novel, for most people, is a realistic fictional narrative dealing with commonplace forms of experience. Anything else is simply not a novel. Third, and most importantly, the experience of reading a novel is different in kind from that of viewing a painting or play or film—a difference that works against the acceptance and effectiveness of illogical or anti-realistic content.

The "unwritten" arts work directly on the passive spectator, set in action responding emotive mechanisms both conscious and unconscious without any necessary intervening effort of will or intellection. One need not work, actively, to look at a painting or film: if the disoriented images (or non-images) of a Chagall or De Chirico, a Picasso or De Kooning duplicate some essential structure of our own unconscious, a felt resonance, rich with overtones, can be struck with efficient directness. The magnificent resources of the cinema render it the ideal medium for the re-creation of dream-experience, a potential that has been exploited by creative directors from Sjöstrom and Dreyer to Bergmann and Resnais. The classic surrealist films—Weine's *The Cabinet of Doctor Calegari* (1919), Bunuel's *Un Chien d'Andalou* (1928) and *L'Age d'Or* (1930), Cocteau's *Le Sang d'un Poète* (1930)—are perhaps best experienced, in fact, in a state approaching total though still receptive passivity, the state of the dreamer. Although the drama has traditionally been a literary form, more and more strongly is the "anti-literary" drama, the Theater of the Absurd (lately and handsomely chronicled by Arthur Esslin) rising in force and acceptance. As we have seen in the case of Beckett, here too the directly sensuous "outside" nature of the experience makes possible an immediate emotional communication, involving a minimum of conscious effort on the spectator's part.

By contrast, the experience of reading a novel—any novel—is necessarily one of willed and conscious effort. We cannot simply "dream" our way through nightmares-in-print, however desirable this may seem. We must stay awake, at least detached and rational enough to *read:* to keep translating the alphabetical symbols on the page into ideas. Only after this is done can any emotional communication take place. The process, obviously, is going to take more work than the passive ingestion of a film. And when added to this original effort is the often-frustrating task, common to all the "surrealist" arts, of trying to elicit sense and significance out of apparent nonsense or distortion, it is perhaps less surprising that the anti-realistic novel remains, so generally, unread and unregarded.

What, then, about modern poetry? Are not precisely the same efforts demanded by the works of Dylan Thomas or Wallace Stevens or Ezra Pound? Indeed they are; and this similarity reveals one of the most important critical points that can be made about anti-realistic fiction. It is not, except in the most general sense, with the painters and playwrights and *cinéastes* that these writers ought most validly to be compared; it is assuredly not, as we have seen, with the traditional "novelists." The anti-realistic novelists are poets, primarily, and their methods, their outstanding technical achievements—the rhythms of Beckett, the images of Hawkes, the diction of Djuna Barnes—are the methods and the achievements of poetry.

This granted, the reader as well as the writer of anti-realistic fiction may be able to readjust his expectations to more reasonable terms. The reader should approach an anti-realistic novel anticipating all of the difficulties, but also all of the rewards, of abstract-impressionist, post-Poundian verse. And the writers and defenders of anti-realistic fiction may stop feeling cheated by the narrowness of their reception. The most, reasonably, that they can expect is the audience and acceptance of the Thomases and Stevens and Pounds, which is fairly limited itself.

But even on these narrower terms, are the anti-realists receiving their due? Joyce is surely read as much as T. S. Eliot, and Kafka more than Pound; but what of their offspring to the second and third generations? If it is true—and I suppose it is—that today's anti-realistic poets-in-verse receive, by and large, more attention than the poets-in-prose, one could of course explain that the latter simply aren't as good. That they show, on the whole, less polish, perhaps less precision, less finesse, I would grant; but I would claim also that they have more to say, and a greater richness of experience to communicate.

Another possible explanation is the comparative length: poetry, generally, comes in much smaller, more digestible pieces. Again, the alienating sordidness already discussed of so many anti-realistic novels has not yet so thoroughly overtaken modern verse. More fundamentally, we have not yet developed a critical language of any precision, comparable to that of the best new critics of poetry, to deal with the poetic qualities of *Nightwood* or *The Cannibal:* unable to discuss them, we ignore them.

Most fundamentally—to return to the point from which we started—there is a problem of names, of generic walls no one is yet quite ready to break down. A novel, Sir, is a novel; and poetry is poetry. And these are neither. Until the millennium proposed thirty-four years ago by Edmund Wilson (in "Is Verse a Dying Technique?"), when we shall drop such distinctions altogether, the anti-realistic novel will doubtless continue to find its way blocked by this inbred prejudice against literary bastardy.

The ideal solution, perhaps, for those authors who can achieve it, is to adopt the best of both possible worlds: to combine the expected satisfactions of realistic fiction—the tensions, suspensions, and resolutions of a plot, identifiably human characters and responses—with the rich resources of subconscious power in the anti-realists' domain. Monsters and humans can dwell in the same fictional world, and the world be the richer for it, as Dickens and Dostoevsky have shown. The "marginal" anti-realists of our time, particularly Lawrence Durrell, have been notoriously more successful than most of the writers discussed above; and a great part of their success is due precisely to this ability to combine the two realms, to draw on the power of subconscious visions in the midst of a detailed and recognizable world. Even so "traditional" a novel as *Ship of Fools* obtains remarkable added force from the presence of the two diabolic and other-worldly Latin children—nightmare-creations comparable to anything of the anti-realists.

The anti-realists' audience will continue to be small, at least no larger than their verse-writing confreres'; but one can surely hope that their means and materials, so powerful in their own difficult and disturbing works, will begin to feed more freely into the mainstream of traditional fiction.

2

The Tropics of Miller [1962]

The most lasting, affecting experience of fighting one's way
through the tropics of Miller is meeting the man who built
them. Everything he has ever written is a piece of ever-in-
progress autobiography, a continuing *roman-fleuve* of The
Life of Henry Miller. He quoted Emerson for the epigraph to
Tropic of Cancer: "These novels will give way, by and by, to
diaries and autobiographies—captivating books, if only a man
knew how to choose among what he calls experience that
which is really his experience, and how to record truth truly."
And he has been trying to live up to the prophecy ever since.
Tropic of Cancer, first published in 1934, is the story of his
days (and nights) in Paris and Dijon in the early 1930's. *Tropic
of Capricorn* returns us to the five years he spent working in
New York, from 1920 to '24. *Black Spring* records, among
other things, his turn-of-the-century boyhood in Brooklyn.
The Colossus of Maroussi and *The Air-Conditioned Nightmare* are "travel books" of a sort, recollections of trips through
Greece and America made near the beginning of the war. *The
World of Sex* and *The Rosy Crucifixion* trilogy now in progress take most of their material again from New York in the
1920's, and in *Big Sur and the Oranges of Hieronymous Bosch*
Miller tells of his life on the California coast since 1944. The
articles and short stories collected in several other books are all

equally autobiographical, all pieces in the ever-growing puzzle of the whole.

In an age of pervasive and overwhelming social integration, Miller has achieved the all-but-impossible stance of total detachment. He is an Individualist so extreme as to seem at times prehistoric. He is above or below, or beyond, or apart from all our most intimate social concerns. Clashes of ideology, affairs of state, scientific achievements, "progress" in every sense, the whole complex of reservations and deceptions and expectations that makes social living possible—with all of these, Miller is uninvolved.

So total a withdrawal has its cost: Miller has been epically unsuccessful, both denounced and unread for most of his adult life. But if the position of detachment has its misfortunes, it has also its rewards, rewards of no small consequence to the reader of Henry Miller. His lifelong "commitment" has yielded a unique and devastating quality of honesty in almost all of his works. There is no hesitation, no withdrawal, not the slightest touch of reticence; neither does he boast of all his sordid adventures and criminal emotions. They are simply there, for better or worse. This is how it was. No other author has seen fit to record as such ugly matter-of-fact every last crumb of existence. Few admit such things to themselves. For the reader, the experience is likely to be disturbing and totally new.

A second advantage of this unenviable commitment is the faculty of "pre-civilized vision" the artist acquires. He becomes able to *see* with a stunning, primordial strangeness. The effect, once again, is devastating. Most of the scrofulous images in the *Tropics* result from this pre-civilized vision, this faculty of seeing latent correspondences which shock the civilized sensibility: a face "nothing but a skull perforated by two deep sockets in which there are buried a pair of dead clams." . . . Civilization "rotting like the toenails of the saints," worshippers "like a million heads of cauliflower wailing in the dark," "asses smooth as the skull of a leper." We are shocked (and the shock is every bit intended) partly because we are not used to seeing such things in print—we cannot, that is, share the author's freedom from a civilized sensibility. But also because the author has penetrated to an elemental and singularly effective source of imagery—the deepest-lying levels of consciousness.

A third result of Miller's epic egocentricity is a blessing somewhat more mixed. He is first and always writing for himself; but like his grandfathers Lawrence and Whitman and Blake, he feels compelled time and again to speak out to the abandoned world. Miller the doom-shouting apocalyptic critic, Miller the arch-romantic idealistic prophet can be somewhat less than convincing. At best, his own eloquent and evident conviction can move, stir us "as if" we believed.

> If at intervals of centuries there does appear a man with a desperate, hungry look in his eye, a man who would turn the world upside down in order to create a new race, the love that he brings to the world is turned to bile and he becomes a scourge. If now and then we encounter pages that explode, pages that wound and sear, know that they come from a man with his back up, a man whose only defenses left are his words and his words are always stronger than the lying, crushing weight of the world, stronger than all the racks and wheels which the cowardly invent to crush out the miracle of personality. . . . Let us have more oceans, more upheavals, more wars, more holocausts. Let us have a world of men and women with dynamos between their legs, a world of natural fury, of passion, action, drama, dreams, madness, a world that produces ecstasy and not dry fucks.

This Blakean-Lawrentian ideal, the eternal shout of the earthman, is as hopelessly unattainable as the Marxist millennium or universal Christian love. It is moving beyond question. But few readers will feel impelled to start smashing the looms or dissolving their civilizations.

What is experienced by the reader in these visions and denunciations (in such few of them, that is, as are vivid and coherent) is, once again, simply "the miracle of personality"— the large and lasting fact of Henry Miller.

When a man like this sets about to write, the result is something altogether strange. There is no shred of a sense of direction either spatial, temporal, or logical to be found in all the chaos of the *Tropics*. Anything ordered, organized, expected, is untrue for Miller: "It is counterfeit," he says. "I felt compelled, in all honesty, to take the disparate elements of our life . . . and manipulate them through my own personal mode, using my own shattered and dispersed ego as heartlessly and recklessly as I would the flotsam and jetsam of the surrounding phenomenal world. . . ."

There is a felt quality of "writing-in-progress" in Miller's works, of the author impulsively improvising at the type-writer, letting a wide-open imagination take him wherever it will. "I have made a silent compact with myself not to change a line of what I write. I am not interested in perfecting my thoughts, nor my action."

Writing oneself out freely and uncritically, as the Surrealists discovered, may produce only page after page of tedium and incoherence. At its liveliest, though, Miller's semi-automatic writing yields a captivating "musical" quality. Theme merges into theme, and image into image, exploding at last into wild surrealistic fantasy.

This same careless directionlessness results in Miller's books becoming unlikely portmanteaux packed with the oddest ac-cessories. Even *Tropic of Cancer*, which, when it has a plot, is a picaresque succession of panhandled beds and mindless copu-lations, finds room for theories of art, a review of Matisse, the end of the world, Hindu mysticism, Proustian memoirs, and the thought of Oswald Spengler. In Miller's own terms, such "digressions" and intrusions are scarcely to be criticized, any more than the copulations.

Like his character Moldorf, like his friend and champion Lawrence Durrell—and he can sound *very* like Durrell—Miller "is word drunk." He delights in characterization by catalogue, circling round a character or a place with evocative chains of words or phrases. Like Whitman's endless roll-calls, this can become simply a device for marking time while the mind is disengaged. But here is Tania:

> . . . *les voies urinaires.* Café de la Liberté, Place des Vosges, bright neckties on the Boulevard Montparnasse, dark bath-rooms, Porto Sec, Abdullah cigarettes, the adagio sonata pa-thetique, aural amplificators, anecdotal seances, burnt sienna breasts, heavy garters, what time is it, golden pheasants stuffed with chestnuts, taffeta fingers, vaporish twilights turning to ilex, acromegaly, cancer and delirium, warm veils, poker chips, carpets of blood and soft thighs.

Like Durrell, too, are the telegraphic scene-setting para-graphs—"Twilight hour. Indian blue, water of glass, trees glistening and liquescent. The rains fall away into the canal at Jaures"—and the fascination with exotic colors. "Vermillion, saffron, mauve, sienna, apricot, turquoise, onyx, Anjou, herring, Corona, verdigris, gorgonzola." . . . "The sun is settting fast. The colors die, they shift from purple to dried blood, from nacre to bistre. . . ." Lines like these could almost serve as parodies of *Justine*, 22 years in advance.

Humor is another quite unexpected reward. Miller alternates in his narrative sequences between droll exaggeration and satire and the wildest of high-humored gusto. The whole chapter on the visiting Indians in *Cancer* is a priceless example of the first; the mad weekend at Le Havre at the end of the book is perhaps the best of the second. The brilliantly bitter "Via Dieppe-Newhaven" in *The Cosmological Eye*, the outrageous Telegraph Company office fantasy in *Tropic of Capricorn*, his life as a school teacher in Dijon in *Cancer* are masterpieces of comic art. Miller lists in his "genealogical line," along with Lawrence and the Surrealists, the likes of Rabelais, Boccaccio, and Petronius; and the presumption is justified. The best of Miller's pornography, like the best of theirs, is blessed with ludicrous exaggeration.

It is interesting to note that all of these sequences comprise extended, almost uninterrupted sections of straight narration. The Dijon episode takes up 20 pages, the longest unbroken piece of narration in *Tropic of Cancer*. The Telegraph Company occupies the greater part of the first 50 pages of *Tropic of Capricorn*. This is not, as we have defined it, Miller's natural mode. This is the way of the novelist. What is more, although none of Miller's "reminiscences" escapes exaggeration and distortion—"Every word I say is a lie"—these are clearly the most invented, least autobiographical passages.

In a word, Miller is perhaps most successful, surely most readable, when he adopts the method of the craftsmen of fiction. The most memorable of his characters, too, whatever biographical antecedents they may have had, were certainly born again in Miller's creative imagination. Obscene, unhappy Van Norden, for example, the real Colossus of *Cancer*, is surely too rich and fantastic to have happened anywhere else.

But conscious craft is not the whole of art. There is also that "creative imagination," at once the faculty that sees and the faculty that invents. These surrealistic visions may well be the ultimate reach of Miller's accomplishment. The best of them combine the startling immediacy of the "Miller eye," his unique free way of seeing, with the rich rhythms and diction and organization of his art. The best of them, unfortunately, are better left unquoted. But they are like this:

> The earth is not an arid plateau of health and comfort, but a great sprawling female with velvet torso that swells and heaves with ocean billows; she squirms beneath a diadem of sweat and anguish. Naked and sexed she rolls among the clouds in the violet light of the stars. All of her, from her generous breasts to her gleaming thighs, blazes with furious ardor. She moves among the seasons and the years with a grand whoop-la that seizes the torso with paroxysmic fury, that shakes the cobwebs out of the sky.

Which leaves only three things to consider, the three things that are still likely to put most people off from considering Miller at all: the Miller world, the question of pornography, and the tedium.

The Miller world is a rather repulsive place. People with bits of food sticking to their lips are always swabbing themselves for venereal disease in flats smelling of rancid butter. Even exempting the sexual *malaise*, this becomes a little hard to take. The imagery, as we have seen, partakes of the same fetid odor of disease, particularly (as witness the title) in *Tropic of Cancer*. Even spring—"There was a touch of Spring in the air, a poisonous, malefic Spring that seemed to burst from the manholes." Of course. It is so pervasive an atmosphere that, once we learn to breathe, sudden intrusions of the "other" world—*our* world—have the shocking quality of an unexpected grotesque. "A letter arrived from America. Moe is getting A's in everything. Murray is learning to ride the bicycle. The victrola was repaired."

The source of all this, and its justification in Miller's terms, is easy to seek. It derives in part from his unashamed, open-eyed recording of precisely what was: this may well have *been* what was for Miller. It comes, in second part, from the pre-civilized, subconscious correspondences he is particularly apt to discover —at some cost, to conscious, post-civilized sensibilities. And finally, as part of his apocalyptic scheme of regeneration, he has, quite frankly, every *intention* of shocking us out of our Puritanic skins. "A man who is intent on creation always dives beneath, to the open wound, to the festering obscene horror. . . . When a hungry, desperate spirit appears and makes the guinea pigs squeal it is because he knows where to put the live wire of sex, because he knows that beneath the hard carapace of indifference there is concealed the ugly gash, the wound that never heals."

These same sources help to explain the unparalleled content of obscenity in Miller's work. "From the point of view of both its happenings and the language in which they are conveyed," Edmund Wilson wrote of *Tropic of Cancer* in 1938, "it is the lowest book of any real literary merit that I ever remember to have read." He might only have wished to revise that judgment the following year, when *Tropic of Capricorn* appeared.

Miller seems to have three approaches to his pornography: the factual, the humorous or hyperbolic, and the truly salacious. The first, which is all too common, is also deadly dull. Matter-of-fact recordings of who, how, and how many times are likely to arouse few erotic impulses. The second escapes the same indictment by taking the opposite extreme. Some of the most agreeable fantasies in the *Tropics* take off from the rankest obscenities; they exploded quickly into cosmic exaggeration far out of reach of the lecher.

The third, I suppose, must remain a matter of taste. In this respect, the almost mystical sexual experiences of D. H. Lawrence are often far more affecting, simply because they *are* idealized. Honest Henry Miller is always hearing springs squeak or belching or wondering how he can get his money back, and shattering the dream.

As for "those words," it is perhaps simply a question of accustoming oneself, or not. In an amusing passage from a story called "Astrological Fricassee" (in *Remember to Remember*), set at a Hollywood party, Miller gives us fair warning not to take them too seriously:

> "What's *your* game?" she asked suddenly.
> "*My game?* Oh, I write."
> "Go on . . . do you mean it? What sort of stuff? History, biology . . . ?"
> "Naughty books," I said, trying to blush deeply.

"What kind of naughty books? Naughty-naughty—or just dirt?"

"Just dirt, I guess."

"You mean—Lady Chatterby, or Chattersley, or whatever the hell it is? Not that swill you don't mean, do you?"

I laughed. "No, not that sort . . . just straight obscenity. You know—duck, chit, kiss, trick, punt. . . ."

Still, perhaps Oscar Wilde was right: the only sin is to bore. At least for a writer.

That a book is nearly impossible to read through need not rob it of critical esteem. *Finnegans Wake, Remembrance of Things Past,* and James' *The Golden Bowl* have all survived without the grace of ready readability. If we are balked by works like these, however, it is because our minds cannot keep up; there is too much. In Miller's books, there is too little to keep the mind nourished and awake: malnutrition, and not fatigue. Miller's works are stretched with great deserts of *longueurs,* unshaped visions and tedious, unintelligible preaching. "The air pockets, the alkali wastes" will leave the reader dried, disinterested, bored for chapters on end.

Henry Miller is obviously not for every reader. He is a difficult, deficient, and outrageous writer. He ought to be approached, if not with sympathy, at least with some awareness of what it is he is trying to do. The fully achieved artistic experiences—the verbal mastery, the humor, the extended narratives, the imaginative visions—can be, when plucked from their surroundings, rich and satisfying enough. For those who are prepared, however, the really enlarging experience will be that of the man himself. There isn't likely to be such another.

Sexus, Nexus, and Plexus [1967]

I am not a friend of Henry Miller's, nor (I should confess at
the start) a persuaded admirer of his work. I undertook, six
years ago, a critical study of all of his writings then available in
the Harvard University Library, to coincide with the first
American appearance of the *Tropics:* all of his writings, that is
to say, except *The Rosy Crucifixion.* So in a way this is a completion, a fulfillment of that earlier essay. Later, in the midst of
an early passion for The Alexandria Quartet, I wrote on the
Miller-Durrell letters, an experience that substantially in-
creased my respect for the senior correspondent. Miller is notoriously not accorded in America the critical respect he is
given abroad, and I share, as regards his "novels," that want of
respect. Yet among the tenets of my critical creed are that
every serious and talented writer merits a full hearing, and I
grant that Miller is serious and talented, and that careful, informed, and dispassionate criticism should illuminate the work
of any such writer.

Miller has received very little criticism of this sort. He does
not encourage it, his work does not invite it. "Honest criticism
means nothing; what one wants is unrestrained passion, fire for
fire." We of the enemy tend to ignore him, to leave him to the
mercies of the pornographers, the censors, or, worst, of his
own disciples. This essay is my attempt to redress the critical
imbalance, to see whether "honest criticism"—criticism classi-

cal, rational, and cool—does indeed "mean nothing" in the case of Miller, and to determine whether he must, after all, be left to the "unrestrained passion" of his fans.

In a way my evaluation *is* doomed to failure, or at least to a serious incompleteness. Miller's books are not things apart, to be judged by themselves; they are more, even, than autobiographies. They are a function of his being, a natural and necessary emanation of the thing that he is. Ultimately, it is that "thing" that matters, and not the books: the human phenomenon called Henry Miller. The books are only a means of access.

Much of the honest critic's energy, therefore, must be spent in trying to ascertain this man, to reach, seize, extricate the human fact. But three books will not suffice for that, all the books will not suffice. We must leave it to those who know Henry Miller, or who think they do, to complete the picture. Let me only say that, on the basis of his letters and the testimony of others, I *do* imagine him a finer, a more complete man than the partial and unlovely self his writings reveal.

One way to begin a critique is to try to describe the object of criticism. *The Rosy Crucifixion* is a trilogy of Miller's "autobiographical fictions," *Sexus, Plexus,* and *Nexus:* written between 1941 and 1959, published in France (in five volumes) between 1949 and 1959, in the U.S. in 1965. The American (Grove Press) edition runs to 1590 pages, something over half a million words, or about forty per cent the length of *À la recherche du temps perdu.*

This is about as far as one can go, in scrupulous honesty, in describing what the trilogy "is." Its content is simply Henry Miller. But, granting this, let me approach this unorthodox work in orthodox fashion, and treat first of its "plot," its characters, its style, and its thought.

"I could never formulate a plot," writes Miller in *Plexus.* And yet there is the ghost of a direction, of a tendency forward pervading the trilogy, despite a radical shift in manner between the first volume and the latter two, despite the vast formlessness of the whole. Miller is "remembering" in these many pages seven years of his past—"the most crucial years of my life"—from his first meeting with June (=Mara/Mona, the second Mrs. Miller) in 1921 to his departure for Europe in 1928. In the autobiographical pattern of his works, *The Rosy Crucifixion* would come directly after *Tropic of Capricorn* (the Western Union years) and just before *Tropic of Cancer* (the Paris years). Its major direction, or theme, is that of escape —escape from a wife, from a job, finally from the spiritual prison of America, to Europe and, he imagines, freedom.

With fine psychological logic, a second direction is the reverse of this, a growing tide of sentimental nostalgia for childhood years, which reaches its crest as escape approaches.

> The desire to strengthen the ties which bound me to the past, to my wonderful childhood, was becoming ever stronger. The more insipid and distasteful the everyday world became, the more I glorified the golden days of childhood. . . . I realized I had lost something precious.

A third trace of pattern in this apparent chaos is the story of Miller's development as a writer, "my struggle to express myself in words." This reaches its fulfillment at the end of *Nexus*, with his discovery of a voice (his own), a subject (himself), an audience (Henry Miller), a purpose ("to smash things," "to curse and blaspheme," "to make of Culture an open sewer, so that the stench of it would remain forever in the nostrils of memory"), and a tone:

> *You* there, pretending to be dead and crucified, *you* there, with your terrible *historia de calamitatis*, why not reenact it in the spirit of play? Why not tell it over to yourself and extract a little music from it?

Still another theme that runs through all three volumes is "Mona," the wife he found and couldn't keep, the mystery of her life and her past. A fifth might be found in all her predecessors and substitutes, the great chain of remembered female names that Miller so often uses as a trigger for salacious or sentimental reminiscences, or as a goad to keep the words flowing. Una Gifford! Ida Verlaine! Ah, Valeska! Carlotta! Rebecca! and the rest, all the various and forgettable objects of the thirty-five copulations of *Sexus*, and the miscellaneous encounters thereafter.

*

But to talk of themes and patterns is to suggest order and design, and this is deceptive: there is none, except that provided by the unconscious. Miller writes without plan, without taking thought; takes great pride, in fact, in having let his millions of words come as they would, "up from below." There *is* a kind of chronology to the reminiscences—Henry's meeting Mona, living with her, divorcing Maude in order to marry her; finally quitting his job at Western Union (at the start of *Plexus*) to give all his time to writing; the sequence of their residences, their attempts to earn money, the Lesbian triangle with Stasia; the girls' departure for Europe, and finally Henry's. But this is constantly broken by vague time shifts into past or future. And for the most part these Grub Street recollections have *no* time, and little reality. The reader's impression is of sixteen hundred pages of talk, endless, pointless talk, of desultory 3 A.M. barroom conversations that never stop; of begging money endlessly and typing words endlessly and fucking endlessly, of drab nights among Village cranks and misfits, all poured out in great waves or spurts of spontaneous Millerian prose.

This is an "impression," not an exact account. There are one or two hundred pages in the trilogy of authentic human life, neither flat nor artificial. But rarely does Miller search for the significant experience, or try to transform the past into present meaning. It is all simply told, because he must tell it. The events may be exaggerated, decorated, painted in all the violent colors of rhetoric; but they are rarely selected with art or re-created into life.

The same holds true, with exceptions, of the "characters" of Miller's world. To this day I cannot remember which is which. The anonymous underground of perverts, pimps, geniuses, cripples, holy men, *et al.*, either inside or out of the Cosmococcic and Cosmodemonic Telegraph Company, Miller rarely identifies beyond an incantatory catalogue. Others, scores of others are introduced for longer sessions; but few ever stay around long enough, or are developed deeply or honestly or sympathetically enough, for us to believe in or care about. They have, it would seem, no insides. They indulge in meaningless, trivial talk with the Master, relate the corny, empty banalities of their lives, praise and wonder at the man who created them. They share Henry's women, contradict his opinions, let him pick apart their psyches and encoil them in insults. Ulric, Kronski, O'Mara, so many others: they are seen but never felt, they are itemized, analyzed, outlined: but they do not exist.

There are, as I say, exceptions. Mona, Maude, Stasia, and Henry's mother are all relevant to the question of the *human* Henry Miller, so I shall reserve them for later. But of those "outside the family," two at least stay in the mind.

Mr. Elfenbein, who breathes for a scant eight pages of *Nexus*, is Miller's one truly Dickensian creation. The grandest Jew of them all, he is a character made entirely out of *talk*, out of the rhythms and allusions and associations and ironies of his splendid Semitic harangue.

MacGregor, who comes and goes through the books, poses more of a problem. He is Miller's pet bourgeois boor, a flat-souled, canting vulgarian whose loud-mouthed Yankee talk is reproduced with excruciating precision. This is, if not genuine creation, at least remarkable photography: MacGregor exists. But the exact imitation of vulgar commonplaces is not satire: it is vulgar and commonplace. One wonders why Miller needed this creature; the occasional idolatry of a MacGregor is no compliment. I suspect that he is primarily being *used*, like every other character in the book, used for the complex purposes of the immense and absolute ego of Henry Miller. He puts into MacGregor's mouth the anti-Miller insults, the nasty half-truths, the criticisms we ourselves are on the verge of making ("that Theosophical shit!"), in the hope, perhaps unconscious, that no one will believe, or care to share, the opinions of this patently stupid ass. He may be trying to silence (and ignore) his own conscience by dressing it as a fool.

Another approach to the "content" of a book, an approach more radical still, is to begin by admitting that it is made out of words. Miller's trilogy often appears to be made of nothing else. The man, like Moldorf in *Cancer*, is word-drunk, word-mad. It was this madness, put to the service of an insatiable ego, that made him a writer. It is the texture, the spangly, scattered surface of his books that makes them so unusual; not the depths or the design, since they have neither. As I tend to believe that any real writer may be finally tracked down in his words, his style—given infinite critical skill and patience—this may be our best point of departure. The style *is* the man—a glowing, glittering, widely varied, gay, disordered, purposefully shocking surface.

Miller's own account here of the stages in his writing career makes clear how fundamentally it was an affair of words. Most writers, no doubt, begin with the same rapture, the same fascination with language and its infinite diversity. But the stronger and saner among them usually mature into a distrust of mere words, and grow more dry and scrupulous in their style.

Not so Miller. For him it all began with words, it all too often ends with words. Voracious childhood reading, a seeking out of fathers and homes in books, in library reading rooms, a voluptuary's fondling of the sounds and shapes of favorite words: until he could admit, "More in love with words than with psychopathic divagations, I could spend hours at a stretch with Walter Pater, or even Henry James, in the hope of lifting a beautifully-turned phrase." We learn of the wall charts "on which were listed the exotic words I was endeavoring to annex to my vocabulary." Later came the gift of tongues, the orator's or raconteur's ability to *hold* his audience, to pour forth effortlessly, eloquently:

> The strange thing was, I reflected, that most everybody I knew already considered me a writer, though I had done little to prove it. They assumed I was not only because of my behavior, which had always been eccentric and unpredictable, but because of my passion for language. From the time I learned to read I was never without a book.

Here is the origin of the Miller style: a taste for words, like a taste for olives or the color green. Preferably unusual, juicy words, words in unlikely combinations, words in long, comma-spaced series of sheer display.

> I believe in God the Father, in Jesus Christ his only begotten Son, in the blessed Virgin Mary, the Holy Ghost, in Adam Cadmium, in chrome nickel, the oxides and the mercurichromes, in water-fowls and water-cress, in epileptoid seizures, in bubonic plagues, in Devachum, in planetary conjunctions, in chicken tracks and stick throwing, in revolutions, in stock crashes, in wars, earthquakes, cyclones, in Kali Yuga and in hula-hula.

A similar case of bravura display is his fondness for meta-phors and similes, sometimes at the rate of an image a line. Not the illuminations of poetry, but rather decor-imagery, imagery encasing nothing, imagery gratuitous, prosaic, strained, and often meaningless.

> It was as if my ear were a dandelion and each little thistle an antenna which caught the message and relayed it to the roof of my brain where it exploded with the dull splash of a how-itzer. . . .

> It was one of those thoughts which scud through the mind like a thin moon through mutton chops. . . .

> She had stirred those grape-like bunches of emotion which were strung like a garland on the skeleton of my ego. . . .

> You can push yourself clean through the filament of life and come out at the wrong end of the telescope.

All this is learned and conscious; it has very little about it of the unconscious imagination. More revealing for us may be the *sources* from which his word-pictures are drawn, his unique predilection for the unspeakable physical image, the scrofu-lous, the diseased, the scatalogical. I once thought this some-thing profound and preconscious, the result of Miller's singu-larly unrepressed way of seeing—his "pre-civilized vision," I called it. I now tend to think it a matter of conscious "*épater-isme*," the desire to shock and disgust. But the truth may lie in between. Many artists want to shock and disgust, but no other makes such use of Miller's palette of snot and pus and vomit. None shares his freedom, even gusto, in telling us of dirty toe-nails, unwiped assholes, mangy foetuses, and "menstrual sauce." Now our response to all this may reveal something of us; but surely its presence tells us something of Miller: of a confused sexuality, perhaps, a discomfort with the body, a se-cret disgust for the physical as deep-rooted as Jonathan Swift's.

Much of this is inwrought with his dealings in sex, an issue I reserve for later. It may find expression as a chain of diseases, or as a grotesque, degrading inventory of the bodily parts and organs. Other examples *do* suggest something primeval and pre-civilized in Miller's way of seeing.

> These are the fluid, solvent egos who lie still as a foetus in the uterine marshes of their stagnant self. When you puncture the sac, when you think Ah! I've got you at last! you find nothing but clots of mucus in your hand. . . .

> It was a depersonalized glut or slop, a hangover from some archaic condition of ecstasy—the residual memory of crabs and snakes of their prolonged copulations in the protoplasmic slime of ages long forgotten.

There is present in these, of course, something consciously comic, something intended to disgust. But I am not yet ready to concede that it is only the "sick" who are disgusted, and the "healthy" who laugh. Miller is attracted to what the world has deemed repulsive. These quotations bear his unmistakable imprint, and tell us something about his spirit as well as his style.

His common rhythm is that of the breathless, comma-cumulative, long-rolling sentence, building up through wave upon wave of overlapping series.

> He would go back to his people, suffer with them, raise them up if he could, and if not, die with them, die as they died, in the street, naked, homeless, shunned, despised, stepped on, walked over, spat upon, a bundle of bones which even the vultures would find it difficult to feast on. He would do this not out of guilt, remorse, or repentence but because India in rags, India festering like a maggot, India starving, India writhing under the heel of the conqueror, meant more to him than all of the comforts, opportunities and advantages of a heartless country like America.

In this example, the sense of organic compulsion is driven through four verbs in series, the last repeated twice, giving on to nine adjectives; then a sequence of three objects, another of four (each repeating "India"), another of three. The effect is that of impassioned rhetorical outburst. This accumulative, self-repeating rhythm may be explained by Miller's typing freely away, never looking back, never seeing a sentence as a whole but only as an on-going stream.

These elements of diction, imagery, and rhythm are mingled, extended, and orchestrated in the longer prose passages, some-

times a paragraph, sometimes several pages, of which Miller is
quite openly, often deservedly proud.

> I have made extensive use throughout these books of irruptive
> onslaughts of the unconscious, such as dream, fantasy, bur-
> lesque, Pantagruelian word play, etc., which lend the narra-
> tive a chaotic, whimsical, perplexing character—in the mind of
> many critics.

This critic, who finds that last phrase just slightly disingenu-
ous, thinks Miller's narrative chaotic enough, whimsical
enough, even perplexing enough *without* the fantasias; and
wonders just how unconscious the source of such carefully-
staged irruptions can be. There is, beyond question, a vivid
quality of verbal freedom in his explosions. But the overall
effect remains one of a studied and aureate *manner*, no more
"unconscious" than the poetry of Crashaw or Gongora. Except
on the rarest occasions—most striking of which is the conclud-
ing chapter of *Sexus*—I think Miller far too self-conscious to
have ready, re-creative access to his own subconscious materials, however rich they may be. What look like wild outbursts
of the imagination are, for the most part, only word-play—
sometimes brilliant word-play. He is more in the tradition of
Joyce than of Dostoevsky.

There are outbursts of many sorts, of many levels of reality:
from attempts to render a psychological state in impressionistic
prose to celebrations of the slums of New York in paragraphs
of random imagery; daydreams and night-dreams, from a literary fancy of castles and monsters—an excellent piece of surrealism—to the very personal nightmare of *Sexus'* last chapter
—an even greater one. These fantasies can explode out of rollerskating, women's genitals, a burlesque show, the Roseland
Dance Hall:

> Here the baboons in full rut swim the belly of the Nile seeking
> the end of all things; here are the ancient maenads, reborn to
> the wail of sax and muted horn; here the mummies of the sky-
> scrapers take out their inflamed ovaries and air them, while the
> incessant play of music poisons the pores, drugs the mind,
> opens the sluice gates. With the sweat and perspiration, with
> the sickening, overpowering reek of perfumes and deodorants
> all discreetly sucked up by the ventilators, the electric odor of
> lust hung like a halo suspended in space. . . .

Flutter and froufrou, camphor and fish balls, Omega oil . . .
wings spread full preen, limbs bare to the touch, palms moist,
foreheads glistening, lips parched, tongues hanging out, teeth
gleaming like the advertisements, eyes bright, roving, stripping
one bare . . . piercing, penetrating eyes, some searching for
gold, some for fuck, some to kill, but all bright, shamelessly,
innocently bright like the lion's red maw, and pretending, yes,
pretending, that it's a Sunday afternoon, a floor like any other
floor, a cunt's a cunt, no tickee no fuckee, buy me, take me,
squeeze me, all's well in Itchigumi, don't step on me, isn't it
warm, yes, I love it, I do love it, bite me again, harder,
harder. . . .
    . . . weaving, sidling, pushing, rubbing, and everywhere a
sea of faces, a sea of flesh carved by scimitar-strokes of light,
the whole pack glued together in one vast terpsichorean stew.
And over this hot conglomerate flesh swirling in the cake bowl
the smear of brasses, the wail of trombones, the coagulating
saxophones, the piercing trumpets, all the liquid fire going
straight to the glands.

At its solid base, Miller's prose is serious, honest, and clear.
The vocabulary is correct, if sometimes stilted, the syntax
fluid, the manner crafted but not baroque. The effect is substantial, sinewy, "chewy," recalling the studied, self-conscious,
very personal styles of nineteenth century English essayists,
neither sparkling nor spare. The diction (converse, deed, dis-
port, enkindle, the timeworn visage) and high rhetoric add to
this slightly archaic strength.

At its best, his language can do spectacular things. Examples
of this best are the explosive impression of Arthur Raymond at
the piano (*Sexus*, XIV, 397), the prose-poem of the lower East
Side ghetto (*Sexus*, XIX, 536), and the wild game of words on
the Polish language (*Plexus*, VII, 315). The "literary" dream
sequence in *Plexus* (IX, 396ff.)—a magnificent piece of sensuous surrealism—can bear comparison with Keats' *Lamia*, and
outdoes Lautréamont. Another small triumph is Elfenbein's
grand lamentation (*Nexus*, XV, 230–38).

Sometimes the prose efforts *do* reach poetic truth, the truths
for which there are no words. I think especially of two fine
passages on writing and creation (*Sexus*, IX, 265–68 and *Nexus*,
XVI). Here communication is, virtually, mystical: the fanta-

sias, so apparently abandoned and illogical, are charged with
creative truth.

But to see Miller's prose here at its very best I would turn to
the last two chapters of *Sexus*. A burlesque house fantasia,
which begins in the customary Millerian slime, rolls first into
nasty caricature, then to genuinely evocative surrealism; and
finally explodes into a devastating, clear-headed outburst on the
cultural implications of this quintessentially American institution. The chapter closes in an attempt, not wholly successful, at
a nightmare tale in the manner of Dostoevsky. The reader then
moves directly into the *real* hallucination of Chapter 23, the
finest thing in all three books. I shall look at this last chapter in
more detail later, since it provides in its excellence a focus for
many key problems of *le cas Miller*.

And at its worst? At its worst there is no worse. Fulsome,
overblown, self-indulging, Gargantuan-voluptuary prose with
no earthly significance, a muddy clogged stream all green and
stagnant, bubbling thinly on and on. Mixtures of Rosicrucian
fatuity, snot-and-vomit *épaterisme*, bits of greasy sex, larded
with Doom-of-Civilization inanities and rendered in the worst
of Millerese: a prose hyperadjectival, sesquipedalian, insistently
cosmic, crammed with bloated, irrelevant, ungainly similes and
undigested erudition: this is the worst. Every hoary American
cliché finds its place, every bit of archaic, toplofty woman's
magazine prose.

I am not so resistant to mysticism, I hope, as to be unable to
tell better from worse. One of the reasons I distrust it, and its
advocates, though, is the wretched nuisance they commit on
language. Miller's ventures into the mystical can sound the
most meaningless, meandering, fake-profound claptrap—*because* of the prose: an orotund, baggy prose that pretends to all
and says nothing.

From these heights to these depths: and between, what Anaïs
Nin has characterized as "the air pockets, the alkali wastes."
However to explain these fantastic variations? And however
explain why, for all the extremes, for all the fireworks, the jer-

emiads, the sum result is still one of almost-unbearable boredom?

Miller himself provides the answer, in an eloquent defense of his *l'art brut* aesthetic. The integrity of this defense I cannot but respect. But it only makes it the more lamentably clear how irreconcilable are our concepts of art.

> Myself, I have never understood poetry as poetry. For me the mark of the poet is everywhere, in everything. To distill thought until it hangs in the alembic of a poem, revealing not a speck, not a shadow, not a vaporous breath of the "impurities" from which it was decocted, that for me is a meaningless, worthless pursuit. . . .

Word-mania explains much of the worst, *and* the best, of Miller's style. The narcissism occasioned by his absolute self-assurance, the exhibitionism engendered by its very reverse—these may lie behind his remarkable freedom and display. But technically, our explanation for the dismal depths, the boredom, the "air pockets, the alkali wastes," the great baggy artlessness of it all lies precisely in this anti-poetic creed. "To write . . . must be an act devoid of will. The word, like the deep ocean current, has to float to the surface of its own impulse." There is, Miller believes and insists, to be no editing, no pruning, no restraint—no "taste," if you like, no art, in anything so crucial (to the author) as this epic act of personal catharsis, of self-revelation. *Every* smeared, dangling impurity must be left in, or the work will not be honest: it will not be Henry Miller. This was the issue in the dramatic exchange of correspondence between Miller and Durrell (over *Sexus*) in the fall of 1949. It marks a division of opinion—a division of temperament, of spirit, of soul—so absolute that I still wonder whether Durrellian standards of art, of taste and craft and discretion, have anything at all to do with the work of Henry Miller.

There are moments when I sympathize with the poor pornography hunters who buy Miller's books. Duped by his notoriety (and the use his publishers make of it), they must find their search balked at every turn by the "Thought" of Henry Miller. To bite in, expecting juicy flesh, and taste only the ashes of metaphysic: it could drive one mad with frustration.

For *The Rosy Crucifixion*, like all of his books, is as much didactic tract as super-autobiography. I do wonder if Miller, in the quiet center of his mind, really thinks himself a thinker; or does he know, and admit secretly to himself, that he is just a high-spirited, verbal child prodigy, playing with ideas? With all his faults upon him, he is so much more interesting than they are. His mock-profound ideas are a sort of borrowed, adopted clothing that suits his temper and his taste, and no essential part of his character or value.

I should like to be able to pass off much of the "thinking" as Rabelaisian parody, or snickering farce. Sometimes Miller seems half to admit that this is the case, to mock his own "senseless jeremiads" and "theosophical shit." But on the whole —and his letters support this—I am sadly convinced that he takes all his philosophizing with dead seriousness, from racial generalizations to Rosicrucian astrology. He trumpets out his "thoughts" with all of the impotent dedication of some self-educated American engineer, floundering giddily out of his depth in the Great Books of the Western World.

For he is *not* a thinker of originality or depth. He simply has not the equipment. His is a better than average intellect, but undisciplined, shallow, and immature, immature like a greenwood violin. He has not the mental discipline or muscle required for prolonged, deep, rigorous thought, nor the maturity of intellectual imagination, the patience, the broad vision of a real creative thinker. He is too devoted by turns, moreover, to romantic unreason; and far too indiscriminate in his judgments, too dilettantish in his momentary passions to be even a good *anti*-cerebral mystic.

What of the vast erudition? Poured into such a receptacle, never assimilated, never properly digested, it forms only the shallowest pool. Big names and big ideas float at random on the surface.

> Naturally I had read Cellini, Vasari's *Lives*, the history of the Inquisition, the lives of the Popes, the story of the Medici family, the Italian, German, and English dramas of incest, the writings of John Addington Symonds, Jacob Burckhardt, Funck-Brentano, all on the Renaissance . . .

Naturally. This sad, self-pluming display shows Miller's to be the image-in-little of America's *own* cultural inferiority complex, the busy insecurity of the self-educated. All the hundreds of thinkers, authors, artists in his bag are so many sequential, unexamined private passions. He has the same passionate, alcoholic's thirst for "Ideas" (the more "abstruse and recondite" the better) that he has for words, just as indiscriminate, just as unsystematic, just as ultimately solipsistic. What value his public thinking may have remains expressionistic, personal, in what more it tells us of Miller; and not at all in its autonomous and usable strength.

This judgment made, let me try to synthesize the Thought of Henry Miller here displayed.

"You're a metaphysician, by crikey!" exclaims one of his learned friends, after witnessing, spellbound, Henry's exposition of a text from Nostradamus. ("The only response I could make was to blush deeply.") Miller obviously agrees. But one might also consider a cruder remark of Marcelle's: "For an intelligent person, you do talk a lot of nonsense." In Miller's case, to begin at the metaphysical does not necessarily mean to begin at the deepest or most profound. This level is as arbitrary, as much a matter of taste as any other. But it is a useful place to start.

It is difficult to get Miller's supernatural world to sit still, since it is always presented in dynamic, hortatory contexts— usually amid a vaguely uplifting, affirmative sermon berating the reader into some new order of being. A God is occasionally referred to, and the words of Christ may be used, but Miller's cosmos is neither theistic nor Christian.

He does acknowledge and insist upon a transcendent order of being, which has its effects on this one; with which, ideally, this one would be merged and identified.

> It is for us to put ourselves in unison with this world order. Until we have the humility to acknowledge the existence of a vision beyond our own, until we have faith and trust in superior powers, the blind must lead the blind.

Sometimes his vision takes on specifically astrological properties. "One becomes aware of those invisible rays which emanate perpetually from the most remote parts of the cosmos

. . ." His own final vision of the cosmic harmony, at the end of the trilogy, begins with a "picture of the world as a web of magnetic forces."

At other times this surreality takes the form of a Shavian "life force" within us, which we must trust and release and never deny. For a time in late *Plexus* and *Nexus*, it takes on an Eastern cast, as Miller longs for the transcendent serenity and radiance of the Zen or Hindu sages.

So the details of the Force Beyond (or Within) are not clear: but there is one. Miller, with his "astral effulgences" and "cosmic fluids," may simply be drawing on traditional sources, a key to which is given in the title of the trilogy. On the one hand it suggests his miserable life, seen and sung with joy ("My life has been one long rosy crucifixion"); but on the other, it clearly alludes to the Ancient and Mystical Order Rosae Crucis, the "Rosicrucians": the esoteric order of seventeenth century (or Egyptian) origins whose language, symbols, and beliefs Miller frequently echoes.

Miller twice relates what may clearly be called "mystical experiences" of his own (*Sexus*, XIII, 369–75, *Plexus*, IX, 316–22). Now it is of the nature of mystical experience to be inexpressible. All accounts of it must be inadequate, at best metaphoric, and much here does remain in a state of non-denotative approximation. But we can remark clearly his experience and conviction of this other, more harmonious reality— "that which embraces, sustains, and exalts life," "the world of (our) true substance," "the mysterious world from which (we) sprang." Suddenly . . .

> one is divorced from the illusory world of material reality. . . .
> Death has no meaning. All is change, vibration, creation and
> re-creation. . . . What was dilapidation, decay, sordidness is
> transmuted. The microscopic eye of the angel sees the infinite
> parts which compose the divine whole; the telescopic eye of
> the angel sees nothing but totality, which is perfect.

Here one can see the germ of a next stage in Miller's thought —the optimistic, affirmative, uplift-sermonizing in which most of his metaphysics is enclosed. The world, to the "angelic" eye, is perfect, its harmony absolute. If you see it otherwise, the fault is you. You lack faith. Be yourself, be gay, be free, be fully alive, and all will be well. Fie on the faithless pessimists and prophets of doom.

These exhortations are legion, sometimes eloquent, sometimes inane (Take the everyday world and embrace it! Drink of Life's undying essence!). Always following the same pattern, they are of much more importance to Miller than the static descriptions of Being. He was clearly born to preach, not to think.

It is remarkable that a writer who consistently takes as his subject the dregs of human life, who insists so on his own miseries and the ugliness of his surroundings, should be such an incorrigible optimist, "always merry and bright." He positively hates the unhappy. "Who said that everything was all fucked up? Where? When? On the seventh day God rested from his labors. And He saw that all was good. *D'accord.* How could it have been otherwise?"

> *But,* you quibble, how can I sing when the world is crumbling, when all about me is bathed in blood and tears? Do you realize that the martyrs sang when they were being burned at the stake? They saw nothing crumbling . . . They sang because they were full of faith. Who can demolish faith? Who can wipe out joy? . . . Joy and faith are inherent in the universe. . . . The bogs and quagmires, the marshes and sink-holes, the pits and snares, are all in the mind.

This is, I suppose, a supportable proposition. To deny the tragic view is a mark of all positive idealists. Unfortunately, Miller's Cosmic boosterism is unlikely to convince those who find the world less agreeably simple. But our interest is less in Miller's philosophy than in Miller: where does this cosmic optimism *come* from? If you will bear with another quotation, I think I have the answer.

> A man who has confidence in himself *must* have confidence in others, confidence in the fitness and rightness of the universe. When a man is thus anchored he ceases to worry about the fitness of things, about the behavior of his fellow men, about right and wrong and injustice.

"I wanted a world made in my own image, a world that would breathe my spirit"—and so he made one. It is what we

all do, no doubt. But this does bring us back to the center, to
the *real* source: "a man who has confidence in himself": Henry
Miller. *Out* of self-assurance, into cosmic affirmation. And
damn the complainers, the whiners, the suffering, the less-
assured.

Down, from these lunary realms, to the more mundane orders
of Miller's thought. From self-assurance, and cosmic optimism,
to a sort of egocentric radicalism, a primitivist idealism. And
from there to the softer manifestations of romanticism and sentimentality.

I was impressed, six years ago, by the apocalyptic social radicalism of the *Tropics*. Today I find myself less moved and
more suspicious. There is clearly so much of mere rhetoric
about it, of self-displaying verbalism and painless anti-bour-
geois insult. It is not easy to be a real social radical, on the
model of Blake and Lawrence. But to ape their attacks on cere-
bral Western civilization is anyone's game. Miller is simply not
serious enough about it, or consistent enough, to be accepted as
authentic. "Fundamentally," he announces, "everything is cock-
eyed." He talks of an Ideal Universe ("made in his own
image") without money, property, police, government,
schools, prisons, etc. "Secretly, I *did* hope to reform the
world." So far, fine: all very properly radical.

But he really doesn't care. "I don't give a damn about the
misery of the world."

> "And what about crime, injustice, tyranny, and those things?"
> "Well, what about them? What can you do about such
> things? You might as well ask me—what about the weather?"

He mocks the socially conscientious, despises those who forever "take on the problems of the world." As he remarks in
perhaps the most self-revealing sentence in all *The Rosy Crucifixion:*

> The man who is forever disturbed about the problems of hu-
> manity either has no problems of his own or has refused to face
> them.

And once again we are dropped back on the target of absolute egoism. The mind reels at the fixity of it: the I is all.

What then of our reformers of cock-eyed worlds? Perhaps the reform he propounds is internal. Perhaps our preacher is a moralist at heart. Putting aside those lessons difficult to interpret, like "Be what you are," and a few unconvincing nods towards Brotherhood and Love, he does, from time to time, offer pearls of pseudo-Lawrencian morality. "Don't throttle your impulses." "Nothing would be bad or ugly or evil if we really let ourselves go."

> I don't give a damn about the misery of the world. I take it for granted. What I want is to open up. I want to know what's inside me. I want everybody to open up. . . . I know that underneath the mess everything is marvelous.

In direct descent, then, from the egoistic radicalism, one can trace his attacks on rationalism and Western civilization. Sometimes, in the manner of Blake, or of Wordsworth, he condemns "the sterile intellect," laments the lost clairvoyance of childhood or the Dawn Man ("We had it once"). Sometimes, in the manner of Lawrence, he denounces all the agents and artifacts of modern civilization (especially American civilization), in the usual terms—rat race, gadgetry, the megalopolis. But it is all too transient, too smug, too easy to do. It recalls the shallow, on-off, stagey spleen of a right-wing journalist.

From here, by easy decline, to still softer cushions of thought. "Thought," in fact, is too hard a word: we have dropped to the realm of feeling. And it is here, I think, in this undistinguished emotional stew, that we reach the real and genuine center of Miller's mind; and not in the elaborate artifice of intellection just discussed. This is the constant man; that is a public act.

The sentimentality, the soft center, takes many forms. He indulges in the most golden-aged, romantic visions of the past —*any* past, Egyptian, Renaissance, his own boyhood; of Europe; of artists, authors, dozens of individual heroes, Russian mystics or American millionaires; of Jews, Negroes, Indians, Poles, Italians, and other non-Anglo Saxon races by turns (even his fat, beer-drinking German uncles); of every sort of adolescent ideal. If his erudition recalls that of Eugene O'Neill, clumsy, graceless, unassimilated, but defiantly displayed for all that, his big soft-hearted American sentimentality reminds one of Whitman. If you admire these two authors, without serious reservations, you may well admire Henry Miller.

This whole investigation—as I warned at the start—has been oblique; "by the way"; instrumental. I have confessed that the books do not matter—only Miller does. And that our long analysis of them was meant in part to prove this, as an intentional exercise in futility, in part to help us on our way to a discovery of the man. Now we are there: all we have left to talk of is Henry Miller.

But which Henry Miller? One never tells all the truth. I have, up till now, used the name "Henry" for the I-character in the trilogy (who could be split again, into present-narrator and past-actor); and reserved "Miller" for the man who created him. They are obviously not the same. For one thing, Henry rarely takes on even a credible fictional existence: as a sentient, feeling, dynamic human being, he is not. What he *is*, most of the time, is a necessary, self-supporting, wish-fulfilling ideal self projected by Miller, cool and controlled, merry and bright, beloved and admired, virtually omnipotent. We can, I think, learn a great deal from him about the "real" Henry Miller.

There is an *a priori* point from which all analyses of the real Henry Miller must begin. We have already bumped into it several times. This is what he calls his "self-assurance": ego-awareness raised to such a pitch that I know not its equal in all literature. He is possessed of a baffling, near-absolute conviction of his own genius and importance—a conviction which precedes any achievement or testimonial or ratiocination. It is the unstated presumption beneath all of his works: that I, Henry Miller, *matter* so much and so obviously that my every word, thought, and action merits publication.

Where this conviction comes from I have no idea. His success at school, his way with words, the wonder of his friends: these alone could never explain so immense a self-esteem. It may owe something to his early life, to his mother particularly; but I know too little of psychology to make the assertion. His proud if unsure status as a self-made intellectual, in a country of deep anti-intellectual roots, a country which provides no special place or respect for the thinker, surely has something to do with his defiant self-sufficiency. (When a man is out of step with his whole people, he must decide that he is right or that they are; and when his towering ambitions receive no external support, then they must be shored up from within.) Or it may be all only an extrapolation into other domains of his Jovean sexual prowess, which I have no reason to disbelieve. From potency, narrowly defined, to Omnipotence: it seems a natural enough Freudian conceit. James Boswell, whose sexual potency appears comparable to Miller's, displays in his Journals an equal egomania.

Wherever it came from, there it is: an Olympian self-assurance, the *fons et origo* of all that Miller is and has done. And, generated by this self-assurance in its meeting with the world, of equal and opposite force, a simultaneous *lack* of self-assurance, a nagging doubt, a feeling that this conviction is unjustified—the latter more often unconsciously than consciously revealed. Hence, in these books, the immense efforts at self-defense, self-display, self-justification; *and* the poignant human cracks in the monument. (If pride at sexual potency lies behind the former, perhaps fear of impotence is the root of the latter. The pattern, again, is Boswell's.)

The evidence is difficult to parcel out. Any display of egotism can be made to look like "compensation" for some secret inadequacy. But I can make my case clearly enough. The books alone, by their numbers and their nature, should be proof of Miller's unique and absolute self-fixation. Not Gide or Montaigne, not Casanova or Boswell, not the vainest, most long-winded of the great diarists or memoirists can equal his undiverted dedication to self.

Convinced of election (in the Calvinist sense), one need not work to achieve it. One simply *is*, glowingly. The visible proof of election for Miller (not that he needed it) lay in his sexual freedom and his gift of tongues, proofs that were sustained and kept afloat on the wind of his disciples' praise ("It was always easy for me to create these 'believers'") and his inflated, factitious reputation. Perhaps even by the condemnations of the righteous: what surer mark of holy integrity than to be despised by the despicable?

From this self-satisfaction, self-captivation, one can deduce much that we have already discussed: the automatic, unedited style; the refusal to accept discipline; the scorn for logic, rules, science, or lyric precision; the unwillingness (or inability) to understand another author in his proper terms, or to make a book on any subject external to himself. This egoism, as we have seen, lies behind his cosmic optimism ("He who has confidence in himself *must* have confidence . . . in the fitness and rightness of the universe.") and his radical idealism.

From it also, in the moral realm, comes his inability to love or sympathize with other human beings, his refusal to acknowledge the demands or claims of egos other than his own. From it comes his violent disgust for, his childish revenges on those who will not support him—even those he has insulted and injured. From it comes his happy brutality, sometimes to the point of sadism, especially to the female animals whose lust he deigns to satisfy. Exceptional egoism is probably a necessary adjunct to exceptional art; but for many who knew Henry Miller, the price may have seemed too high.

But the underside of self-conceit is insecurity. And time and again, all unintentionally, Miller betrays the uncertainty of his pretensions.

His virility fantasies are endless. There is nothing his famous penis cannot do, in the book, no woman it cannot force to her knees in adoration. *He* is always dispassionate, patient, cool, playfully sadistic, mildly surprised at his own magnificent prowess; *they* are slavering beasts begging for his weapon, his brutality, his commands. The elements here of compensation, of self-serving fantasy, of fictions generated by just-buried fears seem to me manifest. Similar insecurity may be betrayed in his manly American hatred for the homosexual.

Other sorts of exhibitionism strike me as no less suspicious. Elaborate contrivances are arranged so that he will be "forced" to display his ingenuity—the Nostradamus speech, the Three Little Bears parody, so gratuitous and inane. He is "trapped" into confessions of his own generosity. Nor is it enough for him to be a sexual, literary, and mental prodigy; he must also be a wizard at the piano, at cycling, at rollerskating, a master gourmet.

Henry's insulting mockery of all his "friends" and associates

—especially those whose claims against him are strongest—strikes me as far beyond their desert; but so does his religious idealization of the learned and travelled man. In both cases, I think, what we are hearing is the undercurrent of Miller's own insecurity, his self-dissatisfaction.

Far surpassing all of these, though, as evidence of Miller's secret doubts, of his anxious need to prop up his pretensions, are the quoted testimonials. It is not only the narrator who talks inexhaustibly about Henry Miller: so does everyone else. I have counted at least forty separate instances of third-person testimonials, invented and written by Miller (what could he have been thinking as he wrote them?); and spoken, purportedly, by characters of every sort in *The Rosy Crucifixion;* spoken either to Henry directly, or to another person in his presence. In either case, his usual response is "to blush deeply," though rarely to protest.

I grant that he tries to make light of some excesses of praise ("another Jesus," "another Dostoevsky"). I grant that he pretends, on occasion, to doubt them ("I never considered myself a remarkable talker, though they insisted I was."). I grant that many of these self-contrived testimonials acknowledge not so much his greatness as the traits of his character—his gaiety, idealism, insouciance, venturesomeness. I even grant that two or three are negative and frankly critical.

But the overwhelming lot are commendatory, admiring, even awestruck. It is one of the strangest performances in literature: *Hommage à moi; Advertisements for Myself.*

> "I have a hunch you're cut out for something big."
> I blushed and tried to pass it off.
> "Come," said Fletcher, "don't be so modest. You've got qualities, anyone can see that. I don't know what you're going to become—saint, poet, or philosopher. But you're an artist, that's definite. And what's more, you're unspoiled."

" 'I don't know any writer in America who has greater gifts than you.' " "He used to say my talk could send him home drunk." " 'You were made to walk through the fires. You have Mongol blood.' " " 'You can't be spoiled. You only take what you need.' " " 'You too old! I can see you burning up the cinders at eighty. You're another Bernard Shaw. You'll never be too old for anything.' " " 'I feel almost as if I were with a god,' " says one of his bed-partners, after. " 'It was a wonderful performance,' she said. . . . 'You almost killed me. . . . Can you fuck like that every night?' "

A strong, whole-hearted egomaniac-artist, I feel, would not need this artificial support. A man of normal self-esteem would be too embarrassed to quote (or create) anything but the smallest fraction of it, too aware of the hyperbolic effect. But a minor egotist-artist, whose achievement and reception fall far short of his ideal self-image, might well try to pad them out with such stuffing; self-praise given the veneer of objectivity; borrowed props for a top-heavy ego. See the posthumous memoirs of Proust's friend Robert de Montesquiou.

At rare and precious moments, Miller *is* able to admit consciously his own failings, his own sham, his own self-doubt. One such examination of conscience occurs in the last of his letters to Durrell in the published correspondence: the clarity of his vision of himself there is enough to stop the heart. Putting aside the false blushes, the "Me-the-little-shit-from-Brooklyn" pose of humility, one can discover such moments of self-revelation in the *Crucifixion* as well, glowing like diamonds in the mud.

> What have I got to tell the world which is so desperately important? What have I to say that has not been said before, and thousands of times, by men infinitely more gifted? Was it sheer ego, this coercive need to be heard? In what way was I unique? For if I was not unique then it would be like adding a cipher to an incalculable astronomic figure.

Sometimes these take the form of outspoken criticism by others. Maude, MacGregor, and Kronski are all allowed to tell Henry painful truths. There is a woman seer of sorts, early in *Sexus*, whole merciless analysis of his faults and virtues makes it clear that Miller does indeed "know himself."

The real break-through of self-awareness, though, coincides with the episode of the highest art, the most intense and affecting drama of the trilogy: the final chapter of *Sexus*, to which I have already made reference several times; and to the more conscious, untransformed version of the same story—Henry's place in a tri-sexual *ménage à trois*—in *Nexus*.

The question of the genuineness of these memoirs, of the equivalence between the lives of Henry the character and Miller the writer, is one I have generally left alone. I have no sure way of knowing the facts in any case, and by my artistic standards the question should be of secondary importance. For the most part I believe "Henry" to be a semi-fictional character, an earlier self revised, improved, and used for the needs of a Miller twenty or thirty years later. He might have made a good character in someone else's novel, but the demands of the writing-Miller were so imperious that his alter ego was rarely allowed the freedom to break into life.

Rarely: but not never. There are occasions when present-Miller *does* try to step out of the picture, and let the real life, the real emotions of his past self take over.

Certain bits of Brooklyn boyhood nostalgia, very small, very sad, are also very real. The vivid scenes of his prodigal-son returns to the family *foyer*, the exact etchings of his mother, are done with fine filial hate. The Christmas Dinner in *Nexus*, for example, has an authentic, bitter American accent. It is so obviously real it leaps from the book. So do several scenes with Maude and Mona, the two women (with his mother) who are something more for him than voids to be filled. The final break with Maude, his grim marriage to Mona, his guilty attempts to see his daughter—these are totally credible, undistorted by authorial egoism. Some descriptions of his early attempts at writing also have the unalloyed ring of truth.

But it is in recalling the intrusion into his life of his wife's friend Anastasia that he unites the finest art with the deepest self-revelation.

I have asked myself why I am so profoundly struck by this story, both in its emblematic guise at the tail of *Sexus* and in its more attenuated, narrative form in *Nexus*, when almost nothing else in Miller's writing can produce in me the *frisson*, the indelible internal reshaping that is the mark of sure creative art.

The story is first told in surrealistic metaphor, so far out of chronological sequence that one does not yet know who "the big woman" is; what Henry's situation is; how and when it all came about. But the very fact of its sudden, so clearly compulsive relation, out of all order, at the end of *Sexus*—like the key memory, so long buried, that at least breaks out after protracted months of fruitless psychoanalysis—this, *and* the irresistible *rightness* of the surrealism, the unconscious metaphors (the cellar, the dog, the rides in the dark, the rats, the shooting, the beating that is and is not real, the marrow bone-ring): these stun the reader with the authenticity of the event. It is as real as nightmare, as Hitler, as human evil, as Gregor Samsa's transformation; as real as the broken beat of a heart. If it has been transformed, surrealized, it is only so that the *whole* truth might be told, as only art can tell it: not to let us know what happened (the banal facts behind it are revealed 640 pages later); but to make us feel what Henry felt. If you know and can detect the beat of alive, confessional art, art that is a necessary, life-saving creation of the artist's unconscious, as opposed to willed, schooled, conscious art; if you can hear the purgatorial, personal accents of truth behind the fictions of Proust or Kafka, Strindberg or Beckett: then I think you will hear them in Chapter 23.

I ask myself whether my response to this chapter is only a piece of aesthetic/moral prejudice. Do I simply *prefer* an episode where the present-time narrator, the 1949 Miller is entirely effaced and absent, where the semi-fictional 1927 character is allowed full and absolute rule, in the traditional manner of the novel? Yes I do. But because, in this case, the "real" Miller so often lies, whereas the artful fiction tells the truth. Do I simply prefer a Henry Miller insulted and injured, facing despair, *not* smug, *not* "merry and bright," because that suits my own temperament, my own philosophic vision? Do I regard him as honest and authentic, and the "gay sage" a sham, because *I* am faithless and pessimistic? Perhaps: but what of Miller's professed kinship to Dostoevsky, to whom he has never been closer? What I am responding to here is the accent of truth: what I resist elsewhere is the hollow note of sham. I cannot put it more clearly.

The details that follow in the opening chapters of *Nexus* are, in a way, anti-climactic, like the painstaking job of reintegration that must follow the key "break" in a psychoanalysis. It is proof, I think, of Miller's art, of my aesthetic of truth, and of the particularly *living* truth of this story that it loses no whit of its force in a sequential, mundane retelling. This is not to say that Miller tells it easily. The key fact of the story—that his wife is a Lesbian, at least in part, that he must now share her with, even relinquish her to a mannish Bohemian—this he ignores, hides, resists in a score of ways: by releasing the evidence but rejecting the conclusions; by pretending to content himself with her or her brother's denials; by letting it be said explicitly—"your wife and her friend: a couple of bull-dykers"—only by another, and *in a dream;* even by trying to deceive himself with prickly verbal screens:

> "We know how to make our own way . . . giving exhibitions . . . pretending that we're Lesbians . . . pretending that we're make-believe Lesbians. Pretending pretending . . . I'm sick of it."

But this resistance only tightens the tension. It makes it all the more painfully clear that what he is telling—or trying not to tell—is true; that it is, in fact, one of the radical truths of his life.

> Once I thought that I had been wounded as no man ever had. . . . Because I felt thus I vowed to write this book. But long before I began the book, the wound was healed. Since I had sworn to fulfill my task I reopened the horrible wound.

This passage comes from the end of *Plexus,* and makes no direct allusion to the nature of the "wound." But the words that follow, the first words of *Nexus,* are exactly the same as the last words of *Sexus.* And the effect, on the reader who can remember back 640 pages, is devastating. The truth of truths, denied for two volumes, is about to be told, the horrible wound reopened. This egoist of egoists, this tower of self-assurance, this monumental, self-celebrating phallic symbol was, for several hellish months, passionately, degradingly enslaved to a Lesbian wife, and forced to live *à trois* with her mistress.

> . . . there must be something wrong with a man—at least so the world reckons—when his wife is violently attracted to another woman.

There is the wound. Little by little, he reveals the whole story: Mona's devious, Proustian insinuations to "poison his mind"; his own diabolical schemes against Stasia; his manic attempts to win back his wife; his hysterical nightmares of despair; his animal degradation; the Pirandellian "play" he writes, each of the three playing his own part; his total collapse when the girls finally run off to Europe together.

> I saw in every phase and moment of his pitiful weakness the utter wretch I had been, the blackguard, nothing less, who had striven so vainly and ignominiously to protect his miserable little heart. I saw that it had never been broken, as I imagined, but that, paralyzed by fear, it had shrunk almost to nothingness.

One day he finds himself writing of it; and suddenly realizes that his torture must be over, that the wound has crusted closed.

This is the story that Miller had to tell; and only here is it told. It could be, it almost was made into a great novel. But I have artificially reassembled it, according to my taste for truth and design, out of the bits and pieces sown through the 1600-page mélange I have already too extensively described. It exists, in this shape, nowhere but in my own imagination. *Si sic omnia dixit:* Had he always written thus.

I had planned to conclude with a moral assessment of the man, based primarily on my interpretation of the thirty-five fucking-scenes of *Sexus*. But I am tired of this work, and find I have neither the Godlike presumption for final judgments, nor the stomach to wade through that ocean of semen again. I do think Miller sick (at least while writing *Sexus*), self-imprisoned, unable to love or know tenderness, unintentionally cruel, impotent in the most serious way. But the passionate responses of my reading grow dilute and mechanical, as more and more days pass since I closed the books; and I am far more inclined now to sympathy than to censure. Maybe I *have* no business here. Let me turn, with more mercy than justice, for a hail and farewell, to the one Henry Miller I have ever been able to admire—perhaps another fiction—the friend and correspondent of Lawrence Durrell:

. . . Perhaps in the summing up, my life will be seen to be a huge pyramid erected over a minus sign. Still, nevertheless, a pyramid.

. . . Looking back over my tumultuous writings, I begin to wonder if perhaps I was not trying to hide something? Or perhaps I was hiding from myself . . .

Henry Miller and
Lawrence Durrell [1963]

Lawrence Durrell and Henry Miller have been writing back and forth for twenty-eight years, ever since the young Englishman wrote an exuberant, Millerian fan letter to the author of *Tropic of Cancer* in 1935. By now, one would think, they should understand each other. But the obvious and near-tragic fact that emerges from the selection of their letters is that neither does, or ever has. For twenty-eight years, despite occasional glimpses of the truth, the two writers have been trying to make one another over into images of themselves. That their friendship has maintained itself undiminished through all these years of mutual nonrecognition is simply a triumph of the men over the writers.

At first glance, these painfully honest letters appear to chronicle the spectacular rise of the junior correspondent and the pathetic decline of the senior. Miller's only really "famous" work was written before the series began, and year by year, shrinking into his sullen exile, he finds himself less and less regarded—except by Durrell. One reads the book, in fact, not as Miller's story but as Durrell's, plotting his growth against the sadly static image of his early mentor and master, from the early, Miller-aping *Black Book* to the international celebrity of the *Alexandria Quartet*. But, though Durrell indeed has grown, Miller, against appearances, has not declined: he has simply never moved.

Durrell kept expecting Miller to change, to "write his great work," kept hoping he would, while all the time Miller kept insisting he *could* not and never would. It was integral to his primitivist credo, as man and as writer—for him, there is no distinction; one's writing is simply a function of one's life—that one established a position and stayed there, rock-hard, unyielding, and unmoved. There is a certain stern nobility in his attitude, and, as one hears the same unflinching principles repeated over and over in Miller's letters to an ever less sympathetic, ever less comprehending Durrell, one begins to acquire the respect he feels this long-misunderstood man deserves. In one way, *because* of this monolithic sameness, because, in part, of the suffering and neglect it was certain to bring him—as he well knew—Miller is actually the better served by this revealing exhibition. Of the two, he is, there is no question, decidedly the lesser writer; but he is, as Durrell himself seems to recognize, the greater man. These letters may help one to forget all of Miller's tediously blathering books and to focus on the far more important fact of the man himself.

What Miller is not, first of all, is a "man of letters"—he has nothing to do with "art," with "literature," as most of us regard it. He writes only as a necessary means of self-discovery, as part of his lifelong search for the truth; because he must: "I am doomed to write perpetually." "Literature!" he quotes Balzac writing to George Sand: "But, my dear lady, literature doesn't exist! There is life, of which politics and art are part. And I am a man that's alive, that's all—a man living his life, nothing more." And later, "Where does creation lie—in the one thing done or in the effect? What and how a man does, acts, thinks, talks, everyday is what counts, no?"

With standards like these, one cannot expect much in the way of "art." Miller has almost no sense of "taste" or discrimination, in his own work or that of others—though his five-page critique of *Clea* and, looking back, of the *Quartet* as a whole, is surprisingly keen. But he was even more enthusiastic about *The Black Book*—or the work of Céline ("Still the best writer alive today . . ."), Cendrars, Powys, Giono—or Kerouac. He revels in Hindu arcana, Zen, astrology. He delights equally in the best and the worst of his own voluminous autobiographizing, and insists, against Durrell's hopeless pleas that he develop *some* critical sense, that the most unreadable of his surrealistic fantasias are every bit as important as both the *Tropics* together. And, of course, they are.

The pity of all this stern anti-literary nobility is, unfortunately, that for almost anyone but himself Henry Miller has precious little to say—or precious little worth reading. As Durrell developed, year by year, his own critical sense, discovered the controlled, artistic self that was to dream *Justine* and its sequels, he began, perversely, trying to read Miller's works as "literature," to judge them as "art." When he got to *Sexus* in 1949, the first volume of the three-volume gargantua that Miller calls *The Rosy Crucifixion*, he balked:

> But my dear Henry, the moral vulgarity of so much of it is *artistically* painful. . . . All the wild resonance of *Cancer* and *Black Spring* has gone, and you have failed to develop what is really new in your prose, and what should set a crown on your work. The new mystical outlines are all there; but they are lost, lost, damn it, in this shower of lavatory filth which no longer seems tonic and bracing, but just excrementitious and sad. One winces and averts the face. What on earth has made you slip back on a simple matter of *taste*—artistic taste?

Five days later, having waded through all twelve hundred pages, he desperately cabled: "SEXUS DISGRACEFULLY BAD WILL COMPLETELY RUIN REPUTATION UNLESS WITHDRAWN REVISED LARRY."

Miller, with remarkable grace, accepted his friend's "defection," and patiently tried to explain once again what he was doing. Before this rare display of tolerance and benignity, Durrell retracted at once, and begged the Master's forgiveness; and the crisis passed. But Durrell was obviously right. As books, as "literature," so many of these things of Miller's are very nearly worthless. The gory, gratuitous obscenity that so dismayed his dearest friend is, of course, Miller's most notorious "inelegance"; but the pages in between can be equally distressing. Miller is committed, for one thing, to an autobiographical, "ego-protagonist" mode—it is all he has ever used: "all this Brobdingnagian experience must be vomited forth." Which would be well enough, except that most of Miller's life, for all the sex, has been awesomely dull. His motley associates, the "heroes" of his "novels," have been for the most part a sordid grab bag of crackpots and cranks, panhandlers and astrologers and undiscovered writers—the sort of people who simply cannot retain one's interest through twenty or twenty-five books.

His "philosophy," if it may be called that, often rambles off into untrackable pseudo-mystical realms, but at core it is and always has been an apocalyptic doom-shouting condemnation of the whole of civilization. He simply doesn't like it: we were better off in caves. Since almost none of this, however, finds its way into the letters, one begins to wonder just how serious it all is. The Miller here revealed, the same, almost, from first page to last, is this unyielding anti-literary Ego, writing himself out laughing in book after rambling book.

"If one lived long enough the whole man would come through in the work—ideas, sensations, experience, philosophy, aesthetic, and everything . . . All these 'new trends and directions' which the critics discern with each new work—all this sort of apperception is false." He is childlike, sensitive, very proud, high-spirited, totally uncritical, alternately gay to the point of euphoria and despairing to the point of suicide. He curses a civilization that he does not understand, reviles a country he is unable to leave, and dismisses as worthless all the major authors he has never taken the trouble to read. He refuses to make any effort to commercialize himself, to "earn a living," but harasses his acquaintances to support him ("You call yourselves my friends.") in petulant open letters—and they do. I do not pretend wholly to understand such a man—even Durrell, who should of all people be able, all too obviously fails. But his letters here, cleared of the cant and rhetoric of his books, offer as clear a picture as we are ever likely to get. They prove, at least, if proof were needed, that the Dirty Old Man who still represents the greater part of his public image is really only a fractional, though integral, fragment of the whole —a whole that is huge, unchanging, probably unique, and the closest thing our century is likely to produce to a genuine Noble Savage.

But one reads this correspondence, as I say, not so much to piece together the picture of a Henry Miller as to trace the growth of Durrell—a growth seen, increasingly, as one moving away from the fixed and unfertile point of the Master. The first stage in this development extends from the original exchange of adulatory letters to the completion of Durrell's *The Black Book* in the spring of 1937. So far, they are virtually step in step. The already notorious, middle-aged author of the *Tropics*, up in Paris, could not say enough fine things about *The Black Book:* he thought that he had discovered another Henry Miller. "Your commercial career is finished," he chortles. "From now on you're an outlaw . . . You are *the* master of the English language. . . . This is way beyond Lawrence and the whole tribe."

The new master of the language began to show signs of rebellion, however, signs of what Miller could only regard as a dangerous and spineless truckling to the world. The artist, he had warned Durrell, was committed to becoming "a traitor to the human race"; but his new disciple was giving disquieting evidence of wanting to rejoin it. For one thing, he appeared willing to expurgate *The Black Book* in order to get it published. Henry stepped in at once, spoke of "conscience" and "moral responsibility," and Durrell backed down, awestruck and ashamed. Next came the more serious question of Durrell's "double life," his insistence, as it were, on eating the cake of bourgeois security and spitting it out as well. This Miller could *not* understand. The following exchange, from July of 1937, dramatizes in an essential way this difference between the two men. Durrell writes:

> . . . I CAN'T WRITE REAL BOOKS ALL THE TIME. . . . Already the B.B. has played havoc with me. What I want is this, frankly. Once every three years or more I shall try to compose for full orchestra. The rest of the time I shall do essays, travel books, perhaps one more novel under Charles Norden [his Dr. Jekyll pseudonym]. . . . I think you will probably feel this is traitorous or something, but you must understand that I need my friend Norden in order to keep my peace of mind and be happy a little and love. . . .

And Miller:

> Don't, my good Durrell, take the schizophrenic route. . . . what is the penalty, after all? What can they do to you—THEY? . . . If, as you say, you can't write REAL books all the time, then don't write. Don't write anything . . .

The warning was heartfelt and strong, but of course ineffectual. Durrell, literarily, is still happily schizoid, writing spacetime continua with the right hand and diplomatic low comedy with the left. ("All this is very perplexing to my fans who don't know whether I am P. G. Wodehouse or James Joyce or what the hell.") The disciple, already, was drifting away.

Through the late 30's, when the two finally met in person, first in Paris and then in Greece (see Miller's *The Colossus of Maroussi*), the breach widened, as Durrell took more and more a part in the human race from which Miller was more and more retreating. Miller writes that he must withdraw, to meditate and write; Durrell writes back, from his once-despised England, "I have written nothing but grown in humanity half a cubit." Miller raves to him about Tibetan yoga and the Zen masters—"It drives me wild, delirious with joy"; while Durrell discovers the Palladian green loveliness of Warwickshire, rediscovers the grandeur of Shakespeare—he even loves the swans and the tourists of Stratford. They are writing at, not to, one another, from two different worlds.

The crucial years for Durrell, for Miller too, in a way, for so many people, were the war years. Miller retreated—from civilization, if you will—to America. He drove sixteen thousand miles, first, about this "Air-Conditioned Nightmare"; then, shrinking as far off to the edges as he could, settled into a borrowed, ramshackle cabin at Big Sur, California—one of the most spectacularly beautiful seacoasts in the world.

While he sat there fending off the tourists, playing Pingpong, and spewing out reams of *The Rosy Crucifixion*—the sum of his activity, virtually, for the next fifteen years—Durrell had actively rejoined the world, and was working for the British Information Office—in Alexandria! "I have a wonderful idea for a novel on Alexandria . . . ," he writes one day in August, 1944; and from then on we are reading paragraphs and pages from the embryonic Quartet in his letters to Big Sur.

But more important still, for Durrell, was the experience of war, of statecraft and public starvation, of "history as reality" —the sort of drastically maturing experience that Miller had purposely fled. He tries, over and over, to explain to Henry what it is all about. "We live in an atmosphere of privation,

spiritual as well as physical; and from all over Asia and Europe
the famine reports are pouring in. It's hard to feel anything
until you've seen the effects of the war. It's lucky you have
been spared them. Athens would make you weep: smashed
currency, labour shortage, dearth of raw materials, hunger,
syphilis, and the ruin of the common man. Only the rich still
glitter." Later still, from Yugoslavia—Durrell is on the Foreign
Service circuit by now: Press Attaché, Director of Public Re-
lations; Buenos Aires, Belgrade, Cyprus—

> . . . my dear Henry, you are crazy. You cannot have the
> faintest idea what a communist country is like. . . . No, but
> you won't understand even now. BUT IF YOU CAME HERE FOR
> JUST A WEEK, you'd realize that even a great war would be jus-
> tified to prevent THIS, and liberate the millions under the yoke
> of this tyranny, this moral prison. . . . But you will disapprove.

After the war, Durrell finds himself more and more reconciled to England, and has become fast friends with—of all people—his publisher and new mentor, T. S. Eliot. One wonders
what Miller must have thought. Durrell even presumes now to
advise and to criticize; the roles are beginning to reverse. ". . .
Like all American geniuses you have no sense of form whatso-
ever . . . you have lost a good deal of critical control . . .
quite half of *Murder the Murderer* [Miller's nihilistic response
to the war] could have been blue-pencilled out. It seemed
repetitive and platitudinous." Something less than subtle has
happened to the relationship, although neither yet seems entirely aware. "I occasionally read your frenzied appeals to
reason in the avant garde papers—sounding but so remote . . ."
The oceanic gap that now divided them was suddenly and
cruelly laid bare, as we have seen, by Durrell's outspoken condemnation of *Sexus* in September of 1949, and as frantically
covered up again. Although they quickly pretend it never happened—they were, after all, friends first and critics only a far
distant second—this ugly episode discovers just how very far
Durrell had grown from Miller since his return to America,
how much he had forgotten what it *was* that Miller had devoted his life to doing. Otherwise, how could he possibly have
troubled Henry over questions of "moral vulgarity," "critical
sense," "failing to develop"—of "taste," for heaven's sake, of

"ruining his reputation"? These were now, of course, among Durrell's own major concerns, but they had never been Miller's. That Durrell was "bitterly disappointed" in the book was perhaps to be expected; but that he could have so lost sight of the Master as to expect him to heed, even to understand, his so-"literary" critique is astonishing.

Durrell is more careful after this; one feels more and more the tension of benevolent reticence, of remembered praise and ritual congratulation. Miller is, he realizes, simply too fine a man to be hurt like that again: there are more important things than "taste." *Sexus* comes up for a hesitant, more kindly review, eight years too late. "I found somewhat to my surprise that *Sexus* which I was once so shocked and disgusted by is really as great as *Tropic*—only it is very unpruned." Even his desperate, so sensible attempt to convince Miller, through four successive letters, of the cheap, pretentious-sentimental banality of the Kerouac & Co. Beats ("They need a week at a French lycée to be taught to think and construct"—the *new* Durrell talking—Eliot's Durrell)—even this, so obviously serious and sincere, backs down at last into respectful, filial acquiescence. "Don't be angry with me for not going along on this book. Maybe it has fine things in it which are not on my wavelength. . . . I may have been unjust . . ."

Proposing his own Quartet, which so evidently satisfies *him*, Durrell is to Miller uncertain, apologetic: "(Christ, you will say disapprovingly. The conscious artist.)" Of *Mountolive*, he is positively ashamed. It is so "naturalistic," so un-Miller. "You may yawn your head off . . ." (Henry, of course, loves it, effusively. "My dear man, don't say such things, ever, not to anyone. That book is a perfect gem." Two can play the same game.)

On matters not directly concerned with the now off-limits grounds of their writings, the two can still serve as each other's best conscience—as they have since the letters began. Uproot yourself from America, Durrell insists. It's ruining you. ". . . America is really harming you, making you critically soft. . . . I feel that a visit to Europe is essential to you for your work . . ." In return, Miller kept nagging away at Durrell to get out of the Foreign Service, to quit everything else and write. "Is it so impossible? You'll always be working for someone, if you think it's 'necessary.' Take a good think some day. Map out your life as you'd like to live it. Then jump!" Durrell did "jump," at last, in December of 1952, and from here on the book is his—his and Justine's, Pursewarden's, Narouz's, Melissa's.

With that, as the world knows, he was in: Henry, at the end of his fine critique on the *Alexandria Quartet*, handed over the crown. Translations, prizes, Book-of-the-Month Club, Durrell's own problems with fans and reporters, honors from the Queen Mother followed in order. Durrell was now writing introductions for Miller, trying to pay back a long-standing debt. Miller responds—an exchange typical of their later relationship —with a gracious preface to the French *Justine*.

Against the triumph of Durrell, the tragedy of Miller, now juxtaposed letter for letter, stands out all the more starkly. It is with a certain pain that we watch as this sixty-eight-year-old monument comes at last to the kind of bitterly honest introspection in depth that monuments should never have to make:

> What I feel like saying sometimes—when the whole bloody *Crucifixion* comes to an end—is "Ladies and Gentlemen, don't believe a word of it, it was all a hoax. Let me tell you in a few words the story of my tragedy; I can do it in twenty pages."
>
> And what would be the story? That, wanting desperately to become a writer, I became a writer. In the process I sinned. I became so involved with the Holy Ghost that I betrayed my wife, my child, my friends, my country. I fell in love with the medium. I thought—if one makes a stroke on the blackboard that is the thing in itself, the reality. I almost fell in love with myself, horrible thought. I recorded what I saw and felt, not what was.

Or perhaps the triumph, as well as the tragedy, is really Miller's. He raises, in the last letter here, Yeats's central question: "Perfection of the life, or of the work?" Pleased, proud of his onetime disciple's success, he is still not sure. "All I was trying to say, bedazzled as I was, and it was like trying to put a knife into a crevice, was: 'What's it all about?' After the last line, *what?* After the television appearances, after the Académie, *what?*" What, indeed.

The Permanence
of Durrell [1965]

Critics who have ventured to revisit and review Lawrence Durrell's *Alexandria Quartet* in the five years since its completion have been remarkably hesitant, however strongly (or reservedly) they profess their admiration, to make any claims for its longevity or future acceptance. The best of them did go so far once as to risk putting it somewhere between *Green Mansions* and *Wuthering Heights,* which seems to me hedging one's bet so safely as not to be betting at all; there is a tolerably vast region between. The oddity is that most of them *have* liked it, have found great wonders to sing of in this four-storied monument to the imagination. They have also found, again almost universally, defects and deficiencies—a certain lack of seriousness, a thinness of "content"—but very few seemed to doom it altogether for these. The French, in fact, who consider Durrell more theirs than ours, were delighted at the escape it offered from their own increasingly, distressingly overcerebral fiction.

There is an unconfessed suspicion of impermanence in this very sort of welcome, however, and it is striking how many critics, French, English, and American, have tended to regard Durrell in these terms—as a "refreshing corrective," a healthy antidote, a brief interlude in the sun before going back to Beckett and Camus; or as the herald, with Nabokov, of a "renaissance of Prose"—which, while high praise, seems somehow not high enough. Heralds tend to be forgotten once the renaissance begins.

One means of eluding a final judgment on Durrell has been to insist on the need for the years of distance required for subsequent, more objective rereadings. Perhaps here my experience with the *Quartet* can save us some time: I have, for five different very good reasons, read it through five times already —the equivalent, let us say, of ten years distance in time. Much of the monument, I can tell you, *does* disintegrate under repeated attack, and not only the pot-boiling plot-making of *Mountolive*. The whole elaborate substructure, in fact, becomes increasingly less interesting, and one begins to remember the *Quartet*, as one reads it, in brilliant bits and pieces. Durrell once wrote to a friend, "If the *Quartet* remains readable in ten years I believe that the form will interest you more than the content"—an odd thing for any author to say, even one so compulsively interested in form. However, if by "content" Durrell meant his famous multi-sexed and many-faceted "investigation of modern love," his prediction has come true. *That*, for all its high pretensions, wore through rather quickly; while the complex game of narrators and time-shifts—the "form"—if not as exhilarating as the first time (when one had no idea how it was going to come out), is still fun to play.

Still it is, after all, somewhat academic to think of content only as the schematic or philosophic justification, the "meaning" or message of a novel. One can reduce, and many—including Durrell—have reduced the *Alexandria Quartet* to an exotic and intricate dramatization of certain Ideas, ideas like the relativity, the shifting multiplicity of truth and the non-existence of discrete personality; the disintegration of directional time; the belief in an unwilled, sensual *Élan Vital* that propels human actions and renders sexual union our most certain means to knowledge (this his ostensible excuse, as if he needed one, for all the sex). But this is certainly not defining the *Quartet*. The *Alexandria Quartet* will remain readable in ten years, if my abridged-decade's worth of reading is any indication, but not for any such rationally-distilled content as this. These overinsisted and (here, at least) uninteresting ideas, either platitudinous or unconvincing, have already, most of them, become something of a bore.

If we think of content, rather, as what happens in the books, the events, the episodes—or better, what happens to *us*, the in-process fact of the reading experience—then we must take issue with the author. These, the events, will assuredly last; and the labyrinth of form will one day be seen in its true, its instrumental value, as little more than the device that Durrell found necessary to "set his novel free to dream." All the Chinese boxes of narrators and editors and emendators, the fictions of Darley's Greek-island manuscript and Balthazar's great Interlinear and Justine's Diaries and Pursewarden's notebook, the letters-within-letters and novels-within-novels—all this, and perhaps all the Gnostic-cum-Einsteinian philosophy as well will be recognized as the elaborate means Durrell was forced to use, for whatever unconscious reasons, to release the fantastic imaginative energy of his Alexandrian visions. These and the sensuous, evocative language with which they are built, unquestionably represent the content of most lasting value in all the *Quartet*. It is on these, and not his tendentious "meanings" and convoluted form, that Durrell's one strongest claim to permanence must rest. It may be worth looking into just how strong a claim this is.

The Durrellian Imagination is a creative organ of awesome fertility: its equal for power and inventiveness has rarely been seen since Dickens. It can charge a single word or phrase or image into stunning surreality; it can capture all Alexandria with a play of random notes.

> And when night falls and the white city lights up the thousand candelabra of its parks and buildings, tunes in to the soft unearthly drum-music of Morocco or Caucasus, it looks like some great crystal liner asleep there, anchored to the horn of Africa— her diamond and fire-opal reflections twisting downwards like polished bars into the oily harbour among the battleships.

> At dusk it can become like a mauve jungle, anomalous, stained with colours as if from a shattered prism; and rising into the pearly sky of the sunset falter up the steeples and minarets like stalks of giant fennel in a swamp, rising up over the long pale lines of the sea-shore and the barbaric cafés where the negroes dance to the pop and drub of a finger-drum or to the mincing of clarinets.

Like the heroes of Dickens novels, the title-characters of the *Quartet*—even that Zionist sphinx, the near-mythical Justine—tend to pale somewhat, to elude one on rereading. But again like Dickens, the minor characters—Scobie of course, De Capo, Melissa, Memlik Pasha, Pombal, Leila, the Virtuous Samira—Narouz!—are the surest signs of their author's imaginative powers, and destined to at least some kind of immortality. (George Steiner, in an excellent essay, called Scobie "the finest comic invention in English since *Tristram Shandy*." Durrell is nowhere more at ease, nowhere is his imagination in higher gear, than in the all-too-few pages of Joshua Scobie. If Pursewarden represents the most distasteful, the most personally unpleasant aspect of his author, Scobie is surely his richest, most ingratiating self.)

The Durrellian Imagination in action is capable of even grander things. As epic in stature as is Narouz, alone and standing still with his camel's harelip and his great *kurbash*, how much greater an achievement is Narouz breaking the wild Arab horse in the desert; Narouz confronting the Mazgub; Narouz gone prophetically mad, flicking bats to death with his whip in his brother's face; Narouz, like some apocalyptic monster, dying surrounded by all the sensuous nightmare of the East. It is scenes like these one remembers as the Alexandrian visions. It is these scenes, even more than the language or characters, and far more than the "Form" or "Ideas," that represent Durrell's most convincing claim to posterity. Such visions can be richly, romantically humane, like the duck-shoot that closes *Justine* or the fish-drive that opens *Mountolive;* like Nessim's great hallucinatory dream, like "Mountolive in Nighttown"—the drunken ambassador trapped in the house of child prostitutes—they can be madness itself.

What is it like, the imagination that can conjure up such visions? At first glance, the *Quartet* seems easy to parody: one has but to catch the musing, nostalgic, *fin de siècle* Darleyan tone, construct a vocabulary around words like "etiolated," "vertiginous," and "languor," and crowd the canvas with enough images of scorpions and dead foetuses done in amethyst, nacre, and mauve. But (though Durrell would be the first to appreciate a really good parody) one would still be a long way from reproducing the imagination behind. For one thing, and this many have seen, Durrell's sensitivity to language is something more than preciosity or affectation. He has a feeling for the quiet music and the tactile sensuosity of words that recalls Forster or Fitzgerald at their best, that recalls, as they do, their master Keats, or his master Virgil. He can, to choose the outstanding example, recreate sounds in a way unequalled by anyone writing.

> From the outer perimeter of darkness came the crisp click of sportsmen at singlestick, dimly sounding against the hoarse rumble of the approaching procession with its sudden bursts of wild music—kettle-drums and timbrels like volleys of musketry —and the long belly-thrilling roll of the camel-drums which drowned and refreshed the quavering deep-throated flute-music . . . the peristaltic measures of the wild music—nibbled out everywhere by the tattling flutes and the pang of drums or the long shivering orgasm of tambourines. . . .

The deathwatch over Narouz that closes *Mountolive* becomes a whole *symphonie fantastique* of such images of sounds.

The key to much of this success is not, as it may seem, any curious hypersensitivity to sensation—Durrell is probably inventing most of these sounds—but the author's remarkable knack for discovering the image that so vividly seems to create it. Durrell took issue once with the English critics who were "scoring him," he complained, "like boxing referees (two points per good metaphor)." But there is no question that it is the texture of Durrellian metaphor that creates the "heraldic world" of Alexandria, a world in which the images, the insects and diseases and mythical figures to which characters and objects are compared, become at last at least as real, often far more real than the characters and objects themselves. (As he confesses. "I want to frame them [the Alexandrians] in the heavy steel webs of metaphors which will last half as long as the city itself." *Justine*.) Durrell is the most lushly, effectively metaphoric prose writer of our time; and the *kinds* of images he chooses to use do a great deal to create the world he would have us wander in. A diplomat looks "glum as a foetus in a bottle"; Hamid shuffles about "like a boa-constrictor muttering softly"; "events crawling over one another like wet crabs in a basket," "soft cobweb voices," dirigibles like greasy buttocks, a hand running across the counterpane like a frightened rat, clouds growing like a scab or turning black like an ink-squid, huge faces "like the belly of a whale turned upwards in death," "the palpitating viscera" of a watch rupturing the fine membrane of consciousness, Narouz' prostitute "like a huge caterpillar nibbling a lettuce," Narouz himself some great hairy spider and Capodistria more a snake than a man. The images, whether consciously or unconsciously chosen, create a weirdly non-human fantasy-world, existing as if parallel to and above the world of the Alexandrians: a world, precisely, of scabs, buttocks, viscera, whale bellies, and caterpillars, a world of pure imagination not far removed from nightmare. One has only to imagine the *Quartet* stripped of such monstrous metaphors to realize how important to the total experience this Other World is.

Although the exoticism of the setting and the skillful control of dramatic tension contribute strongly to the fully-achieved Alexandrian visions, even here a great part of the effect may be attributed to the subtle dream-distortion of metaphor. Nessim's great historical dreams in *Justine*, the Carnival in *Balthazar*, Narouz and the Bats in *Mountolive* all realize their full potential of nightmarish intensity through the infusion of this other world of imagery. At best, such scenes are grounded in the sort of affecting and honestly-achieved psychological tension that makes the nightmares believable, that make the dreams *our* dreams. The most successful of these anti-realistic interludes is the "Mountolive in Nighttown" sequence, the effect of which, in a very few pages, is remarkably similar to the "Circe" episode of *Ulysses*, or the carnival scene in Lowry's *Under the Volcano*.

Concentrating on Durrell's purely imaginative achievement, I do not want to undervalue his skill as a dramatist, as a craftsman of dramatic encounters. The brief Nessim-Melissa affair in *Justine*, even Darley's with Clea in *Clea* are handsomely sustained relationships of a poignant and very credible intensity. Time and again Durrell sets for himself "encounter"-scenes that would be a challenge for the most skillful of psychological novelists—and brings them off: Darley and Cohen, Narouz and the Mazgub, Narouz insane and Nessim, Mountolive and the aging Leila; or he maintains a gripping, almost (again) Dickensian suspense in episodes like Clea's near-drowning or the murder of Narouz. But he can fail quite as easily, and, in the larger drama of "plot," he will sink to the level of the cheapest Foreign Intrigue film. While admitting, then, the presence of occasional skills such as these, I would still be unwilling to risk a vote for Durrell's permanence on the basis of anything short of his unique and prodigious imagination.

One has still not fully defined this imagination, however—and this point *must* be made—until he has added the irresistible, all-fusing element of humor. Durrell simply cannot take himself seriously, or when he seems to, when he adopts his pretentious, aphorizing Pursewarden pose (the one character in the *Quartet* he seems unable to laugh at), then attention wanders, and sympathy dissolves. One of the great differences between Durrell and Henry Miller, a writer he often recalls, and much admires, is Durrell's continual ability, or perhaps necessity, to laugh—or at least to snicker impolitely—at himself, his obscenity, his imagination, his creations. He *knows* that all his *fin de siècle* decadence, even his precious Gnostic cerebration, is nothing but a giant game. He delights in it—he delights, it would seem, in our knowing it too: he is forever giving it away. " 'Truth,' said Balthazar to me once, blowing his nose in an old tennis sock, 'Truth is what most contradicts itself in time.' "

On occasion, the accusation leveled by otherwise favorable critics—Edmund Wilson, Bonamy Dobrèe—of a tasteless overindulgence in the grotesque, the sadistic, the revoltingly sexual seems to be justified. But more often this Baudelarian excess is relieved, like the cryptic, heavy aphorism above, by a strange streak of comedy down the center.

Pursewarden, for example, writes of "the famous womansaint (alleged by the way to have three breasts)." Leila, like Madame Rosepettle of *Oh Dad, Poor Dad*, becomes incensed when the boy forgets her pet cobra's saucer of milk. The Swedish vice-consul's wife is gruesomely beheaded by Bedouin raiders, and we learn directly after that "they had been trying to extract the gold teeth which had been such an unpleasant feature of her party smile."

We begin to listen for this tone, to see almost always this shadow of a smile. A dress "the colour of hare's blood," the Cervoni's family crest (a Pan raping a goat), "a silver hinge flies open upon heavy white (like the thighs of Egyptian women) cigarettes, each with its few flecks of *hashish.*" Of course. The little horror stories Balthazar tells (like Capodistria's experiments in Black Art) are on a level of ingenious non-seriousness with the classic Tales of Scobie or Pursewarden's really first-rate dirty poems. Or listen to De Capo, on the Nature of the Universe: "The world is a biological phenomenon which will only come to an end when every single man has had all the women, every woman all the men. Clearly this will take some time. Meanwhile there is nothing to do but to help forward the forces of nature by treading the grapes as hard as we can."

The straight-faced, almost pouting "decadence" of a Huysmans or De Sade cannot hold up long under this kind of treatment. The trouble is, neither can the more serious intentions of the *Alexandria Quartet.* It may be this very compulsive, self-conscious self-irony, this laughing at sex (along with his refusal to provide unnecessary Millerian detail) that has laid Durrell open to the otherwise surprising charge of prudery. Whatever the cause, it creates very serious problems, and may well be at the root of the whole question of Durrell's survival.

Again, the example of Dickens rises to hand. Dickens, like Durrell, had a multitude of "selves" he felt forced to push forward, a multitude of voices: high-comic, low-comic, ironic, sentimental, suspenseful, reformist. The sentimental-serious self was forever being tripped up by the ironic-intrusive, and he finally gave in in *Bleak House* and divided himself in two. With a century of narrative experimentation behind him, Durrell can more comfortably split his intentions among a dozen *personae*—though essentially, perhaps, only three: Darley, the romanticist; Scobie, the comic; and Pursewarden, the serious, cynical critic. Behind them, as with Dickens, there is a confusion of intention that keeps the *Quartet* from ever cohering into a single, memorable experience; a confusion that allows each reading to be a sequence of varying *kinds* of experience of undiminished imaginative intensity—but that leaves us with nothing solid to hold onto in between.

Henry Miller, a much lesser artist, D. H. Lawrence, perhaps a greater one, at least maintain a single voice throughout all of their works, and leave us, when we are done, with the memory if nothing else of a rather overwhelming personality, firm in its monolithic convictions. Durrell leaves us pleased, vaguely nostalgic for, unhappy to leave Alexandria; leaves us thinking that this *has* all been quite wonderful—but . . . where do we go from here? The *Quartet*, at last, rich as it unquestionably is, strikes me as totally self-directed, as experience for experience's sake, saying nothing more, and moving us nowhere further.

On occasion Durrell does try to sound as firm as Miller or Lawrence through one of his "selves," usually Pursewarden, blasting out at the English Disease or proclaiming the Gospel of Animal Man. But half his heart just is not in it, and he cracks it with a Scobeyan snicker, or drowns it in a wash of Darleyan romance. He can play romance, warm, human romance, by the way, with a thousand violins: the entrance of Amaril and Samira at the *Auberge Bleu*, to the strains of a favorite Viennese waltz, must be the warmest bit of pure human joy since the sleigh-ride out to the Uncle's in Tolstoy. But the pathos, the romance, like the other conflicting, contradicting strains, is not allowed to develop into anything outside of itself, and ends where it began.

Durrell appears not to have known what he wanted to do, to have been unable to choose among his voices and intentions. As a result, while each leads a vigorous life of its own as long as our reading is in progress, they seem to cancel one another out when the reading is done. Even the stunning images, the surrealistic visions, demanding (and receiving) as they do such total attention to themselves, *for* themselves, participate in this same functionless, narcissistic, self-defeating limitation. They are only present, so very much present, as long as they are there before us: gone, they contribute to nothing beyond.

My own verdict, ultimately, on Durrell's survival is probably as ambiguous as anyone else's. The intensity of the separate imaginative experiences of the *Alexandria Quartet* will remain in glorious, undiminished force as long as there are readers to take them up; but left as they are with nothing tangible to hold onto in between, nothing solid to remember, the great danger is that future generations may very well not take the trouble.

3

Three Glimpses of Scott Fitzgerald

3

One [1962]

Few writers' lives are so well worth the telling as F. Scott Fitzgerald's. His own story, his and Zelda's, has all the brilliance and glamour, all the pathos and symbolic force of the best of his fiction. His fiction, in fact, *is* his life, but life with the edges trimmed, given point and precision, a precious concision, a sense of ordered direction that his real life never had. The backgrounds of his novels—Princeton, New York, Long Island, Paris and the Riviera, Hollywood—were the settings he himself had danced and died through; each of his heroes in turn is another, deeper view of the author.

Half of the pleasure of a good biography, in fact—and the latest is a good one—is the shock of recognizing events and characters out of the novels. Everything that ever happened to Fitzgerald, and this was a man to whom things happened, wild, incredible things, seems to be happening again somewhere in the novels and stories.

This alone might make a biography richly entertaining. But Andrew Turnbull's *Scott Fitzgerald* is vastly more than that, as Scott Fitzgerald was vastly more than a writer. He invented in his fiction the metaphor of the 1920's, and then led the dance himself. He and Zelda, his mercurial, magical bride—"so obviously, romantic lovers," wrote Van Wyck Brooks—waltzed drunkenly around a world the color of his dreams and the size of millions, "A Diamond as Big as the Ritz" come true. "He recorded the age he was helping to form," writes Turnbull, "and his work and his play became hopelessly intertwined." He recreated, as someone seems to do every generation, the American Romantic Ideal—"the ever-witty, the ever-beautiful"; and, of course, above all else, the unthinkably, gloriously rich.

The ideal went out of fashion, though, in 1929, and so did he; the age he invented had died. "It was now fashionable to consider him passé, buried with the foolishness of the twenties." "But to die," Fitzgerald once mourned (a few months before he did in fact), "so completely and unjustly after having given so much." Trying desperately to live, or live down, their Grand Illusion, Zelda went hopelessly insane, and Fitzgerald died a forgotten, alcoholic, Hollywood hack.

The Grand Illusion survived, however, and men have come to agree that Gatsby and Gatsby's parties represented something far more essential than the twenties. The shift of attention and acclaim to the richer, if less meticulously carved *Tender is the Night*—Fitzgerald's, not Jason Robard Jr.'s and Jennifer Jones'—suggests, moreover, that his highest achievement was not the nostalgic evocation of an age. It was not even the recreation of an essential American myth: the green light Gatsby believed in at the end of Daisy's dock; not even in the exquisite and affecting prose he found to communicate the dream—at its best, the finest that American fiction can offer. Fitzgerald's genius, an almost tragic genius, as *Tender is the Night* gives witness, was fully to understand the hopelessness, even the appalling viciousness of the romantic ideal he created. In a way not unlike far greater artists, he could both wholly believe in the ideal—in Gatsby, Gatsby's green light, the drunken butterfly world of the twenties, the whole grand American dream—and consciously recognize its ugliness and folly.

Perhaps oversimplifying, we like to apportion our novelists into "romantic" and "realistic" realms: on the right we place the suprasocial, unrealistic visionaries, on the left the involved and conscientious critics. The now famous "Crack-Up" may have been the result, but Fitzgerald, alone among the great American novelists, seems to have been able to live, totally and effectively, in both worlds; "to hold," as he put it, "two opposed ideas in the mind at the same time and still retain the ability to function"—to have been able both to dream and to criticize his dreaming.

Andrew Turnbull is not the first to realize the extraordinary potential for drama in the life story of Scott Fitzgerald. Fitzgerald himself discovered it first. Budd Schulberg, who worked with the aging Fitzgerald on a movie assignment the year before he died, turned this grotesque experience into *The Disenchanted*. Sheila Graham, his friend of the Hollywood years, paid her respects in *Beloved Infidel*, a notebook for the notebooks of *The Last Tycoon*. Most interesting, though, is a comparison with *The Far Side of Paradise*, Arthur Mizener's prize-winning, "pioneering" biography of 1951, surely a key document in the "Fitzgerald Revival."

For one thing, of course, Turnbull knows more. He has interviewed a selected four hundred and fifty people ("and corresponded with several hundred more"). He can dare, now, to name Miss Graham outright as Fitzgerald's mistress, and get straight the name of Zelda's French airman. He revises, even dismisses, not a few of the classic Fitzgerald anecdotes "on the basis of new information," and adds a fair handful of his own. But more to the point, he has simply written a far better book.

Turnbull has caught, one feels, the very curve and contour of his subject's life; he seems painstakingly to have traced a "significant form" in this shapeless mountain of detail. His book "reads like a novel" in the very best sense. It has, over-all, the inexorable "rightness," the necessity of sequence and structure and thoughtfully chosen incident that makes the experience of it a pleasure, and the final effect one of unity and a meaningful coherence. He has communicated the totality of the man—only Fitzgerald's collected works could do it better —and has done it (for this one is grateful) in scarcely over three hundred pages.

Mizener's work, on the other hand, seemed to have no underlying pattern, no developing form, no standard of choice: it is to Turnbull's in this respect, as the novel whose name it paraphrases is to *Tender is the Night*. Attempting a "critical biography"—something of a bastard genre to begin with—Mizener was forced to break into the already uneven pace of his narration with extended (though often valuable) critiques of each of the novels in turn. Digression, in fact, digression on vast and vague questions of the man and his work, was the rule rather than the exception in this earlier work, and the subject was often all but lost in the rambling and indiscriminate prose.

Mizener's book is unquestionably the better documented, the more "scholarly," if you will—though this is somewhat to impugn good scholarship. But Turnbull's (while depending, as he confesses, a good deal on his predecessor's) brings us the man. If much of Fitzgerald's life has in fact the quality, as it shares the content, of the best of his fiction, Turnbull maximizes the effect by his own thoughtful and judicious presentation. Fitzgerald, whose comments on the craft of fiction are among the most valuable quotations in the book, might almost have been speaking of his biographer when he insisted on "the enormous moral business that goes on in the mind of anyone who writes anything worth writing . . . the mental speed that enables you to keep the whole pattern in your head and ruthlessly sacrifice the side shows."

There are lapses, of course, and they hurt. The single chapter of "memoir" (Turnbull, as a boy of eleven, knew Fitzgerald as a tenant of his parents' Maryland estate) is over-detailed far beyond its significance. The author's analysis of Fitzgerald's Catholicism—even worse, of his "Irishness"—is weak and unconvincing. Ideally, he might have woven in more effectively biographical passages from the novels and stories. "Babylon Revisited," one feels, tells us more about the man and his time than twice its length of "real-life" anecdote, however carefully researched. Even more embarrassing are Turnbull's occasional attempts at a "poetic" style.

But by and large the man is thoroughly in control of his weapons, and his weapons are those of the craftsman of fiction. He sets his scene with admirable, and economic, effect: the Princeton of 1916, New York in 1920, that dazzling crowd at Antibes. He brings characters to life with just the right touches; Zelda, that most elusive of beings, is before us in a paragraph, whirling mindlessly around a deserted Casino floor. Never, to my knowledge, has such full justice been done to the massive,* Johnsonian "father-figure" of American letters, Ed-

* *"Massive.* I have also written before of this stupid and oppressive word,

mund Wilson—the man Fitzgerald called "my intellectual con-
science" for twenty years. So for Monsignor Fay, John Peale
Bishop, Christian Gauss (all characters in *This Side of Para-
dise*), Maxwell Perkins, Ernest Hemingway, the rich Riviera
Murphys, Irving Thalberg ("The Last Tycoon"), Sheila
Graham, the whole *dramatis personae:* they are there.

Most importantly, of course, so is F. Scott Fitzgerald. When
all is added up and analyzed, the real reason his story seems "so
well worth the telling" is that it is our story too, the American
ideal, even to the tragic ending: the life we would all somehow
like to have lived. "I remember," he wrote—*we* remember—
"riding in a taxi one afternoon between very tall buildings under a mauve and rosy sky; I began to bawl because I had everything I wanted and knew I would never be so happy again."

---

which seems to have become since then even more common as a ready
cliché that acts as a blackout on thinking. . . . I myself, I am sorry to say,
have lately been described as 'massive': in an article called 'Fitzgerald's
Grand Illusion' by David Littlejohn in the *Commonweal*, I am referred
to as 'the massive, Johnsonian "father-figure."' And, apropos, let us not
only scrap *massive;* let us be careful about using *Johnsonian*, which has
been so inappropriately applied to so many people from G. K. Chester-
ton to Alexander Woollcott; and I much object to *father-figure* even in
quotes. It makes me feel as if I resembled that colossal wooden statue of
Hindenburg that the Germans used to stick nails in."
(Edmund Wilson, "A Postscript to Fowler: Current Clichés and Sole-
cisms," *New Statesman*, February 8, 1963.)

Two [1963]

The Fitzgerald Question, the puzzle that so haunts the critical imagination musing on the man and his works, is precisely that of The Man and His Works: How on earth could this man, this madcap, egotistic, alcoholic hack, this dollar- and publicity-crazy International-Set butterfly ever have produced works of such artistry, depth and crystalline tragic vision? Knowing the man as we do, or think we do, it seems to us impossible that he could ever have found it in him to set in balance the profound and exquisite ironies of *Gatsby* or *Tender is the Night*.

Andrew Turnbull's new edition of *The Letters of F. Scott Fitzgerald* provides, let me say first, materials that may seem only to magnify the first term of the dilemma: there is all the evidence one could ask here of Fitzgerald's brashness, his egotism and folly.

He thought his play (*The Vegetable*, a less-than-impressive affair abandoned after a week in Atlantic City) was "about the best American comedy to date . . . 'undoubtedly' the best thing I have ever written." He ventures, with notable self-assurance, to write his own advertisements, calling himself one of the half-dozen masters of English prose now writing in America. What other writer has shown such unexpected developments, such versatility, changes of pace, etc., etc."

These letters give witness to the grossest commercial-mindedness, a pathological readiness to criticize others, a dis-

graceful and so obviously fraudulent foot-licking of the established Great. The collection is filled with apologies for the night
before, and vows of sobriety for the days to come. "I don't
blame either of you for being disgusted with our public brawl
the other day—but the manhole is on again; we are sober . . ."
In the disastrous years 1935–37, scarcely a letter goes by without one guilty, compulsive protest that he is now, at last, "on
the absolute wagon."

It is perhaps as a father that Fitzgerald appears at his most
unfit and unflattering, and Mr. Turnbull has done him the dis-
service of offering this particular view to us first, by beginning
his collection with Fitzgerald's letters to his daughter from out
of his declining years. Brought up in the sordid atmosphere of
"Babylon Revisited," Scottie was later packed off to boarding
schools out of reach of her insane mother and alcoholic father;
but the latter continued to monitor her life by a nagging, pretentious series of Chesterfieldian letters.

There is more, of course, than this; this is the black, the expected side. For these letters also go a long way to answer our
opening question, in the overwhelming evidence they afford of
a depth and subtlety of conscious artistic skill we may have
known, until now, only by deduction.

This man may have *been* egocentric, foolish, degenerate,
vain—although, even morally, that is far from the whole story.
But he was also a trained, committed, and intelligent artist, per-
ceptive and articulate about his literary craft. His comments,
collected here, about writing and the writer; his judgments of
classic and contemporary authors mark him, to this reader's
stunned surprise, as one of the more insightful and discriminat-
ing critics and literary theorists of our time. Most illuminating
is the running commentary and criticism he provides on his
own works—his influences, his intentions, his methods and
effects, his realizations and failures. It was not, after all, the
result of gin-fired inspiration: he knew, at every stage, precisely what he was about.

Moreover, Fitzgerald's comments on writing go beyond
mere criticism and craftsmanship, and begin to suggest the
origins of the far-more-than-superficial greatness of his work.
He convincingly describes style as a function of truth; he talks
of the *inner* source of sensation. He writes, to a young author,

of the cruel and anti-human commitment of the artist, pledged
forever to dragging out and using all that has most wounded,
since that is what will mean most. "Maybe someday I'll get a
chapter out of it," he concludes his account of a hapless love
affair. "God, what a hell of a profession, to be a writer. One is
one simply because one can't help it." "Often I think writing is
a sheer paring away of oneself, leaving always something thin-
ner, barer, more meager." Why go on? "It is simply that,
having once found the intensity of art, nothing else that can
happen in life can ever again seem as important as the creative
process."

To be an artist, he once wrote, required "the egotism of a
maniac with the clear triple-thinking of a Flaubert"—in which
phrase he came close, in black-and-white terms, to describing
himself. But "maniacal egotism" will not suffice to describe
Fitzgerald; the depths here uncovered in his artistic awareness
remind us that the folklore Fitzgerald, the Scott of the movies,
is only the sour and shimmering surface.

For his was, after all, a tragic story and not only a pathetic
one, because he was a man great and opened-eyed enough for
tragedy. Most of these letters are from the last ten years, from
1930 to 1940, and magnify by this accident of survival the
tragic character of Fitzgerald's person and career. He is here
looking back, wondering how it all came about: Zelda's crack-
up, his own, his decline to neglect, to this ignominious drudg-
ery for *Esquire* and Metro-Goldwyn-Mayer.

He wrote then: "I am not a great man, but sometimes I think
the impersonal and objective quality of my talent and the sacri-
fices of it, in pieces, to preserve its essential value has some sort
of epic grandeur. Anyhow after hours I nurse myself with
delusions of that sort. . . . But to die, so completely and unjustly after having given so much! . . . in a *small* way I was an
original . . . I have not lost faith."

There are letters, understandably, of self-defense, of self-
pity, petulant patchings of his shreds of ego—much that *is* only
pathetic. He has, for one thing, to keep reminding people bitterly of who he was; he weeps at being out of print. He knows
he is a failure, and hates it. By 1936 he was trying to write skits
for Burns and Allen, to sell "Babylon Revisited" to Shirley

Temple to pay off his debts of more than $40,000, and hocking his car to eat.

The tragic greatness emerges, however, not from the lamentations, but from his adamant and impossible combination of awareness and faith. He had measured to the inch the depth to which he had fallen, knew precisely the blackness of his pit and the forces, self-caused and other, that had driven him in—it is all detailed in "The Crack-Up." And yet he keeps on, believing, trying to climb back out—the next book; the next one. "I have not lost faith. People will *buy* my new book," he wrote, seven months before his death, at forty-four.

He expressed, more than once in these last bitter years, the shape of mind that had made his fight possible. It was what he himself called, "for lack of a better phrase . . . the wise and tragic sense of life . . . the sense that life is essentially a cheat and its conditions are those of defeat, and that the redeeming things are not 'happiness and pleasure' but the deeper satisfactions that come out of struggle." His life had been a sodden tangle of unhappiness; but "what do you care about happiness," he wrote to the editor (then twelve years old)— "and who does, except the perpetual children of the world?" Despite the myth, he was not one of them. "Our united front (he was writing of his and his wife's) is less a romance than a categorical imperative."

This is the dimension of greatness: the ability, ultimately, not to *care* about happiness; to work when there is nothing left to work for; to overcome the poisoned, polished hardness of the world with the triumphs of the self. And it is the wonder of this eloquent collection that it transports us so completely— more completely, even, than Turnbull's handsome biography of a year ago, which drew so dramatically on these very letters —into the creative and poignant vigor of so real and so valuable a life.

Three [1965]

This richly edited collection of Fitzgerald's prep school and college stories* may strike the outsider, the unconverted, as just a bit foolish. But to genuine Fitzgerald-nuts, and they are legion, it will afford a source of illumination and delight.

The fifteen stories begin with "The Mystery of the Raymond Mortgage," an absurdly (and charmingly) crude detective story of 1909, when Fitzgerald was twelve; they end with two Princeton tales of high society which already suggest that balance of tone, that poise between romantic indulgence and ice-cool critique which defines the maturest of vintage Fitzgerald.

Artistically, his development is fitful, though no reasonable devotee will be reading these stories for their art. "Reade, Substitute Right Half" (1910) is written in the purest high school prose, the purple-slang jargon of the amateur sportswriter. It is undiluted daydream-heroics, and fun to read. "Debt of Honor," a corny Civil War piece, is the first of Fitzgerald's experiments with the detached, dramatic opening, one of his fortes.

By "The Room With the Green Blinds," a sort of B+ horror story about John Wilkes Booth, he has already moved far beyond the first mystery in control, setting, and pace. Two

* *The Apprentice Fiction of F. Scott Fitzgerald, 1909–17*, ed. John Kuehl. Rutgers.

rich-boy-and-rich-girl stories end the prep school series. The first, "A Luckless Santa Claus," is really strongly assembled, an ironic social survey, with the beginnings of psychological analysis and cynical distance. The second, "The Trail of the Duke," is a silly thing with a cheap twist-of-lemon ending, but is of interest for its arty opening paragraph, its tintype of New York, and—again—its cynical detachment.

The first Princeton stories seem a setback after this, marking a probably necessary stage of literary and philosophic posing. "Shadow Laurels," like "The Debutante" later, is written as a purple playlet with lush stage directions ("far away in the twilight a violin sighs plaintively"); it reveals a great deal about Fitzgerald, but not through its finesse. "The Ordeal" is his Catholic story. It is cloyingly overwritten, full of neurasthenic imagery, philosophic namedropping, and vague maunderings about the Infinite—very much a hothouse affair, very much a sensitive sophomore's, despite another of his truly professional openings. It, too, tells worlds about Fitzgerald.

Mr. Kuehl, the editor, thinks that "no apprentice work shows better form" than "The Debutante," Fitzgerald's first real Jazz Age effort (*The Nassau Lit*, 1917, printed in Mencken's *The Smart Set* in 1919). It does "observe the unities," as he notes, but it is not much elevated by the observance. It is this sort of thing people thought Fitzgerald was writing, this sticky, slick, slangy, dated teenage *femme fatalism*, long after he had transcended it, long after he has seen through the "miniature silver flasks"—a perfect symbol—and moved on to where he was only *using* what he here only describes:

> "From below, there is a sudden burst of sound, as the orchestra swings into 'Poor Butterfly.' The violins and faint drums and a confused chord from a piano, the rich odor of powder, and new silk, a blend of laughters all surge together into the room. She dances toward the mirror, kisses the vague reflection of her face, and runs out the door."

"The Spire and Gargoyle," the story that follows, overromanticizes college days, the collegiate mystique, as "The Debutante" does the fast young flapper—two myths Fitzgerald had a large part in creating, and the devil's own time escaping. It is done in a fatuous, beery, Halls of Ivy style, the very self-indulgent emotionalism over varsity spirit most undergraduates want, at some stage, to entertain. If the two tales recall *This Side of Paradise*, it is because they were later incorporated into it; and because the novel, for all its vogue and its 44,000 copies, may still be called "apprentice work," too.

This editor is not too happy about "Tarquin of Cheepside," a neat little joke on Shakespeare. He thinks it faked and ahistorical, and it is; but Fitzgerald retained a perverse affection for it and so do I. On the other hand, Mr. Kuehl gives his most serious attention to "The Pierian Springs and the Last Straw" (one thing Fitzgerald had not learned was how to write titles), the last story here; but it strikes me, for all its correspondence with *Gatsby*, its cynical sheathing, its offhand narration, as artificial, overliterary, and greenly melodramatic.

Far more interesting, I think, are the two stories before it, "Babes in the Woods" (another two chapters-to-be of *This Side of Paradise*) and "Sentiment—and the Use of Rouge," which begs retitling. "Babes" begins as a *Seventeen* magazine story, playing around a high sexuality that never quite emerges. But the author moves to a cool, keen analysis of the dance of social poses, and hovers near the true Fitzgerald mark. *Style* here is everything, in the actors and in their creator; and he nearly brings it off, makes this affected adolescent flirtation take on music and meaning.

"Sentiment" is a stranger thing yet—but it is the real find of this collection. The analysis is sharp, the judgment meticulously balanced, the subject freighted with a graver social weight than any other story before "May Day." It makes the butterflies look poor indeed. This is Fitzgerald, fully the artist, taking the true temperature of his time.

"No, I'm a romantic. There's a huge difference; a sentimental person thinks things will last; a romantic person hopes they won't." ("Sentiment—and the Use of Rouge.") One of the more tantalizing games a reader can play with these early stories is that of estimating the quality of this young romantic's romanticism. Fitzgerald notoriously retained the ability to dream adolescent daydreams long after most people outgrow them, or think they do; to dream them, that is, but to know he was dreaming, and to criticize the dream.

How wholehearted, we ask, *was* his idealization—at sixteen, at twenty-one—his longing idealization of the graceful rich of Society, of football, of soldierly heroics, of the South, of New York, of the knowing flapper, the Halls of Ivy? And when did this romanticism divide itself, take its analytic, then tragic turn? ("A romantic person hopes they won't.") "I, for instance, am both a romanticist and a psychologist. It does take the romance out of anything to analyze it." ("Sentiment.") Or does it?

Another consequence of the reading is the jarring sense of distance and change it asserts. It all seems so archaic, so uncool: the blushings, the flirtations, the dreams, the storybook responses of these "fast" collegians. Were eighteen-year-olds *ever* so quaintly naïve? Without the hard art of the later novels and stories, the full pressure of an all-aware imagination, the flappers and philosophers of these early stories turn unmagically back to windup historical dolls in period dress. If young men are still dreaming such dreams, there is no Fitzgerald around to prove it.

Special praise must be given to the editor, John Kuehl of (naturally) Princeton. His efforts deserve a less oppressive, less scholarly-sounding title (Why not *Fitzgerald's Early Stories?*); because his book is so readable, so accessible. In his preludes to the stories, he assembles tiny essays on the themes and issues they engage: Fitzgerald and his Father, Fitzgerald and Football; and Catholicism, and the South, and the Rich; his reading, his women, the reception of his stories. One may question, at times, his emphases, his interpretations, his judgments; but all his information is useful and unobtrusive. And how good of him it was to include the complete text of Fitzgerald's bizarre "teen tips" to his younger sister, to append a facsimile of the strange six-page manuscript Fitzgerald called "The Death of My Father."

4

Portraits

Robinson Jeffers [1962]

Robinson Jeffers, the doom-shouting Inhumanist Poet of two generations, died early this year at Tor House, his hand-built hermitage on the California coast. It took his death to remind most readers that he had in fact still been alive.

Even to the tiny world that pays attention to poets, Jeffers had effectively been dead for years. Less attention was paid to his last two books than to any before. The critics, such as Mark Van Doren, who had hailed him twenty and thirty years earlier as the great hope of American verse, had nothing to say. They had, one suspects, changed their minds.

The triumph of Jeffers' earliest works, like *Roan Stallion* and *The Tower Beyond Tragedy*, had been equalled again only once, when his adaptation of Euripides' *Medea* made Broadway in 1946; but that was Judith Anderson's *Medea*, and not Robinson Jeffers'. The big *Selected Poetry* has been out of print for twenty years; his little Modern Library collection slipped off the lists a year or two ago. And now he is gone.

No doubt, one of the reasons men seized on Jeffers in the twenties and thirties was that he was writing readable poetry, coherent and powerful narrative verse. He still cared very much to be understood. Jeffers explained later that "the most 'modern' of English poetry seemed to me thoroughly defeatist, as if poetry were in terror of prose, and desperately trying to save its soul from the victor by giving up its body. It was becoming slight and fantastic, abstract, unreal, eccentric."

To those who, like him, were disaffected by the preciosities and pedantries of the New Poets, of Eliot and Pound and the Imagists, Jeffers seemed a sound American voice. Here was a sort of disillusioned Walt Whitman, rolling out nightmarish tragedies and harsh landscape studies of the California coast in long rhetorical lines. These were poems to be shouted aloud. Surely *this* was the American tradition: Whitman and Robinson had given in to Sandburg and Frost and Lindsay, to Edgar Lee Masters and Robinson Jeffers. Great poetry, it seemed, could still speak to the people and be understood.

This may be correct, but none of these men has proved it—partly because "the people," at least the American people, no longer read poetry, if ever they did. Thirty-four years ago, considering the question "Is Verse a Dying Technique?", Edmund Wilson concluded that with people like Lawrence and Joyce on the one hand, writing what was called "prose," and people like Sandburg and Jeffers, on the other, writing what was called "poetry," the old distinctions had simply ceased to mean anything. Jeffers' long narrative poems of tortured blood-and-lust passions on the primeval, hawk-haunted coast were only D. H. Lawrence novels reset in dithyrambic verse, Wilson claimed—and scarcely the more successful for being in verse. The best of these narratives, most of them long forgotten—*Roan Stallion*, perhaps; *Thurso's Landing; Cawdor; Give Your Heart to the Hawks* (a Jeffers title if ever there was one); certainly *The Loving Shepherdess*—might at least be read today and still in print, had they been written in prose.

Jeffers has been buried, however, not so much by the style he chose—Frost is still very much with us, to say nothing of the abstract and eccentric New Poets—as by what he had to say. "God-if-there-is-a-God is neutral"; for him at best the source and summation of his everlasting rocks and hawks and oceans. Man is vile and valueless, a chance bit of cosmic dust caught between spectral epochs. Soon he will be dissolved and scattered again so that primeval Beauty can reign, eternally undisfigured by his excremental acts, in "the enormous dawns of time after we perish." "A day will come when the earth/Will scratch herself and smile and rub off humanity."

Jeffers may have been the only public spokesman of our time actively anticipating the equivalent of a nuclear war. Man's story, for him, has been one of the pettiest, most hateful cruelties; his narrative poems are a bloody sequence of violent crimes, his "lyrics" are screaming with majestic birds and beasts whipped and mangled by their master Man. The second World War, to Jeffers as grotesque as it was predictable, gave the occasion for his most scornfully misanthropic verse—and probably his worst.

. . . The earth is a star, its human element
Is what darkens it. War is evil, the peace will be evil, cruelty
    is evil; death is not evil. But the breed of man
Has been queer from the start. It looks like a botched experiment that has run wild and ought to be stopped.

The depths of Jeffers' repetitive, ranting abuse were reached in the title poem of *The Double Axe* in 1948. Not since Lemuel Gulliver met the Yahoos has the human race been quite so despicably dismissed.

. . . I am sick tonight, I am human:
There is only one animal that hates himself. Truly the sweating
    toad and the poison-gorged pit-viper
Are content with their natures. I'll be a stone at the bottom of
    the sea, or any bush on the mountain,
But not this ghost-ridden blood-and-bone thing, civil war on
    two legs and the stars' contempt, this walking farce,
This ape, this—denatured ape, this—citizen—. . . .

But Gulliver was not Swift, and Jeffers, perhaps, was not entirely the Old Inhumanist of *The Double Axe*. He could find beauty, if not in the life and pleasures of man, at least in his sufferings and death—in the frenzied high death-defying madness of his Medeas and Clytemnestras, his Tamar Cauldwells and Helen Thursos. Mellowing just a bit at 64, he could go so far as to say

It is easy to know the beauty of inhuman things, sea, storm
    and mountain; it is their soul and their meaning.
Humanity has its lesser beauty, impure and painful; we have to
    harden our hearts to bear it.
I have hardened my heart only a little: I have learned that happiness is important, but pain gives importance. . . .

Or, earlier,

> Praise life, it deserves praise, but the praise of life
> That forgets the pain is a pebble
> Rattled in a dry gourd.

He could find beauty too in the impersonal, glacier-like movements of masses—even masses preparing for war. And like Lawrence, he could find traces of it in our "elemental" sub-nature, the non-human blood-life that the men and women of his Monterey tales tried to share with their stallions and hawks. For the most part, though, and increasingly, he had to turn away from man to find it.

> . . . At least
> Love your eyes that can see, your mind that can
> Hear the music, the thunder of wings. Love the wild swan.

The shock of this message, and the impulsive violence of Jeffers' expression of it may have helped assure him an audience on first appearance. But as years went on, and the self-same fulminations kept crackling out of Tor House—his annual burnt offerings to appease the hungry coastside gods, Jeffers once called them—fewer and fewer were shocked, or even listening. We had other concerns, and other favorites. Jeffers knew well that no one was dancing, but for forty years he never changed the tune. First bitterly, then resignedly—"You and I, Cassandra"—he commented on his *apartheid*.

> Therefore though not forgotten, not
> loved, in gray old years in the
> evening leaning
> Over the gray stones of the tower-top
> You shall be called heartless and blind.

Sixteen years later, he was.

> —As for me: laugh at me. I agree with you. It is a foolish busi-
> ness to see the future and screech at it.
> One should watch and not speak. And patriotism has run the
> world through so many blood lakes: and we always fall in.

"Patriotism" and its follies confounded Jeffers, especially when confronted by the horrors of the War. But never in his many later "public" poems did he attain the finesse in well-wrought Olympian disgust of "Shine, Perishing Republic" of 1925, perhaps his best-known shorter poem—a poem, like so many of Jeffers', that could survive on its title alone.

In fact, this failure to develop, or refusal to change, has probably been one of the most devastating causes of Jeffers' own "perishing." We are appalled, or certainly at least not attracted, by a monolithic, unjointed, unmodulated career. How much of the appeal of Yeats, for example, or O'Neill, or Thomas Mann, to speak only of modern artists, would be lost without the satisfying movement from Early to Middle to Late. Jeffers could only say the same things over and over, from one generation to another; not only do the subjects lose their force, but so does he. After forty years of screeching, Cassandra grows tired.

The deficiencies, the idiosyncrasies, even the original, very personal strengths that one could accept in the early poems became tedious, empty, and unconvincing when repeated for the hundredth time. One begins, probably unfairly, to suspect the poet's own sincerity. The same spasmodic-Gothic grave-yard imagery, the buckets of blood, the everlasting hawk-symbols and rock-symbols and bone-symbols; the inability to evoke any but a small family of mad Jeffersean characters, all incestuous or murderous or parent-hating, all violently rhap-sodic, all death-wishing; the tasteless supernaturalism, the ad-olescent perversions of Christianity, the attempts to translate a misunderstood modern science into modern poetry; above all, the insistent "Inhumanism."

> I have shared in my time the human illusions, the muddy
> foolishness
> And craving passions, but something thirty years ago pulled me
> Out of the tide-wash; I must not even pretend
> To be one of the people. I must stand here
> Alone with open eyes in the clear air growing old,
> Watching with interest and only a little nausea
> The cheating shepherds, this time of the demagogues and the
> docile people, the shifts of power,
> And pitiless general wars that prepare the fall;
> But also the enormous unhuman beauty of things; rock, sea and
> stars, fool-proof and permanent. . . .

Thirty years ago, this had worked; but no longer. Even the most sympathetic critics were disappointed as book after book came out, and no new paths were taken, no change, no self-renewal occurred. Mark Van Doren, who all but "discovered" Jeffers' first major book, already saw, while still affording high praise to his second, the dangers of his *idée fixe:* "He seems to be knocking his head to pieces against the night."

It is hard to say, though, where one would have had Jeffers go. The most benignantly-inclined cannot deny a measure of truth to his ugly Inhumanist visions—and he need not look far beyond himself. Still, since *we* cannot do it, it is hateful to think that another man could stop on that dry rock for a life-time, without even trying to move. There is hope for man at least in Yoknapatawpha, but none on the wuthering heights south of Monterey. We insist on our "Towers beyond Tragedy," even as we realize what they are made of: to know the lie, and yet use it.

Inventing all the objections, Jeffers had his own final word in a testament called "Self-Criticism in February," written in 1937:

The bay is not blue but sombre yellow
With wrack from the battered valley, it is speckled with violent
        foam-heads
And tiger-striped with long lovely storm shadows.
You love this better than the other mask; better eyes than yours
Would feel the equal beauty in the blue.
It is certain you have loved the beauty of storm disproportion-
        ately.
But the present time is not pastoral, but founded
On violence, pointed for more massive violence: perhaps it is
        not
Perversity but need that perceives the storm-beauty.
Well, bite on this: your poems are too full of ghosts and
        demons,
And people like phantoms—how often life's are—
And passion so strained that the clay mouths go praying for
        destruction—
Alas, it is not unusual in life;
To every soul at some time. *But why insist on it? And now*
For the worst fault: you have never mistaken

Demon nor passion nor idealism for the real God.
Then what is most disliked in those verses
Remains most true. *Unfortunately. If only you could sing*
That God is love, or perhaps that social
Justice will soon prevail. I can tell lies in prose.

Sartre's Genet [1964]

Until a few months ago, Jean Genet, to the American public, was known as the author only of two extraordinary plays, and as one of the three French-writing playwrights (with Ionesco and Beckett) responsible for introducing the so-called "Theatre of the Absurd." His two best-known plays, *The Balcony* (1958) and *The Blacks* (1959)—there are also three others—were notable for their spectacular use of perverted ritual onstage, for their heady mixture of the lyrical and the base, for their ingenious, occasionally quite disturbing manipulations of reality and appearance: Genet could, at his best, set into question the whole nature of illusion, theatrical and otherwise.

The Balcony, granted some reservations about its "plot" and the later scenes, was considered a stunning and original theatrical experience. *The Blacks* was still fine spectacle, still shocking, still informed by an ingenious idea; but somewhere, it seemed, Genet had lost hold—it was all so talky, so crude, so overassertive. And with his latest play, *The Screens*, an epic, anal-erotic tangle so far staged only in Germany, he seemed to have attempted far more, and achieved far less. The recreative genius, the taut visionary effectiveness of *The Balcony*'s opening scenes had been washed away in a sea of near-meaningless, meandering scatology. The heyday of Genet, and the Absurdists generally, seemed drawing to a close. He flowered briefly, a strange hothouse plant, and then ran to seed: it was all very exciting to watch.

Such, until last autumn, was the American's Genet. But the recent appearance of two books, one by him (translated after twenty years), one about him (after ten) has expanded the image considerably.* For the French, and the French-reading public, the plays of the last few years represented only the latest chapter, and not necessarily the strongest and most important, in the checkered career of one of their most baffling *enfants terribles*. He cherished, and was cherished for, his position as The Outsider, the outcast, the alien voice of the Underworld. His off-Broadway successes, in fact, struck some continental observers as an unfortunate giving in to the demands of "Art" and of audience, by a man who established his black name by standing for so long so far apart from such concerns.

Genet has been recognized, regarded, held in awe, praised and condemned—"admired" is inadequate—for both his books (five semi-fictionalized memoir-narratives) and the example of his life. In the two books now before us, both masterfully Englished by Bernard Frechtman, we have adequate materials, at last, to judge them both. *Our Lady of the Flowers*, while the first of Genet's narratives—"novels" they are not—is representative of the lot, as good and as bad, and in much the same ways, as the rest. And *Saint Genet*, Jean-Paul Sartre's gothic monument of a "preface"—all 625 thick pages of it—is at least one man's attempt, heroic and unedited, to present "The Man Genet."

Our Lady of the Flowers is not likely to be sold in America primarily for its lyrical prose-poetry, its poignant evocations of a prisoner's soul: it will sell because of its detailed descriptions of homosexual love. This is, of course, not all of the book, any more than his professed and active homosexuality is "all" of Genet. But it would be foolish and dishonest to describe the book without giving full credit to the homo-erotic fantasies, the burning lusts for hot male members that provide so much of its life and motive force.

* Jean Genet, *Our Lady of the Flowers* (Grove Press); Jean-Paul Sartre, *Saint Genet, Actor and Martyr* (Braziller).

This sick, sinful reverie all began in a French prison cell, sometime in 1942. Born a cast-off bastard, Genet had been leading a half-life alternating between prison terms and the sordid vagabond years of beggary, burglary, and buggery that earned them for him ever since he first robbed his foster-parents at the age of fifteen. This career was to continue, with the additional crime of writing now added, for another six years, when (1948) he only escaped life-sentencing, as an incorrigible thief, by the intercession of Sartre and other members of the French intelligentsia. With such a life, no fiction was needed.

He started writing it all out, redreaming it one day on the backs of the brown paper bags the prisoners made: he had plenty of time. He began by musing, half to himself, on the handsome young murderers whose pictures he kept pinned to the walls of his cell. Inspired by erotic daydreams, he wrote on to keep them alive. The smoke-rings of reverie, half-memory, half-imagination, drifted to enhalo other bodies, other boys, to idealize other nights and days; gradually shapes were embodied by sheer onanistic will, and strong sordid characters emerged: his vision of Queerworld came into focus, and the story of Darling, Divine, and Our Lady of the Flowers began.

It is a grotesque little story, like all his stories—though honestly, tenderly told—of the passions and jealousies, the loves and hates, of the bitter sufferings and joys of the Night people, the queers, the queens and their pimps. It all has, until it grows tiresome, the fascination of some absurd and bestial parody of "normal" life and loves—octopuses copulating in a green-lit aquarium tank, a hill of monkeys fighting and posing and chattering in a zoo. But as Genet makes clear, as we are, perhaps for the first time, made to realize ourselves, the octopuses suffer and yearn; these monkeys are human. Genet is, after all, one of them, and not one of us.

The book, for all its hot-blooded invert's dreams, *is* honest, unassertive, non-defensive. Genet is not anxious to escape to our world, or even to defend his own. He does not consider his to be strange, or perverse; sad, if anything, erotic, beautiful, painful, and sad: but true. We may be shocked—but not, yet, because he is trying to shock us. For himself, he is quiet, almost content: poetic, self-contained, self-assured.

We may still reject it all, of course, find it monstrous; we may stand outside the tank and observe. But, as has often been pointed out, Genet is able to evoke the full range of amorous emotions, from the first stirrings of affection to the black cruel hell of abandonment, with as much sensitive and tender intimacy as any "heterosexual" author. We may, despite ourselves, find parts of it hard to resist.

The story Genet invents, despite its title, is effectively that of "Divine," born Louis Culafroy, first male, then "female"; her rise, decline, and fall. It begins, twenty rambling pages into the book, with her entrance into a Montmartre café one 2 A.M. in a champagne-silk blouse and sandals, seeking customers. We trace through the griefs of her various liaisons in a scattering of erotic scenes; moments from her boyhood are interleaved between, in the wry-nostalgic manner of a Faulkner. She grows old, unattractive, dried and hard, as Genet felt himself to be doing ("from myself I make Divine"), and is abandoned in turn by each of her lovers: Darling the pimp, the Negro Seck Gorgui, the adolescent murderer called "Our Lady of the Flowers." Mating off with one another, they recombine their figures in the everlasting dance, and leave Divine to paint her face, beg her favors, grow old and die young alone.

This is a too-clean, too-neat distillation of the book, and does not, I confess, correspond very closely to the experience of reading it. "Clean" because I omit, perforce, the outspoken, subjective (and objective) details of Genet-Divine's longings and loves; genuine, unexaggerated, lyrically-rendered as these are, they are obviously going to affect each reader differently, and some disastrously. Homosexual encounters, for Genet, are a relevant but not extraordinary part of the texture of his life and his work, of a kind with burglary and loneliness and imprisonment and imagination. For many readers, however, these particular words, these particular descriptions may seem to be written in flaming red light. They cannot read them of a piece with the rest of the book, and because of them cannot see the tenderness, the honesty, the pain. They cannot read Genet's book as he wrote it, cannot find Genet in the work: their own selves, their blocks and digusts—this is meant as no criticism—will be too much in the way.

My outline, moreover, is "neater" than the book, as such plot-outlines must be, because it pays no mind to the "movement" of the work, the way its voice wanders in time and in space. The story of Divine is there, yes, at the center; but it is spun out, fitfully, from the erotic dreams of the prisoner Genet, the dreams that are the real matter of this narrative, as he is really its hero. We are forever jerked back to the Cell, the cot, the fevered mind of the poet.

At times he breaks off, for several pages, to tell us of his state, of prison life; or to mingle genuine memories with the fiction, real lovers with their fictional children—if anything is quite fictional, or quite real. ("Truth is not my strong point.") He will mingle characters' pasts and presents, discuss the problems of writing, talk to us, about us, of himself, his reasons for writing. He admits, in fact, that the whole story, the whole book is only a pretext to talk about himself, to indulge his inner longings.

> The longest detours finally lead me back to my prison, to my cell. Now, almost without trimmings, without transposition, without intermediary, I could tell of my life here. My present life.

This scrofulous free-associating may have been very well for Genet, time-filling, stimulating, therapeutic, even lucrative. But what about us?

The erotic, pornographic appeal, such as it is, of the violent anal and oral intercourse scenes, the lovingly described genitalia will most likely lose both its attractive and repulsive power shortly after the first manic skip-reading through. There will remain the mild surprise or disgust at seeing such things in print, but Genet has expressed it all so naturally that one soon begins to take it so—which may, for all I know, be a part of his malicious intent.

The circuitous ramblings themselves begin to annoy, after a while; unlike those of Sterne, Faulkner, Gide, Durrell, they seem to be leading us nowhere—except perhaps deeper into the mind of the prisoner-poet. The intense homosexual introversion of both narrator and characters goes, in time, beyond the point of poignancy and pathos, and becomes simply stifling, distasteful; one can keep one's head under Genet's musty blanket for just so long.

The sordidness, the scatology are another serious block. If it is only my own psychic shortcomings that prevent me from enjoying impassively Genet's rich compositions of excrement, vomit, and sperm, well so be it: the more limited I. I may marvel at how palatable his transforming poetic genius can make them appear, but my tastes, still, lie elsewhere.

What, then, of the "transforming poetic genius"? What of those who would have us read Genet "for the style"? This is, after all, the prose-poet of the dunghill, in the great Baudelairean tradition. Let me grant that he can be a master of language, and that these translations do his mastery justice; there are paragraphs, fine pages, that ring the tone of true poetry. But so detachedly aesthetic a judgment, as Sartre deliciously makes clear, is unfair and absurd. "I know people who can read the coarsest passages without turning a hair: 'Those two gentlemen sleep together? And then eat their excrement? And after that, one goes off to denounce the other? As if that mattered! It's *so* well written.'" It does matter, of course, it is meant to matter. Daintily plucking the flowers out of the evil in this fashion does justice to neither, and certainly not to the author: it is simply a means of keeping the book at sufficient distance to avoid the smell, when the smell is what really matters.

Are the Genet-affirmers, then, only that breed of cultists every intelligent pornographer attracts? Partly, yes. The French have a way of adopting, and then canonizing ("Saint Genet") their outcasts. But there is value in the encounter, in spite of all. So honest and non-defensive a view of another moral world, a world so absolutely alien to ours, *can* be humbling and enlarging. And Genet makes, more in the total of his works than specifically here, as good a case for his anti-world as one could. Moreover, the encounter may serve, in a way, as a test of our own moral responses—their firmness, their flexibility, the nature of our impulses.

Genet's relationship with Us, *les justes, les autres,* has undergone striking changes between his first and his latest writings. In *Our Lady of the Flowers* he was generally content to leave us alone, to let his world speak for itself—or at most only to

suggest the gap between. Subsequent narratives begin to stress
more the alienation; and by *The Thief's Journal* (1949), he had
quite distinctly taken sides.

> I made up my mind to live with my head bowed and to pursue
> my destiny toward night, in an opposite direction from yours,
> and to exploit the inner side of your beauty . . . Since rectitude
> was your domain, I would have none of it. . . .

He had even begun to insult us. "I recognize in thieves, trai-
tors, and murderers, in the ruthless and the cunning, a deep
beauty—a sunken beauty—which I deny you." "You who regard me with contempt are made up of nothing else but a succession of similar miseries, but you will never be aware of this,
and thus will never know the meaning of pride."

The attack in *The Balcony* was devastating, but except for
Madame Irma's parting slap ("You must go home now, where
everything—you can be sure—will be even falser than here"),
it was all kept powerfully oblique. By *The Blacks*, Genet had
given way to open denunciations of his audience, to a ranting
mockery of all the institutions of civilization. And the furious
gibberish of *The Screens*, the gross caricatures of colonials and
legionnaires, the diarrhetic scatology, were obviously intended
to be insulting.

This transformation of the hurt introverted outcast into
screaming extrovert Fury, as the young exile turns increasingly
upon his exilers, upon *us*, is to me the most interesting aspect of
the development of Jean Genet. But even in *Our Lady of the
Flowers* war had been declared, the attack set in motion with
subtlety and skill. In the last twenty-five pages—the most
powerful narrative fragment of the book—Genet presents us
with an image of ourselves, the Just Ones, sitting in judgment
on *his* world, in the person of the young murderer who gives
the book its title—an image so grotesque and convincing, so
dehumanized and enmonstered, that we find ourselves
trapped, betrayed: we find ourselves siding with this cheap
egocentric queer, this thrill-killer, against the judge and jury of
goodmen like ourselves; and *because* of his crude, outrageous
effrontery. The fantasies of the just are shown as more vile
than the crimes of the villain, the judges become the judged:

the subversive evil game of *The Balcony* is played out before
us, within us, sixteen years ahead.

Jean-Paul Sartre's *Saint Genet, Actor and Martyr* is almost as
unlikely a phenomenon as the man who is, ostensibly, its subject.
It was commissioned in 1952 as a "preface" to the French edition of Genet's "Collected Works"—his passport into respect-
ability. But Sartre so spilled over his bounds that it filled all of
the first volume, easily the longest of the three. He had written
a "preface" half as long, and twice as difficult, as the Collected
Works themselves.

The author, at first glance, seems surprising as well—Sartre,
in 1952, was as celebrated as Genet was unknown; Genet's un-
der-the-counter works had been available only in expensive and
limited editions. It was not the sort of perverse taste one ex-
pects a distinguished philosopher and man of letters to confess
to, let alone to defend at such phenomenal length.

Strangest of all is the book itself. It can by no stretch of the
definition be called a critical work. It is not about Genet's
works, but about the "work of art" that is Genet himself—or
that he becomes in Sartre's hands. Genet's writings are never
here considered as things-in-themselves; they are regarded
rather as pretexts, as evidence for the philosophical and biographical points that Sartre is making.

For Sartre is one of those who regard the Man Genet, the
example of his archetypical life, as something far more important than all of his collected works. Now this may be: and our
glance at the works themselves may have already suggested
something of this sort. But it early becomes evident that this
stupendous study is not about Jean Genet, but rather about an
elaborate philosophical construct of Sartre's who passes by his
name, borrows his words, and shares the events of his life.

The method of Sartre's presentation is the give-away. He has
taken a number of events and stages in Genet's career (and
invented a few others), and fitted them together into a dialectic pattern positively awesome in its baroque elaboration; he
has spun out of each word, each gesture of Genet's the most
extraordinary web of mytho-philosophical conjecture, and
then pieced all the pieces together. It all, or almost all fits; like

any decent philosophical system, this fantastic spun-glass geometry of the Sartrean mind holds together. It is truly a wonder to observe, an arduous challenge to follow. But it must not be mistaken for Genet.

Our first suspicions arise from Sartre's unique brand of "philosophical psychologizing," his fantastically excessive, but militantly asserted metaphysical conjectures. Genet's bastardy leads him—at six—to cosmic alienation, explains a score of other characteristics. He feels himself his mother's excrement, not her child, we are told; by which is explained *that* taste. His inability to own things explains his poetic dematerializations. He is motivated not by hunger or loneliness or sex, but by "his austere and feverish quest for Being." His life becomes a metaphysical un-merry-go-round between Being and Nothingness, subject and object. He is forever making difficult existential decisions, consciously evaluating his directions in terms of Sartrean ideals, structuring his life on a perfect Sartrean pattern.

What Sartre has done has been to take the historic Genet as a frame of focus for all that he has himself thought about the human condition. It is as if he had been trying to rewrite *On Being and Nothingness* in elaborate parable form; to give his concepts an incarnate point-of-intersection, an embodiment called Genet. To make the task more difficult, he set himself the challenge of constructing this artifice, this philosophic tale, out of the real Genet's *own* words and actions.

He borrows his building materials from the literary and biographical facts of the real Genet, then restructures them, adds cause and effect sequences, invents motives, and pumps in universal relevances: what results is a carefully-crafted, inner-coherent fictional character, like Lytton Strachey's Victorians, Tolstoy's Napoleon, Gide's Dostoevsky, the Marxists' Lincoln, bearing a sort of squared-off shadow resemblance to the original. The ideas, the stages spin out from one another with fine philosophical coherence; but if one were to stop at any point and measure the construct against this particular French thief and writer born in 1910, the results would be bewildering.

Occasionally, rarely, Sartre's and the real Genet do seem to coincide, and his comments and explanations can be helpful. But such correspondences are infrequent, almost accidental.

"In a *good* critical work, we will find a good deal of information about the author who is being criticized and *some* information about the critic." These terms are decidedly reversed in Sartre's attempt, and he could be damned out of this, his own footnote. But this is to presume that the mind of Sartre is less valuable than the art and life of Genet. If we do not here have Genet, we *do* have Sartre. And that is something. As a sequential construct, a philosophic idea given local habitation and a name, there is still much to be learned from Sartre's Genet: it is suggestive, challenging, enlightening, exhausting. If, as they say, there were not a Genet, Sartre would have had to invent him anyway. As indeed he has.

The pattern of Sartre's Genet—and the structure of his book —is that of an existential Quest for Being in thirteen stages: tracing it through its mathematical jungle of sophistries is itself a good week's work.

The pattern begins with his birth as an unwanted alien, and his ontological christening: "You're a thief," the young Genet is told; and, like a good Existentialist, he elects to be one. From this he moves to a total Will to Evil, *absolute* alienation, both in essence and in act, and the hopeless, 600-page search for a Self is on. Condemned from the moment of his birth, trapped in his own identity-curse, he nobly wills himself to *be* what he must, what he is: "This is his greatness: he has willed his solitude, his exile, and his nothingness."

We follow, or try to follow, this "feverish quest" from the first Will to theft and to Evil (remembering, all the while, that "it is freedom, it is particularity, it is solitude that we are aiming at, and not Evil for its own sake") through homosexuality, solipsism, betrayal (the worst of evils—to harm evil itself); "saintliness" or self-negation, Platonic idealism, and illusionism; to aestheticism, virilification, and, finally, *Art*. At last, we have found our Being.

> Burglary, age, and weariness have slowly and slyly acted upon Genet: without awakening him, their patient action has disgusted him with dreaming; without virilifying him, it has forbidden him to play at femininity. . . . in extending to all domains, this sexual transformation is going to lead Genet from aestheticism to art . . . an austere, lucid, calculating consciousness comes into being, freed from all dreams, freed even from

the dreamer who dwelt in it. This pure freedom of the artist no longer knows either Good or Evil, or rather it makes of them only the object of its art: Genet has liberated himself.

"The consciousness of others is the medium in which man can and must become what he is." There are still two hundred pages to go, but this is, effectively, the end of the quest. It has, for Sartre, his Genet, and for us, been arduous, tiresome, enlightening, maddening.

Sartre's own prose style, the language of his discourse, can ring as hard and clear as fine crystal. So often do we find the right, the illuminate word, the sudden drop to a keen poetic specificity that at last lets us in on his secret; there is, in his drolly perfect examples and analogies, that grounding in the real that is the mark of the effective and communicating, the this-world-dwelling philosopher. Moreover, his elaborate, painstaking progress into the dialectical soul of his Genet is a triumph of creative intellection, of hard-willed, flame-like application. Once we grant what this thing of his is—that it is not, really, "Genet"—it can be a dizzying delight, a brisk and exhilarating exercise to swim in the Sartrean currents, to follow this mind at work. Everything *fits* so well, everything follows; his stages lead so neatly one to the next, ideas are spun out to all possible conclusions with such admirable honesty and thoroughness. And along the way, we will have completed a full course in the existential philosophy of Jean-Paul Sartre. Some of the real prizes in this book—the creation of the "Evil Man," the ferreting-out of the Worst Possible Evil, the "Myth of Nature," the invaluable historical notion of "The Loser Wins"—have nothing, necessarily, to do with Genet; they remain our possessions long after the experience of the progress has been forgotten. We will have been forced, moreover, if we have read honestly, to have dwelt for at least six hundred pages in metaphysical realms, to have thought of life in terms of Being and Nothingness, the absolutes of Self and Other. The extra-mundane awareness is, I think, an ennobling and valuable possession, particularly when it is so grounded in the real; we may—so gruelling is the ordeal of reading the book—find our minds in fact permanently expanded to this extra dimension.

These are the "Beauties" of *Saint Genet;* but the "Faults," in this monster of a book, come near to submerging them. What actually takes place, while reading, is a continuous alternation between disgust and delight: it is all a compound of the most rigorous logical deduction and painstaking dialectic with wilfully indulged personal mythologies, malevolent absurdities, bizarre conjectures and judgments; leaps and turns and twists that leave us half-gasping at the intellectual agility, half-appalled at the hopelessly distorted assertions.

If the style can be crystal-fine, it can also be dissonant, crypto-mythical, sententious and bullying. It can oftentimes seem so padded, so endlessly repetitive, so incredibly unedited. Worst, it is studded with those maddeningly coy, half-meaningless aphorisms the French refuse to stop using: "May it be that poetry is only the reverse side of masturbation?" And if Sartre is an agreeable enough philosopher, a harmless pseudo-psychologist, he is—here, at least—a hopeless literary critic.

The overall logical progress is clean and controlled; but Sartre has a mania for the muddy whirlpools of paradox—*"tourniquets,"* he calls them ("whirligigs," Frechtman translates)—he finds, or invents, en route. Since Evil, for him, becomes "a geometric locus of all contradictions," the nexus of all paradox, we whirl back and forth endlessly on the tiresome, everlasting, and apparently inescapable wheel, as it spins on in space engaging nothing substantial. The purely Evil man must want to harm the Good; which means he must understand and appreciate what is Good; which means he cannot be purely Evil . . . And so on, and on. Sartre claims that Genet has a particular taste for these tail-chasing spirals, these endless sophistries. "Genet constructs them by the hundreds. They become his favorite mode of thinking." The truth is, of course, that *Sartre* does, since "Genet" here is only his puppet-creation.

I have suggested that Sartrean philosophy, at its best, can be enlightening, expanding, and humane. At its neutral mid-point, it can be meaningless, but abstractly fun to follow. At its worst —and there are three major sections here that bring out the worst—it is spiteful, perverse, malevolent, and wrong. In each case, Sartre is simply using his dummy-Genet as a club to flail viciously, stupidly, uncontrollably at his own particular enemies: the bourgeois, the Church, Mauriac, Jouhandeau; sometimes, when a particularly misanthropic fit is on, at the whole world except Genet and himself.

The first instance (24–31) is his "Scapegoat Theory of Evil": "If we want to find the real culprits in this affair, let us turn to decent folk and ask them by what strange cruelty they made of a child their scapegoat." "In the case of those who condemn Genet most severely, I would say that homosexuality is their constant and constantly rejected temptation, the object of their innermost hatred, and that they are glad to hate it in another person because they thus have an opportunity to look away from themselves." This is all very common cant, and one might have hoped beneath M. Sartre. It is all so sophistical, question-begging, fraudulent: a cheap dare that defies us to object: to exonerate the criminal by rhetorically turning on others, making the fact of his imputed vice the evidence for theirs, with no other intention than that of clouding the issue of his crimes.

The second instance is the chapter on "Saintliness" so-called (194–249), where Sartre's social prejudices (pro-activism, anti-quietism; pro-Marxist, anti-clerical) lead him to the most chokingly grotesque mythifications of sociology and economics. Philosophically distorted psychology may be—as so often here —worthwhile, even if it is not honest psychology. But philosophically distorted history is absurd and worse. He sets up puppets called Saint Therese and Jouhandeau, just to knock them down with his puppet Genet: "After the canonized Saint, after the Sinner, what a relief to be with him again. What rectitude he has, what frankness!" What bilge. The whole chapter is shot with a personal spleen that undercuts any pretense to controlled and logical argument.

Most offensive, perhaps—doubtless because directed not at the French bourgeoisie or St. Therese, but at the reader of Genet, i.e., me—are his blithe assertions of what happens to us when we read (499–502). We *become*, it seems, the villain. "Regardless of who the writer is, when the sentence starts with 'I,' a confusion arises in my mind between this 'I' and my own . . . *it is I* who desire the boy." Deny this, and he has you on the hip. You say no? You shut the book in disgust? "What you vomit must in some way have been inside of you. . . . It is your soul that is rotten." Poor François Mauriac, who had the temerity, and in no uncertain terms, to find Genet disgusting, has only revealed his own "loathsome instincts."

*

This is all of course vile, but it returns us to the essential question of Jean Genet: is he really all that evil? Does he really
elicit such loathsome responses, pervert us in spite of ourselves?
   The last, the releasing stage in the philosophic quest of Sartre's Genet not only freed him from his circular search for
Being: it also moved him in his direction toward a militant, evil
attack on the human race. The decision to escape through art
necessarily brought with it the obligation for Genet to establish, for the first time, a relationship with the world of men.
And the relationship he chose—in Sartre's fictional schematiza-
tion, but also, apparently, in fact—was not the most salutary
for us.

> What if he gave himself, by an act, the power of existing else-
> where, in all his virulence, for horrified minds? . . . What if
> he deliberately invented a way of embodying himself in strange
> substances and forced the others to discover him there? . . .
> Hidden behind a wall, this crafty hoodlum could enjoy at will
> the astonishment of decent people.

Is this what Genet has done? Granted, his thievery was criminal, his prostitution base, his ethic of betrayal inhuman. But if
he is to be the epic Master of Evil Sartre has claimed for him,
his books must live up to their reputation: they must have the
power to turn *us*, who have never known him, to evil.

> Genet, who has been a victim and instrument of the good citi-
> zen since childhood, is now able to avenge himself at last. . . .
> He will make that innocent discover the Other in himself; he
> will make him recognize the Other's most improper thoughts
> as his own; in short, he will make him experience with loathing
> his own wickedness.

This alone might lead us to virtue; the true test would be for
us to enjoy the wickedness we discover. In one way, Sartre
points out, the mere act of reading becomes complicity. "The
bamboozled reader starts by following Genet and then finds
himself in the process of affirming the opposite of what he
thinks, of denying what he has always affirmed." Does he? Do
we? "By the beauty of his style, of his images, by the aesthetic
depth of his inventions, by the rigorous classical unity of his
works . . . we find ourselves in the process of accepting for

its formal beauty a universe whose moral ugliness repels us."
This might in fact happen, if one could find all that beauty and
order.

Once, at least, as I suggested, in *Our Lady of the Flowers*,
this very subversion does take place; faintly, infrequently, in
the other narratives. (Sartre makes a good case for *Miracle of
the Rose*.) Again, we may find ourselves willfully indulging
our worst in the opening scenes of *The Balcony; Deathwatch*,
Sartre claims, once moved a spectator to murder. But on the
whole the effect is nowhere near so dire as Sartre pretends. We
may have been momentarily trapped, but we soon return to
our moral selves not greatly shaken. This may be enough to
content Genet, but it doesn't yet make him the Devil; a minor
devil, perhaps, as a minor writer—a truly greater writer with
his will to Evil might indeed do serious damage. But until he
appears, we have devils enough, far more disastrous and subtle
than Genet, to concern us.

Cleanth Brooks' Faulkner [1964]

Professor Cleanth Brooks of Yale has written a long, handsome, and unfailingly sensible book about all of Faulkner's Yoknapatawpha novels. He is obsessed by no thesis, driven by no design: he simply wants to help us to read the novels as sympathetically and thoroughly as he has, and as they deserve to be read. To those who would shrink the novels into histories of the South or tracts on the Negro Problem, or bloat them into symbol-lands, to those who would wrench out his characters' speeches and call them Faulkner's, to all of the many non-readers and misreaders and pushy, perverse interpreters he counters his own brand of humble and illuminating common sense. "The book has its own rights, as it were, and in proportion as we admire it, we shall want to see not merely what we can make of it, but what it makes of itself."

First he clears the messy ground before him, patiently explaining what the books are not. *Intruder in the Dust* is *not* about lynch mobs in Mississippi, *Absalom, Absalom!* and *The Sound and the Fury* are patently not allegories of the Decline and Fall of the South. Gavin Stevens does not speak for Faulkner, Faulkner does not hate healthy sex, Joe Christmas is not a Christ-figure, Ike Snopes' affair with a cow is not the summit of sanctifying love. There is so much nonsense to be shoveled away.

Now he can turn to the novels themselves. To each he gives

a chapter of its own, the tone, direction, the critical intensity and shape of each directly stemming from the novel out of which it grew. Some (*Intruder in the Dust*) are primarily corrective, some (*Sanctuary*) designed to solve particular problems. Some (*The Sound and the Fury*) enter their novel through the coils of narrative technique, in the untangling of which—Faulkner's maddening and extraordinary gift—Brooks has no peer. Others start with thematic considerations—love, honor, the Community, the pathetic grandeur of Faulkner's "plain people"; or ease their way in character by character. Every essay, whatever its peculiar approach, brings us back to the novel, clearly if not completely, with directness, wisdom, and justice.

It is especially interesting to see what Brooks has done for the "major works," the works so tiresomely overdiscussed one would think they had by now been drained dry of useful comment. For each his presentation is clear, respectful, unshrill; aware of others' work, he can still be of help. For "The Bear," he simply "points out a few of the great scenes" for Parts I–III; explains the grand, daring stroke of Part V; and provides, for the deep-winding discussion of Part IV, just the kind of lucid analytical outline we need. On *The Sound and the Fury* he is more hesitant still, perhaps still more aware of the reams of previous commentary. He talks around and about the three crazed brothers, comparing them, gingerly reconstructing the inner maelstroms that merge into this blackest of books. For his favorite, *Absalom, Absalom!*, he modestly offers, in an eight-page appendix, a priceless tabulation of what we know and what we don't, when and where we learned it; a genuine labor of love. The best single chapter, to my mind—perhaps because it was most needed—is that on *Intruder in the Dust*. All of Professor Brooks' peculiar characteristics and abilities—his intelligent Southernness; his keen common sense for the obvious; his respect for the book-as-it-is, unfogged by current social problems or critical modes; his feeling for Faulkner's sense of the community, for his keen comic touch—all of these are employed in the crafting of this sure and brilliant chapter.

No reader of Faulkner will agree with everything Brooks has to say; but in each chapter he will find something he needs: at very least he will find the novel, offered frankly and unstained.

His presentation of *The Hamlet*, for example, is clumsily over-schematized, chopped up into overlapping abstract "themes" with a heavy hand. But there is Ratliff, there are Eula and Flem, there is Ike's idiot-poetry; there, in three pages, is "Spotted Horses." Brooks can, on occasion, become hung up on his own themes, force out strange things that aren't the novel. But as long as he can recreate the *experience* of Faulkner so vividly, so completely, it is pointless to quibble.

For this, after all, is his gift. He takes the novels as they are, sees them, feels them, tries to explain them, brings them back to us—the novels we have read (and those we have not)—richer than before. These are not "interpretations" but *presentations*, re-presentations, every word rooted in the novels themselves. The value of his work, ultimately, is to strengthen our own hold on the novels, to enrich our remembrance and affirm, justify our possession. This may seem a modest achievement, but no honest critic dares try to do very much more.

Not all of Faulkner is open to him: as hugely human as the novelist is, each of us may take to himself his own share, his own Faulkner. Brooks finds, and offers us, primarily the wise, Man-affirming tragi-comedian, the creator of Uncle Ike and the Reivers, the voice behind the voice of V. K. Ratliff (surely the most humanely ingratiating narrative presence in literature). What he most admires are the ancient, smiling eyes behind the triumphs, the clumsy, boorish, inarticulate triumphs of Lena Grove, the Bundrens, the Mink Snopes of *The Mansion*. This Faulkner, conscious, loving, community-rooted Faulkner, the Faulkner who "leaves us not knowing whether to laugh or cry," he understands like a brother.

> One might try to characterize Faulkner's attitude in this fashion: he finds human beings fascinating, so fascinating that the fact that his characters are ignorant rustics in no wise diminishes interest in them. He is not willing to set any limits to what they will do in terms of trickery, mad folly, or even heroism: the human being is obviously capable of almost anything. This conviction springs not from a weary cynicism but from a profound conviction of the powerful mystery that resides in human nature. Faulkner simply does not condescend to his characters, not even—to use a currently fashionable term—by feeling com-

passion for them. His interest in his characters goes far beyond all the modes of condescension.

But his clear and sympathetic vision of Faulkner's "middle range" maintains itself very nearly to the exclusion of any real sense of the depths, the Underground, the irrational blood-currents of passion and horror. It is all, for Brooks, too much in the sun. He is not blind to Faulkner's sense of the spiritual, the non-rational—religion, honor, love, the superhuman endurance of subhuman beings; but to the powerful wellings-up of the creative unconscious, to the inner darkness that one feels in the very roll, the resistless, repetitive roll of the prose, the compulsively sinuous, off-putting plots—to this he is closed. Faulkner *is* all that he says he is, and it is rare and fine of him to see it. But he is more. To balance off *Light in August*, as he does, by celebrating the victory of the enduring Community over the poor "Outsider" is somehow to make the novel a bit too safe, too homey, to mute the felt effect of inner horror. The ocean-floor pressure at which Faulkner's packed, desperate imaginative life was led, the ocean-slow inexorable pace, the drunken roll of words, the more-than-sexual sex; all the mad driven fury *against* which Brooks' humane and affirming Faulkner was so obviously fighting—none of this is here. In making "The Yoknapatawpha Country" too solidly a human "Community," he neglects to remind us that it was also a Region of the Mind.

But this is perhaps simply to substitute my Faulkner for Professor Brooks'. One cannot dwell simultaneously in the clear realms of critical common sense and the subterranean depths. Let me qualify my earlier claim only so far as to say that it is *almost* all here: despite its limitations, its occasionally murky prose, this is the most sensible, most valuable book about Faulkner ever written. I have concentrated on the central chapters (the first three may be skipped): but one's eight-fifty also buys 75 pages of useful critical notes; genealogies of all the big Yoknapatawpha families; a *complete* index of Faulkner's people; and one of the best-looking, most visually and tactilely readable books of the year, with a magnificent Cartier-Bresson bookjacket photo. The publisher may be as proud as the author.

Everybody's Shakespeare [1964]

There are two ways of writing a biography of Shakespeare. The first is to tell all that one knows about the man William Shakespeare. This can be done, and has been done, in ten pages. One notes his Stratford family, his birth approximately four hundred years ago last April, his wedding at eighteen to a pregnant older woman, the names of their children; then his partnership in a company of players, the fairly certain list of his poems and plays, his various addresses, the property he bought and sold, a few minor lawsuits, tax bills, and civic enterprises; the reports of a handful of friends (and one enemy) on his moderate fame, his agreeable nature; some dedications, some deeds, and his will; his death in 1616. With less assurance, the biographer can then take note of the seventeenth-century legends—the deer poaching, Shakespeare's roles at the Globe, his London wenching, the Stratford carouse with Jonson and Drayton that supposedly brought on his death.

This is something, but it is hardly enough. It does not conjure up a man. It is dispiriting, when we try to turn from the writing to the writer, to have England's greatest word-art dwindle to a few property deeds and dedications and a second-best bed. So we try to squeeze out something more.

The second way to write Shakespeare's biography, then, is to guess, conjecture, invent, bluff, digress, fill in "background," and analyze and criticize the poetry for several hundred more pages. Add capsule biographies of Elizabeth, Essex, Marlowe, Jonson, Greene, and (especially) the Earl of Southampton; summarize the social, political, economic, and cultural history of Elizabethan England; describe the Warwickshire countryside, 1588 London, and the shape of the Globe; and discuss Shakespeare's plots and plot sources, other men's plays, and show business, playwrighting, and the printing trade generally at the turn of the sixteenth century. What we have then —we have just got three more—is a book-length "Shakespeare: His Life and Times," but mainly his times.

There is something not entirely genuine, then, about these three new biographies,* or at least about two of them. The third doesn't quite pretend to be a proper biography, and is all the more successful. There is little that is strikingly new. The first, the great historian's Shakespeare, is full to bursting with detail and critique and conjecture; but it is aggressively, offensively written, and almost physically uncomfortable to read. The second, by a professional biographer, is a patch-up of the same general sort. It is shorter, less pretentious, and agreeably readable—if not so miscellaneously informative. The third book, by a theatrical journalist, is the smallest, most modest of all. It is a winning little book, one that actually tells us something new and worth knowing about Will Shakespeare.

A. L. Rowse's great new theme is Shakespeare's sex life, the sonnet business, the ups and downs, the pains and after-effects of Shakespeare's supposedly not entirely requited love for the Earl of Southampton in 1593–1595, an affair triangulated toward the end by the entrance of the famous Dark Lady. For Rowse, there is no problem. It is all simply and unquestionably literal fact, read exactly out, sonnet by sonnet, as obvious autobiography. "The game has now come to an end, for good and all . . . the problem is solved, as is clear for all to see." To this, the heart of his analysis, he devotes forty close pages in the center of the book. He then spreads its color over the rest of Shakespeare's work and life, finding more and more "obvious"

* *William Shakespeare: A Biography*, by A. L. Rowse. Harper & Row.
Shakespeare: A Biography, by Peter Quennell. World.
How Shakespeare Spent the Day, by Ivor Brown. Hill & Wang.

corroborations. Every play now yields nostalgic echoes of the bitter affair.

My objection to Rowse's book is not that this is all false: much of it, most of it may be true. It is rather that his pretensions are so vastly in excess of the facts, his assurances so entirely unwarranted, his manner and tone so pompous, so pushy, so uncivil.

It all begins, he insists, with something called "historical method." "It has enabled me to solve, for the first time, and definitively, the problem of the Sonnets. . . . I have, for the first time, been able to establish the date and occasion of *A Midsummer-Night's Dream.*" "Only the historian" can follow what Shakespeare wrote, "humbly line by line," with an eye to outside events "with firmness and achieve certainty." "Only the historian" can appreciate Shakespeare's conservative political genius, and thus *Henry V;* only the historian can discover all the buried references to Essex.

Rowse's trumpeted "historical method" often seems no more than a thin framework of matched-together dates and patched-together facts, filled in with cubic yards of egoistic bluster and assertion. "We have no reason to doubt that *A Midsummer-Night's Dream* was produced to grace the occasion" (the Countess of Southampton's second marriage). "There is no reason now for doubting that Marlowe was the rival poet of the Sonnets." There are good reasons for doubting both. "All commentators have taken this as a reference to the Armada of 1588. It is not." "There has been some doubt about the dating of the play: I do not see why: it visibly comes between *Troilus* and *Measure for Measure,* and it breathes the atmosphere of early 1603."

Throughout, Rowse pretends that Shakespeare's life, his thoughts, his actions, his motives and meanings are all transparently clear. The only reason I can conceive for this bland and patently fraudulent pretension of "knowing all" is nothing more or less than intellectual pride: Rowse refuses to admit that any Shakespeare can be too paradoxical or ineluctable for a great historian to understand. What we resist, in the end, are not Rowse's facts, not his conjectures, but his shoveling technique, his constant and unwelcome presence in the book. He interrupts the stream of his own thickish prose with silly asides, exclamations, rhetorical questions. There are tasteless inlays of cheap editorializing, of Conservative cant. Each man may indeed make his own Shakespeare; but it takes a grotesquely perverted lack of historical imagination to turn *Coriolanus* or *Henry IV* into splenetic attacks on the welfare state.

It was obviously the fate of Peter Quennell's *Shakespeare* to be everywhere measured against Rowse's. For, despite its disagreeable features, Rowse's book, with its wealth of detail, is the year's most impressive Shakespeare biography. Quennell duplicates his senior's outline exactly, chapter by chapter; he fills up his book with all the same material for a Type 2 biography—lively background material, side biographies, respectable critiques of the works in chronological order. He indulges in Rowse's sport of hunting out quotations to shore up biographical conjectures, sniffing out Shakespeare from his works; and he reaches much the same conclusions as Rowse in regard to Shakespeare's loves.

Several factors make Quennell's effort the more generally readable. He is, first, better trained at quick, graceful, popular writing, and can often say as much in a page as Rowse does in ten: he covers the details of Shakespeare's will and death in two substantial paragraphs, while Rowse is still lumbering through his documents and sources. He can carve out great slices of intellectual history without the professional historian's baroque armory of detail. He is always moving modestly and clearly forward, casting his light.

Secondly, Quennell is a critic of considerably clearer head and commoner sense. Rowse has a tendency to stuffy Bardolatry; Quennell keeps his reader's wits always about him. He can flick the early poems with his nail and hear them ring dead, and then *say* so. His ear for living verse permits him to make keen believable judgments of the Histories—and, more importantly here, of what Shakespeare thought when he wrote them.

Finally, he is far less proud, less assertive, less unkind. "At every stage of his existence, the great majority of statements that we make about Shakespeare's character and private life must be made in a conditional form." His treatment of the Sonnets, as I say, reaches most of the same conclusions as

Rowse's; but he *admits* to their tentative nature, confesses his difficulties, goes no farther than his due. His tasteful and brief account is ultimately far more convincing.

Quennell's freakish hobbyhorse, to correspond to Rowse's sonnet affair, is the Earl of Essex. Together with his Queen, the doughty Essex steals center stage from Shakespeare for a full chapter and a half. Quennell pretends this is all really about Shakespeare, but his very imbalance convicts him. Whenever he gets caught up with his substitute hero, his noble Essex—about whom, after all, we know so much more—he can forget to mention the poor playwright for pages at a time. He was fascinated by the Earl of Essex and decided to tell us about him.

Ivor Brown, before Kenneth Tynan, wrote dramatic criticism for the *Observer* and for the *Guardian;* his wife is a professional director. He is a dedicated, thoroughgoing, experienced man of the theatre. Since, as he makes beautifully clear, this is precisely what Shakespeare was, no one is better equipped than Brown, by temper and training, to reconstruct "How Shakespeare Spent the Day."

His book does not pretend, as I noted, to be a full-fledged biography. It is the story of Shakespeare's conscious workaday world, the competitive, hard-working life of the London stage. With a combination of fine source quotations, of prudent and informed conjectures, and of a spirited theatrical imagination, Brown whips it all back into life—the company and its owners, the directors, the stars, the supers, the ad-libbing clowns, the lively milieu, the company hacks churning out plays like TV writers, the scripts and promptbooks, the costumes and props, the records and schedules, the money problems, the audiences, going on tour; Shakespeare the part owner, Shakespeare the actor, Shakespeare at a casting meeting, Shakespeare at rehearsals, Shakespeare walking to work, Shakespeare busily scratching away at his candlelit desk.

He does daring things in the process—makes counter-reflective conjectures back from twentieth-century practice to Elizabethan, invents little tiring-room scenes of Shakespeare arguing with his colleagues. But he gets away with it all, because he is so obviously right. This *is* how Shakespeare spent the day,

for twenty or twenty-five years. It is right that we be reminded
of it, and a joy to be reminded so brightly, to have it re-created
with such verve. The *esprit* of Shakespeare's company—owners, stars, players, crew, writers together—is evoked with a just
exuberance, and then Shakespeare is planted in the center.

I believe in Ivor Brown's Shakespeare. But convincing and
near-complete as he is, we must not forget how much is missing. Brown has given us as genuine and close-up a motion picture as we are ever likely to get of Shakespeare's typical day.
But he leaves out—he admits he leaves out—"that other world
from which the Sonnets came, a world of intense devotions and
passions, deep pleasures and bitter disenchantments." He leaves
out also, but for a few glimmers, that strange artistic alchemy
down deep inside the head, far below the workaday theatrical
concerns.

It is clear that, for the most part, generation after generation,
we can only rejuggle our few pebbles of fact, respin, reconjec-
ture to suit our peculiar demands. Some minds seem to come
closer to Shakespeare's, however, seem to possess the right at-
tributes to needle their way in: minds no doubt humane, sympathetic, imaginative, the most like his. Keats, in his way, came
awesomely near. In his simpler, no-nonsense, "outside" way,
Brown has reached home too.

I cannot help thinking, though, that it is still the view *inside*
we are after: what did the imagination feel like that could
dream of Cleopatra, could spin out the speeches of Iago? Each
of the three biographers whatever else he may have essayed,
has helped us come closer, has sketched out one or two ideas of
the creative mind in action that strike true when we go back to
the plays, that seem to catch a responding gleam in the eyes of
the ubiquitous Droeshout engraving.

Then, it seems we are near; but only for an instant. Then
back to the frozen face, that locked-up wall of a forehead; or
better yet (as Jonson reminded us in the Folio: "Reader, Looke
not on his Picture, but his Booke") back to the endless design
of the plays. Somewhere, in there, he is hiding: somewhere in
those words we may find him. We are better armed now for
the search, possessed (thanks to our authors) of a new sense of
the view from his window, the scenes of his memories, the fur-

niture of his upper mind; the facts that stood about him, solid as his chair. We should, ideally, try to hold it all, the Warwickshire meadows, Elizabeth and Essex, the London streets; then turn quickly to the plays, and as we read—or listen—try to imagine ourselves writing, try to move into the mind, the hand, the scribbling pen. It is a maddeningly exhausting way, I grant, to read or watch Shakespeare; but it's the only way we'll ever find him.

Professor Pottle's Boswell [1966]

Why a biography of Boswell? And why, since we still have another volume to go, one so long and detailed? One answer (the one given on the dust jacket) is that *something* had to be made of those thousands of manuscript pages in Boswell's private papers, the extraordinary papers that first began to emerge in a Scottish castle forty years ago. McGraw-Hill put up a large portion of the half million dollars it cost to bring this cache to America, and the reduction of it into a "popular" biography may be one way to recover the investment.

Fair enough. But this is still not quite an answer to the question. A more acceptable reason may be Boswell's literary reputation, as himself the author of the most celebrated and most readable biography in the language. There is something to this, certainly, and Professor Pottle makes a strong case for the priceless quality of Boswell's literary gift.

But, although he is already collecting notes toward it in these earlier years, the *Life of Samuel Johnson* is the business of the last decade of Boswell's life, and hence of Professor Pottle's next volume. The great work of these years was the phenomenal Journal.

This Journal, or rather the very fact of Boswell's compulsive journalizing, might be regarded as an even more substantial answer to the question "Why a biography?" The *Life of Johnson* is magnificent; it is matchless. But it was for the most part an

artful job of editing from the great Journal, "the central literary creation of his life"—the Journal that is not only the major
creative effort of these early years but also, in its way, a more
extraordinary document than the *Life* extracted from it.

A case could be made, in fact, that Boswell's compulsion to
write himself out ("I should live no more than I can record"),
together with his absolute mania for veracity, his "almost pe-
dantic passion for circumstantial accuracy," remains his primary distinction. "The workings of his own mind fascinated
him, and he relished every other variety of human nature. But
the experience was not complete, not lived through, not wholly
realized, until he had explored it verbally and written it down."
He remained a fanatic self-recorder, an ego-objectifier all his
life, long after most men outgrow the compulsion to argue
with themselves in diaries. So much a function of his being is
the need to self-record that the reader feels, after one of
Boswell's warm, exact, Richardsonian reproductions of some
tender sexual encounter, that he had relished the experience *in
order* to write about it. "His recourse to orgy to dispel anxiety
has had plenty of parallels, but his recording of the orgy, not
without his usual tone of wonder at his own variety, approaches the unique."

But a genius for journalizing does not alone make a life (or a
biography), and a final justification for this book must be the
unique personality at its center—the very "original character"
that so fascinated Boswell, that he recorded so minutely, and of
which this compulsion to record is only one of a hundred incongruous traits.

Some of the traits are already part of the Boswell myth
(which Pottle tries here to reduce to rational dimensions). Boswell the celebrity hunter, surely the most ardent in history, is
apparent in the *Life of Johnson*. But he laid siege to others than
Johnson, and this volume records his campaigns after the Mar-
grave of Baden-Durlach, John Wilkes, David Hume, Rousseau
(a prize catch, a triumph), Voltaire, the Corsican hero Paoli,
the Pope, at least four Italian contessas, David Garrick, Joshua
Reynolds, William Pitt, General Oglethorpe, and—the one
that got away—Frederick the Great. He "has a rage of knowing anybody that ever was talked of," Horace Walpole

sneered. Boswell himself put it thus: "It is certain that I am not a great man, but I have an enthusiastic love of great men, and I derive a kind of glory from it."

Boswell the wencher is well known to his readers of his *London Journal,* the first volume to be popularly published. He regarded his own prowess as inspired ("Five times was I fairly lost in supreme rapture"), but Pottle ridicules the common diagnosis of satyriasis; to him it seems no more than a "high-rating" sexual athleticism. In any case, this rampant athleticism, from gutter to palazzo (which brought Boswell two bastards and half a dozen bouts of venereal disease in his first twenty-nine years), is here tantalizingly traced and perceptively analyzed, and may gain still more readers for the Journals.

Boswell the melancholic, the morbid, the manic-depressive; Boswell the sadistic, the silly, the all-charming; the madly ambitious, the morally weak; Boswell the restless, the insecure, the volatile and inconsistent, the zestful and self-indulgent—all of these Pottle presents and then attempts to understand, in extended analyses that are one of the book's ablest contributions. He traces puzzling character traits back to infancy, he tries painstakingly to separate out the tangles of conscious and unconscious motives.

I cannot say that Professor Pottle has quite made all this make sense, but he has certainly tried. Back of it all, no doubt, lies Boswell's absolute self-absorption. This adolescent and mirror-walled egoism made an unendurable curse of fathers, demanding mistresses, régimes of self-repression, the prospect of marriage or duty, failure of any sort, in fact *any* limitation of self-expression. At the same time, as Pottle reminds us, it gave us the Journal, and hence the *Life.*

Pottle's presence in the book, like Boswell's in the *Life of Johnson,* is not an unmixed blessing. Like Boswell, he makes no effort at anonymity, but sits most assuredly right in the middle of his narrative. Such biographical self-consciousness, in the robust eighteenth-century manner, may prove a bit vexing to our twentieth-century sensibilities. He tells us not only Boswell's story but a good deal of his own: descriptions of his jobs of research, self-conscious injunctions about "the biographer's duty," arch appraisals of his own rhetoric, defensive justifications of his own theories. He enjoys hiding surprises, delaying climaxes, offering asides to the reader: "We shall not be blackening a hitherto spotless reputation if we cast her in the role of Boswell's mistress." "Who, the reader may well ask, was this Margaret Montgomerie, and why have we not heard of her sooner?"

There *is* something a bit archaic in the manner; and of a piece with it are the Fieldingian euphemisms for sexual matters, the knowing professorial allusions, the facetious and condescending quotations out of context; as well, I suppose, as the tastes for Scott and Shelley.

Disturbing too, and I hope unnecessary, is Professor Pottle's constant defensiveness. The tone is present in everything he has ever written about Boswell for the past forty years; it conjures up a ghostly legion of Boswell haters whom he everlastingly feels the need to rebut. I grant (and Pottle grants) that there is much about Boswell that is hateful, and that "the choice between liking and disliking another human being is legitimately arbitrary." But I really wonder if most readers are as antagonistic toward Boswell as he seems to think.

It is this as much as anything else, this and the quiet note of frustration in his introduction (an account of his lifetime of labor in the Boswellian mine), that leads me to wonder if Professor Pottle might not have been a bit unhappy with the whole job; if the disparity of temperament between biographer and subject was really not too great ("If Boswell and I had met," he once told an interviewer, "we probably wouldn't have gotten along at all well. He was such a noisy, bouncy fellow . . ."); if all these years there has not been a certain honorable, against-the-grain strain to his endeavors, that reveals itself in the vague infelicity of this volume. But the great job is done, and done well, and this is no time to suggest switching biographers.

George Steiner   [1967]

In 1959, at thirty, George Steiner took on the immense rhetorical question of *Tolstoy or Dostoevsky:* a prodigious critical debut. In 1961 he brought his formidable critical arsenal to a proposition larger still: *The Death of Tragedy*. Now, Director of English Studies at Churchill College, Cambridge, he confronts the whole western world of literacy, morality, and communication, its past, its present, and especially its future.

"Now" is not quite right. *Language and Silence* is a collection of 31 essays written between 1958 and 1966 (all but ten of them since 1963), including his now more-or-less notorious polemics on pornographic literature and Hitler's murder of the German language. He included in the book introductions to paperback editions of Merimée's stories and Thomas Mann's *Felix Krull;* contributions to *Festschriften* honoring Ernst Bloch and George Lukács; a program note to the Convent Garden production of Schoenberg's *Moses und Aron*. At least ten of the component essays began as book reviews.

And yet one can fairly talk of the book as a whole, as a single and coherent presentation. It bears everywhere the mark of Steiner's compulsive, even obsessive imagination; it is woven into a tight web of argument, the same strands recurring and crossing, reinforced and refined, in every essay; and it is illuminated by a large, apocalyptic vision. Some of the essays I thought brilliant, most provocative, two or three small classics;

several terribly cheap. But what moved me most of all in the reading was not this or that insight, into Homer or Marxism, but the experience of, the encounter with, George Steiner himself: the gradual revelation or resynthesis of this extraordinary man, *his* imagination, *his* argument, *his* vision.

He was and remains a literary prodigy by Anglo-American standards. He refers several times to the "Central European Humanist," an intellectual type he reveres, and to which he quite clearly belongs. Its distinguishing marks are "a central humanism, classical in background, radical in bias . . . ; a sound knowledge of Goethe . . . ; an uneasy, yet profound admiration of Wagner; intimacy with Heine and Stendhal, with Lessing, Voltaire, and Ibsen"; a rejection of all nationalisms in the interests of a wider, cosmopolitan spirit; a full possession of Shakespeare; an active historical and social conscience.

> The type is recognizable. It is at home, or at least a familiar guest, in several languages. It has its distinctive note of wide, passionate allusion.

Steiner seems professionally familiar with Greek, Latin, Italian, American, and of course German, French, and English language and literature, and at least Russian literature. (He quotes, without translating, Spanish, Italian, and German, as well as French; a small hurdle for the less gifted.) The "distinctive note of wide, passionate allusion" is everywhere evident and occasionally jarring. He writes with assurance of history and politics, with some temerity of music, several sciences, and the visual arts, and with a flourish of uncertain expertise on anthropology, sociology, and economics. As a schoolboy, he tells us, he devoured each issue of *Scrutiny;* as a small lad he puzzled over the identity of Homer, Christ, and Shakespeare. There are 709 proper names in his index.

The breadth of cultural relevance is invigorating. The prodigious erudition can be a guilt-inducing spur to one's own sluggish provincialism. But it can also degenerate into name-dropping snobbery ("he discloses no awareness of Neugebauer"), into a nervous dilettantism or, worse, into a solipsistic bullying that lables as "illiteracy" any cultural equipment less heavyweight than one's own. Learning alone is not enough.

More profound and extraordinary is his imagination—an imagination doom-haunted, of tragic and cosmic dimensions, furnished in a manner as personal as Di Chiricho's or Dostoevsky's.

First, of the past: he is frankly obsessed by a private nightmare of the Nazi death and torture camps, and, correspondingly, by a troubled sense of his own Jewish identity. He grants that his "remembrance of disaster" is "perhaps literary, perhaps masochistic"; "that which haunts me and controls my habits of feeling strikes many as remotely sinister and artificial," but "the black mystery of what happened in Europe is to me indivisible from my own identity." And yet he insists, frequently, that we should all be similarly obsessed ("Men are accomplices to that which leaves them indifferent") and ridden with guilt. At the time of the Warsaw ghetto, "I was fed, beyond my need, and slept warm, and was silent," he berates himself: but he was also eleven years old. He traces feelings similar to his own in Trotsky, Kafka, Schoenberg, and the Anglo-American poet Sylvia Plath.

> Was there latent in Sylvia Plath's sensibility, as in that of many *of us* who remember only by fiat of imagination, a fearful envy, a dim resentment at not having been there, of having missed the rendezvous with hell? [my italics]

Secondly, of the present: young, cosmopolitan, something of a "high journalist," Steiner has a compulsive, love/hate relationship with Now; he cannot leave it alone, remain unaware of or uninvolved in each new piece of *actualités:* the new pornographers, happenings, "camp," Lévi-Strauss, Marshall McLuhan, random music, computer logic. It may be nervous, even neurotic, but it is not a mere display of intellectual *chic:* he honestly and desperately wants to "contain" what matters of the present.

Why? So as to be able to project it into the future. And this, the future, is perhaps the most radical aspect of Mr. Steiner's imagination, the root from which all else derives: the apocalyptic impulse to see ends and new beginnings. His imagination naturally flees the contingencies of today, to "extrapolate" a future in the willingly doom-driven manner of Henry Adams. *Everywhere* he sees the End of an Era, a new world borning, until one suspects something psychologically *a priori* in the very taste for prediction. First comes the compulsion to see (an end or a new beginning); then is collected the evidence to support it. It is this that allies him to Marshall McLuhan, a man who would otherwise fall depressingly far below his intellectual standards:

> He is one of those shapers of the present mood who seem to mark a transition from the classic forms of Cartesian order to a new, as yet very difficult to define, poetic or syntax of experience.

So too all those, from Blake and Nietzsche to Marx and Lévi-Strauss, who look down from afar and see our whole way of being (since 1500, or 1700, or even 5000 B.C.) as contingent, arbitrary, imperfect, non-progressive, and about to end: they are all enlisted in Steiner's army. He himself stands forever at the edge, wishing today away and tomorrow here.

The product of this particular imagination, multiplied by this particular erudition, is what might be called the *argument* of the book. The era whose end he is particularly interested in recording is that of "The Word"—his special province as a man of letters. Other epochal turns—the death of the novel, the end of individualism—are also marked or prophesied; but it is the Retreat from the Word that Steiner takes as his special concern.

> There is a widespread intimation, though as yet only vaguely defined, of a certain exhaustion of verbal resources in modern civilization, of a devaluation of the word in the mass cultures and mass-politics of the age . . .

> Are we passing out of an historical era of verbal primacy—out of the classic period of literate expression—into a phase of decayed language, of "post-linguistic" forms, and perhaps of partial silence? . . . "Who knows," says R. P. Blackmur, "it may be the next age will not express itself in words . . . at all, for the next age may not be literate in any sense we understand or the last 3000 years understood."

His arguments, drawn from every possible realm, are more persuasive individually than in the sum. He tends to find what he looks for, to make the evidence fit his vision; hard logic is sublimed into metaphor in the attempt to make all regions of the earth serve his hypothesis. But the arsenal of support is impressive nonetheless.

He points, first, to the bankruptcy of the classical literary tradition, revealed by Nazi Germany. He notes the superior expressiveness and depth of musical communication. He sees a greater imagination alive in the non-literary arts, as well as a more responsive public. In particular, he points to the dominion of the scientific mode and its rival language of number—a language that is precise, rigorous, objective, and demonstrable, by contrast with the inexact, impressionistic, personal, and unverifiable language of mere words. "Words distort; eloquent words distort eloquently." The language (and values) of science have penetrated history, music, the visual arts, the social sciences, even literary research—to say nothing of the world of politics, production, and consumption. The mere man of letters, unable to "share in the principal adventure of the contemporary mind," the realm that "has drawn to itself the most powerful minds of the time," feels more and more an outsider. His arable field is closed in tighter and tighter, by order of the austere, hard rule of Steiner's favorite philosopher: whereof one cannot speak, thereof one must be silent.

These are the claims of the rivals, the indirect proofs of retreat: what of the word itself? Steiner reaches his own greatest eloquence, ironically, in portraying the verbal decay and corruption that surround him.

> What save half-truths, gross simplifications, or trivia can, in fact, be communicated to that semi-literate mass audience which popular democracy has summoned into the market place? Only in a diminished or corrupted language can most such communication be made effective. . . . access to economic and political power of the semi-educated has brought with it drastic reduction in the wealth and dignity of speech.

He waxes Carlylean on the New Illiteracy and its servant-masters, the thought-controlling, word-deforming mass media, their "confidence tricks" and "hypnotic mendacities."

We are smothered in noise, blunted by the loud, everyday lies of advertising or politics, the loud everyday facts of the "news." We dwell in a "wind tunnel of gossip," at once deluged with cheap words and dependent, more every day, on non-words—on pictures, cartoons, images, loud bright colors.

No one reads aloud; the classics become inaccessible; literary prose shrivels to Hemingwayese, or bloats into erotic fantasia. "Words have killed images . . . words create confusion. Words are not the word . . . words say nothing": Ionesco. Beckett's plays and novels become dramatizations of Wittgenstein's rule. A decade of unprecedented abuse can break the very neck of, can *kill* a living language, Steiner proclaimed of German in 1959. But corrupt commercial means will inexorably attain the same end, sooner or later, in the mass democracies of the west.

Despite his scorn for the market place, his hatred of lie, and his disgust beyond words for fascism, it is not entirely clear where Steiner himself stands. His erudition is substantial, his imagination unique and definable, his argument, if not wholly persuasive, is clear: but his own final moral position is ambiguous. He calls the past dead, yet he tries to preserve it; he despises the present, yet longs to be of it; and as for the futures to which his imagination so anxiously bends, I cannot tell whether he wants to retard them, accelerate them, or simply to describe them neutrally, rolling along with the tide.

Over and again we are reminded of the Retreat from the Word, the end of the novel: but then we are rhetorically asked, in the essay on Durrell, "Who is to say, moreover, that the Alexandria Quartet will not lead to a new pleasure in narrative prose?"

On page 6 we are told that "there is demonstrably more of insight into the matter of man in Homer, Shakespeare, or Dostoevsky than in the entirety of neurology or statistics." And then on page 17 we are told that "Calculus, the laws of Carnot, Maxwell's conception of the electromagnetic field, not only comprise areas of reality and action as great as those comprised by classic literacy; they probably give an image of the perceptible world truer to fact than can be derived from any structure of verbal assertion."

Or observe, his unhappy championing of Marshall McLuhan, "the nervous cheapness" of whose prose obviously makes him sick; or of Claude Lévi-Strauss, whom he confessedly doesn't understand and cannot judge. It is here as with C. P. Snow and science: he stands so in awe of the New and the Coming that he must do honor to all those who seem to be at the head of the line. He treasures, as proper Central European humanist, the fine, honest phrase—but will leap overboard for anyone who seems to be riding the wave of the future, illiterate or not, understood or not.

Just where *is* his own commitment? It is clear that he does not like the quality of the present, or thinks he does not, or should not, or at least enjoys the role of denouncing it: all marks of a good conservative ("a time of fantastic intellectual cheapness, of unctuous pseudo-culture and sheer indifference to values—in the century of the book club, the digest, the hundred great ideas on the installment plan . . ."). But the "future" he posits is vague and unconvincing: never is his forward vision as sure, say, as McLuhan's—who foresees "the greatest of all human ages." Steiner's is a thing of "Pythagorean" books, self-defining, self-questioning, books that defy all general categories; of audience-participation, Brechtian psychodramas; of picture books, and no one reading Shakespeare; of people talking to one another in musical notes, or not at all (antennae, perhaps? or vibrations, like dolphins?); of organ transplants so radical as to destroy all existing notions of personal identity.

A question: Might not his "millenarianism," his strangely ambiguous prophesies derive from his disgust with what is, and his inner urge to hope it away, even if baby must go out with the bath?—and, secondly, from his own peculiar generalizing, future-dwelling, sociological imagination? May his prophetic concerns be psychological rather than philosophical? Another question: may he not be a secret conservative, and his book, secretly (secretly even to him, perhaps), another *Education of Henry Adams*, singing the anarchic future while covertly prizing the humanist past? There are evidently strong impulses in both directions; but I think the resulting vector still points to the past. The very *fact* of this book is, in a way, despite all its futurist assertions, a vote for the right use of words, for the present relevance of a classical culture.

Troyat's Tolstoy [1968]

There are three reasons for the excellence, the peculiarly exhausting excellence of this book. The first is the sheer quantity and quality of life lived by its protagonist (and his antagonist: this is the life of two Tolstoys). With these reaches of barbarism, energy, sensuality, mysticism, notoriety, and disorder none of the subjects of the recent great wave of literary biographies can begin to compete.

The second reason draws on one aspect of this exaggerated, mad vitality: the Tolstoys' compulsion to record every tiny wave of hatred or exhilaration or self-disgust in a proliferating mountain of diaries, letters, and memoirs that must have been at once the blessing and the curse of Henri Troyat's labors.

The third is the genius of Henri Troyat.

The exaggerated quality of Tolstoy's life begins with that of late Czarist Russia; a holy, Dark Ages autocracy, a feudal aristocracy, pogroms, slave beatings, saints and gypsies and madmen, "snarling wolves and bare shoulders": the intensity of life is sometimes obscene. The lives of Tolstoy's Aunt Aline, of the blind poet who lulled his grandmother to sleep, read like tales out of medieval folklore.

Parents and grandmother were seized by death before Leo was ten, and the sensuous richness of a Russian aristocrat's country life was suddenly exchanged for the strangeness of Moscow, 130 miles across the snow. No richer seedtime for a novelist could be imagined than this childhood of death and disruption in a land and a time of extremes. There followed an adolescence of violent enthusiasms, a young manhood of Rousseauvean idealism and epic debauchery; at twenty-two, Tolstoy left home for the Caucasus and war, gluttonous for more experience.

The basic Tolstoyan personality, never radically to be changed, can be identified by his early twenties. He was a man of extraordinary sensitivity—to a scent, to an image, to an insult. He acted always with freakish vitality, showing the same fanatic zest in haymaking as in lovemaking, in riding as in writing. He was still boasting of, and recording, his sexual prowess well into his seventies. But he could also, as one of his daughters remarked, relish with equal lust the dry pleasures of abnegation and abstinence. Sudden and violent reversals, in fact, are the characteristic on which Troyat concentrates as best defining Count Leo Nikolayevich Tolstoy. "His periods of concupiscence and asceticism always alternated in rapid succession," Troyat writes of him at twenty-two. "He was two men—a sybarite and a saint—sewed up inside one skin, each loathing the other."

Erratic, impetuous, primeval in the directness and intensity of his emotions, knowing every passion and its reverse: he had, with all this, a disgust for artifice and decorum, a holy obsession with "honesty," that did not preserve him from his own elaborate structures of self-delusion, for all that it may have contributed to his art. (The classic horrible instance: forcing his eighteen-year-old fiancée to read a detailed account of his past seductions.) He invested all his prodigious energy in school reform one week, gambling the next, astronomy, Greek, hunting, peasant welfare, metaphysics, until his young wife could wonder to her diary, "Am I just another of his passing crazes?" And he had (the final ingredient in this recipe for a novelist) an unparalleled fascination with himself. Add to all this a self-assurance so great that nothing could ever bend or break it down, and the pattern is set. Once this was acquired (at about his thirtieth year), Tolstoy was able to bind up all his contradictions, and impose himself upon the world for fifty years as the embodiment of a new moral order.

In Troyat's account of the public career that followed, Tolstoy's fiction appears of secondary importance: a sort of platform of popularity from which the prophet-reformer could speak to his people. By thirty-four, he was a practicing public crank, a Russianized super-Rousseau drinking foaming goat's milk, making his own shoes, dressing like a muzhik (his version of the Noble Savage), sneering at art, and preaching a vague, anti-authoritarian, pantheistic Christianity. By 1881 he had made the full leap of faith, turned his profits and properties over to his wife, and moved bag and baggage into a rigid, uncompromising private world. Here he was to dwell, battered and battering, for the rest of his life.

To the dense, grand, sensuous masterpieces of realistic epic fiction succeeded holy manifestos, a legion of crackpot disciples, Tolstoyan colonies, rewritings of Scripture, movements of reform. The most celebrated writer in Russia at forty, he became at fifty its most subversive and untouchable idol. His books were banned, and read by millions. He was excommunicated by the Holy Synod and denounced by the Czar, but crushed almost to death by adoring mobs. He was turned to as an oracle, his every word recorded; he was a Czar above Czars. News cameramen, souvenir hunters, the needy, the troubled, disciples and parasites, the famous and the insane swarmed upon him at Yasnaya Polyana, lived in the house, ate at the table. His eightieth birthday, in 1908, became an orgy of celebrity worship. The mob watch at his deathbed, in 1910, could scarcely be equaled even today. It may reasonably be claimed that no author in history has suffered a comparable fury of fame.

The central tragedy of this life, however, was played not in the arena of words and ideas, but in the home—if "tragedy" is not too formal a word for the harness of mutual torment in which Sonya Andreyevna Behrs and Leo Nikolayevich Tolstoy were yoked together for forty-eight years.

Sonya was, at first, the perfect Desdemona to his Othello, an innocent, gay girl held spellbound by this rough-hewn, "experienced" count almost twice her age. (See the subplot of *Anna Karenina*.) But she soon blossomed into something very like her mate: as strong, as selfish, as volatile, as emotional; and very

strategic with her favors. They scratched out rival diaries—
Tolstoyan "honesty" in action—and then showed them to each
other, and then wrote angry replies, and so on, treasuring their
transient resentments like connoisseurs of hate.

Through the six years' gestation of *War and Peace*, Sonya
grew content. As long as she could be her artist-husband's
helpmeet and guard, she could also be his jailer; as long as he
was writing novels, he was in her power. She could write, in
1868, "We still argue, but the causes of these quarrels are so
deep and complex that they would not occur if we did not love
each other as we do."

But when the novelist became the prophet, the battle was
rejoined. "It will pass, like a disease," she wrote hopefully. Instead, she watched with horror as her husband, her noble, celebrated, wealthy author-husband, began to turn in disgust from
all she most treasured: her home, her comforts, her children,
her position, her religion. As a novelist, she could meet him; as
a saint, he was lost. And *he* watched in horror as the necessary
companion of his nights became a living insult to all his sacred
truths.

As she raked in the profits from his profane writings, he
writhed in mortification. "A fight to the finish has begun between us," he declared in 1885. Many times he tried to leave,
but could not. "God's commandment" to husbands held him
back.

When the sex tie was finally broken, in his eightieth year,
Sonya very nearly went mad. Now she had lost all hold. She
threw herself into a vile family scramble for the posthumous
rights to his works, now valued in the millions; but he had
invested all his affections and all his trust in his chief disciple,
Chertkov, a heartless servant-master whose power over her
husband drove the Countess to despair. She countered with
hysterical seizures, tried mock suicides *à la* Anna Karenina.
"They are tearing me apart," Tolstoy wrote of the two rivals,
and finally, on October 28, 1910, walked out to his death.

So thorough, so intimate is the wealth of written record generated by Tolstoy's life that his biographer can at times become
all but omniscient. Tolstoy's courtship of Sonya, for example,
was recorded instant by instant not only by the participants—

master diarists both—but by many observers as well. We have Boswellian recordings of conversations; warfaring diaries of marital tensions and bliss, corrected sometimes several times a day; dreams, fantasies, obsessions, hallucinations all described in minute detail; the combative letters and memoirs and journals of children and associates.

Priceless, certainly; unique. Yet this carload of documentation teems with troubling implications. The very fact of recording one's actions and emotions *changes* those actions and emotions, as Troyat clearly recognizes. In the Tolstoys' private diaries "honesty and candor alternate with insults and self-pity," and much is written in strategic self-defense. "The miracle is that their marriage stood the strain of this continual rivalry to see which could be most truthful." The documents were at once a therapeutic release, notes for novels, and missiles from one side of the bed to the other; later they became the valuable objects of a frenzied family struggle.

Their implications today, for biographer and reader, are almost as complex. Granted that their creation is itself evidence of aberration, of a morbid self-fascination and self-dramatization; granted further that the Tolstoys cannot be said to have discouraged their publication. Still, may they not, by the unavoidable demands they make on his attention, by their semiscandalous fascination, tempt a biographer to focus on the domestic, the conjugal, and to scant the achievements that made Tolstoy worth writing about in the first place? To reduce the author of *War and Peace*, in fact, to the role of a selfish, oversexed, mismatched husband? This temptation is, unfortunately, greatly strengthened by a silence in Tolstoy's diary for thirteen years, from 1865 to 1878, the very years he spent writing his two great novels.

This brings us round to the very special genius of Henri Troyat, for his interest is not that of a critic in novels, but of a novelist in men. If Tolstoy's novels seem to be "missing" from this biography, it is not only because they have little place in Tolstoy's life records, but also because Troyat does not like them very much or analyze them very deeply. He makes ritual obeisance before *War and Peace;* but in his plot-outline critique (the one piece of bad writing in the book), it is very nearly reduced to a web of artless sentimentalities, historical inaccuracies, and philosophic bilge. A great Gallic sneer is turned on Tolstoy's "injustice" to Napoleon.

Anna Karenina scarcely fares better. Troyat concentrates on the analysis of its sources and the demolition of its "ideas," and abandons the question of its art and appeal, after a few remarks on adjectives and details, to Tolstoy's ineffable "instinct, inseparable from life, owing nothing to technique."

Resurrection he finds brutal, crude, hammered together like a shoe. Troyat, a master of prose style, winces at Tolstoy's insensitivity to syntactic efficiency, to "a clash of vowel sounds." This does not mean that he may not say useful, even illuminating things about Tolstoy's fiction. But by and large, his criticism is the surface-skimming of an earlier age.

Nor is this very reasonable Academician particularly sympathetic with Tolstoy's idealist pretensions. Troyat himself is more akin to Turgenev, Tolstoy's favorite enemy: tactful, witty, impeccably suave, apparently disengaged; an aesthete and moralist with a deft, dramatic style, a tendency toward the cynical—and a total unwillingness to acknowledge the irrational, immoralist claims of the Exceptional Man. "Ah, the charms of temporary poverty," he observes of Tolstoy's short ride in a third-class coach. "This special menu suited both his philosophy and his lack of teeth," he remarks of the Master's vegetarian diet—a sleek nastiness worthy of Gibbon. Saints are very hard for the unconverted to live with, be they wives or biographers.

And yet I cannot imagine Tolstoy finding a better biographer. Though he steers clear of Tolstoy's soul, and avoids the lower reaches of the creative unconscious, Troyat has still written a magisterial biography.

The sure, dramatic order—of book, of section, of chapter, of paragraph, of sentence—is almost enough to justify the French educational system. He deploys his vast materials, plans his strategy, shifts his focus or point of view, moves from drama to abstraction, opens and closes his periods or his chapters, with the assurance and finesse of a master. The whole book glows with his intelligence and is articulated by his tact.

Troyat's rhetorical "presence" is as fluid and mature as Jane Austen's. He can energize and judge in the same perfect word, invisibly make the keenest distinctions with just the right detail, the mock drama of a rhetorical question, the wit of a parenthesis, all the while shaping a growing, organic drama that we at once experience as life and savor as art. His play of words bespeaks a lifetime of using them well; his sentences sing—even in English. (The translation, by Nancy Amphoux, is nearly perfect, invisible: she *is* Troyat, for all I could tell.)

As a judge—and biography, of course, is a hugely moral business—Troyat guides us through this jungle of guilt and blame (barring the excesses of skepticism mentioned above) with excellent balance. As a novelist himself, he knows the combination of words, details, rhythms, and quotations to bring these lives back to life, to make horribly clear the high human price of genius.

Turnbull's Thomas Wolfe [1968]

This review has been a long time in the writing. I decided, first, that there was no point in trying to write it until I had come to some terms with Thomas Wolfe's fiction. Although I stopped after the four novels, that still meant reading (in part rereading) 3,076 pages, perhaps a million words. I next decided to review, for purposes of comparison, the biography by Elizabeth Nowell, Wolfe's agent, written just eight years ago (Did we need another so soon?). Then to Mr. Turnbull. My response to the man and his works grew cumulatively, changed decidedly after each of the several courses in this glutton's feast, and I thought it might be useful to describe these changes in order.

One reason for my reading all the novels straight through was that I had never done it before. A second was that I was not at all sure what I thought of those I *had* read, not even of *Look Homeward, Angel.* I was more than a little suspicious—of my own enthusiasms at nineteen, of the continued enthusiasm of certain aging adolescents of my acquaintance, of Wolfe's reputation as the Romantic Young Man's novelist, of the egoism that seemed to lay behind those million words.

Thirdly, for a novelist so notoriously "autobiographical" (and precisely what this means is one of the cruces of Wolfe criticism; *he* insisted he was no more autobiographical than

Tolstoy), one of the duties of a biographer will be to let us know how accurate, how fair, how complete Wolfe's own accounts are; if and how far they should be taken as fact. To decide how well Mr. Turnbull faced up to this problem, I clearly had to know Wolfe's version first.

So, prodded by this autobiography, I turned to the works. Three weeks, three thousand pages later, I made my first assessment.

Look Homeward, Angel, the first book, is far and away the best, I am tempted to say the *only* good one, so different is its nature and quality from the other three. It is a small, sure classic of remembered childhood, of the sensitive child caught in the family trap. Though ultimately less objective, more sentimental than they, it merits comparison with *Sons and Lovers* and *Long Day's Journey into Night*. The determined, smothering cruelty of parents, the unspeakable sufferings (and unspeakable meanness) of the small, the claustrophobia, the tension, the open warfare of Home, Sweet Home; the caged-bird longings, the hot tears, the wincings, the bounds in the air: we have all been there.

The opening chapters of *The Web and the Rock*, Wolfe's second return to childhood, are almost of this level. Though they lack the naked honesty of the first, though they are clearly more contrived and less immediate, they too are poignant and compelling. For the rest—despite good scenes here, good pages there—nothing again is quite so strong. Why is this?

My theory is that only in his Asheville years—the years when he was longing and suffering *unconscious* of any intention to write about it—did Wolfe have a fund of pure experience susceptible to direct and communicable re-creation. Once he fancied himself a "writer," once he saw himself with such egoistic fixity as an "artist," his experience lost its exchange-value for affecting fiction. The Asheville material, experienced in rich, confused, passionate "unconsciousness," was gold; once it had been exhausted, he had nothing else really worth writing about. Once the Proust-game is finished, you don't then set out writing a new series of novels about sitting in bed writing novels.

"He had written out his chief compulsion in *Look Homeward, Angel*," wrote Elizabeth Nowell (in explaining his difficulties getting started on a second book), and I agree: just as I agree with Andrew Turnbull's sanely argued hypothesis that had Wolfe lived past 38, he would not have improved. If anything, I think, he would have repeated and repeated himself, each time more shrill and more shallow. For there is all the difference in the world between writing out of necessity, because one must (which Wolfe only did once); and writing because one wants to be, thinks himself to be, a "writer" (which he did ever after).

After *Look Homeward, Angel,* Wolfe had to draw more on profits than capital: to write in great part about the problems of being a writer—of agents, publishers, reviewers, of his genius and his enemies, of contracts and manuscripts and literary soirées. What extra-literary adventures he did have—his seven trips to Europe, his affair with Aline Bernstein—he describes but he does not *use,* so frozen is he now in self-consciousness. What we have, in the post-Carolina chapters of the last three books, are primarily a writer's memoirs, with all of the sensitive, self-defensive, egotistical bitchiness so often revealed in that form.

The success of *Look Homeward, Angel* released and further inflated, in Wolfe, an egotism of immense and irreducible proportions, an egotism absolute, elephantine; nearly solipsistic. Where it comes from, I don't know: it may be related to sexual prowess. But take this over-inflated ego, this mirror-walled conviction that I Matter Utterly, that my every dit and dot merits proclamation to the world, combine it with an indiscriminate, mock-Elizabethan, drunken lust for words; and you get—as you do, say, in Henry Miller—Wolfe's intense, religious assumption of a "Writer's" vocation. It is something very strange.

The protracted-adolescent temperament that made the story of his *adolescence* so vivid simply could not cope usefully with adult events; with lovers and fame and social classes and foreign cultures and the American character. Such a temperament (passionate, bewildered, hypersensitive, self-obsessed, tossing about the Great Thoughts) makes objective separation of author from hero impossible. It leads to the romantic inflation of every gesture or experience into epic, even cosmic importance. It impells Wolfe to voluptuary daydreams, gross lampoons, and fantasies of revenge. He comes to see himself, eventually, as a Noble Savage, gigantic and all-worthy, and the world about him as a race of vile, tiny vermin. *Of Time and the River,* and much of the two posthumous novels, are envenomed with a neurotic vision of

> . . . all the vile and uncountable small maggotry of the earth, the cautious little hatreds of a million nameless ciphers, each puny, pallid, trivial in himself, but formidable because he added his tiny beetle's ball of dung to the mountainous accumulation of ten million others of his breed.

There is more than this to the latter novels, but it is in this temperament that the rest begins. I did feel the intensity of the German sequences that conclude the last two, and the pathos of his loneliness and nostalgia. The structural imbalance, the lack of editing are failings one anticipates; they are part of the man's nature. I "speed-read," I must confess, most of the poetic or philosophical pages.

> As the great stars of America blaze over them, the vast and lonely earth broods round them, then as now, with its secret and mysterious presences, and then as now the million-noted ululation of the night throngs up from silence the song of all its savage, dark and measureless fecundity . . .

I have too much respect for words used precisely to linger long over words, so many words, used indiscriminately. These are words used not to mean, but to "express," and the self they are expressing is not one we all benefit from knowing. The very refusal to select (never a noun without an adjective, never one adjective when six will do) is an attribute of the Wolfean ego, of which no precious oozing must be lost. At last, I think, he was choked, imprisoned, hallucinated by his own cage of words, which became more real than the objects, the passions, the people, or even the self it pretended to represent. "It is words, words—I weary of the staleness of words, the seas of print, the idiot repetition of trivial enthusiasms" (Wolfe to his editor, on his writing; experiencing a momentary trough of ennui in the summer of 1931).

Reading Elizabeth Nowell's biography of 1960 did little to enhance my image of Wolfe. To the semi-fictional evidence of logorrhea and megalomania, drawn from three out of four of

Wolfe's novels, her book added a weight of semi-factual evidence of moral and mental disorder that only confirmed my attitude of disfavor. I say *semi*-factual because her book, though informative (especially on the latter years, the years of her own association with Wolfe), is not a real biography. It is rather in great part a collation of extended quotations, drawn primarily from Wolfe's own writing, a scrapbook of more or less relevant descriptions of his heroes' thoughts in situations more or less like his own.

This scrapbook-method has several effects. It gives to her "biography" a flat, soft, second-hand quality. It allows her to avoid the task of distinguishing between the novels and the life. It adds little, often, to one's experience of the novels, except to recall their worst features, since the method involves giving over great yards of space to the incongruous unrealism of Wolfe's own prose—the uncritical, whipped-mystic self-inflation it is surely a biographer's duty to cut through. Most seriously, it makes Wolfe seem a nasty fool. As the unedited, unqualified quotations mounted up, as the evidence from letters and notebooks was piled on that of the novels, I found myself turning more and more against the man. The climax was reached in his seventeen-page severance letter to Maxwell Perkins, ostensibly justifying his break with Scribners, which Miss Nowell typically quotes entire. This ugly letter gives biographical solidity to the self-portrait of the novels. It is composed of fantastic self-heroicism; of a necessary mad spectre of surrounding enmity; of the confused emotionalism of an angry child; and of a word-drunkenness in the service of all these, a debased form of language that itself, in great part, creates the sick fantasy world in which Wolfe had imprisoned himself.

> [When I write my *Ulysses*] I will be libelled, slandered, blackmailed, threatened, menaced, sneered at, derided and assailed by every parasite, every ape, every blackmailer, every scandalmongerer, every little Saturday-Reviewer of the venomous and corrupt respectabilities. I will be exiled from the country because of it, if I have to. . . . But no matter what happens, I am going to write this book.

In sum, I saw in this artless portrait a personal moral ugliness, a neuroticism and malice that I could not in the end justify by the merit of his works.

*

All this was only prefatory to reading Mr. Turnbull's new book. Due entirely to its excellence as a biography, his book effected an extraordinary transformation in my response to Thomas Wolfe.

He could not change my judgment of the novels. But he could and did deepen my understanding of, extend my sympathy for the novelist. And this by no tricks: if Andrew Turnbull reduced my resistance, undercut my objections, it was by satisfying so thoroughly the exiguous moral demands of the biographer's art.

He has, simply, brought Thomas Wolfe to life. By an ingenious use of others' memories and reminiscences, woven together with a discreet selection of the *honest* materials from Wolfe's own store, he has been able to reconstruct a vivid, Boswellian motion-picture of his hero; to write, as it were, a kind of objective "novel," with himself as the crafty, creative, all-but-omniscient narrator. He allows us not only to see and hear Thomas Wolfe, talking, teaching, eating, walking, gesturing, even sleeping: but even, gradually, to move *inside* him, to feel, ourselves, the inner pressures and compulsions, to share the activity of his creative mind at work; until at length the rhetoric, the outbursts, even the malice and mania come to seem natural, so carefully and vividly has Turnbull built in us a genuine understanding of his man.

He does, moreover, judge, qualify, and explain; if not with profundity—Wolfe still cries for intelligent *psychological* analysis—at least with tact and sympathetic insight. He sees the man's poses and defenses for what they are, and to each instance of absurd behavior appends an explanation, usually fair and persuasive. His generous sanity undercuts one's sputtering resistance. The long letter to Perkins, for example, that so offended me in Miss Nowell's account, is here reduced to two pages of summary and quotation, fair, judicious, no longer overwhelming. Its rhetoric is rightly defined as "a vein of drink-exacerbated self-pity reminiscent of old Gant." And in going on to speak of Perkins' reply, Turnbull acknowledges "the magnanimity of one who knows he is dealing with a demonic type. For Perkins comprehended, better than anyone ever had or would, the pathos of this great lonely misfit paradoxically crossed with Everyman, whose intensities became self-lacerating when deflected from his work."

Maxwell Perkins, I think, is the key to Turnbull's remarkable achievement. He has done many things well here. In addition to bringing Wolfe to life, and judging him wisely, he has treated intelligently the major questions of Wolfe criticism (the "autobiographical" question, the Asheville reception, the matter of revenge-fictions, Wolfe's anti-Semitism and Germanophilia, Perkins' co-authorship of his novels). He has folded in lively, balanced portraits of George Pierce Baker and Aline Bernstein, of Ernest Hemingway and Scott Fitzgerald (Perkins' other two children), as he did of Edmund Wilson, Irving Thalberg, Monsignor Fay and others in his biography of Fitzgerald.

But his "portrait" of Maxwell Perkins (the greatest editor in history?) is something larger than these. At first I wondered at its extent, its intensity of detail. Not even Wolfe's mother was given this kind of attention. Then I came to see that Perkins was not only the co-hero, but also in a way the co-author of this book. Turnbull is seeing Wolfe through his eyes, writing out of a temperament and perspective wonderfully like Perkins'. He shares Perkins' strictures on the works; but, like Perkins, he tries to point out, to analyze, reasonably to state wherein Wolfe *was* unique and had something uniquely valuable to offer. It was a respect for Perkins' judgment and decency, I am convinced, that led him to attempt this magnanimous assessment, and then to try to persuade us to attempt it too.

Having been thus chastened, led to a larger sympathy by Mr. Turnbull, I would like to turn into my anti-Wolfe self again just long enough to make a small final gesture of defiance. I grant, unhappily, that liking or not liking Wolfe's work may be ultimately a matter of temperament, inbred and inescapable: some like it hot. That for one to say "he does nothing for *me*" will mean nothing to the man for whom he *does* do something, will in fact only betray to him the former's unfitness and insensibility.

> He delighted in pictures [Turnbull quotes] that "showed men drowning their heads in burst hogsheads, tearing wolfishly at a leg of ham, pouring the contents of a wide-lipped ale jug in-

discriminately into a woman's throat and down her neck, while all about the swarming place men fumble in a woman's rich bosom, relieve themselves against a wall (children on the ground), while dogs crawl hungrily to the groaning tables, groups dance drunkenly in a ring, thick-set sweating men rush out of doors with foaming jugs, and in the distance, at a church, a procession winds slowly into a service."

Well I don't. But surely it is not wrong, considering what words have done, can do, are doing, to favor the word exactly used, the thought correctly built, the sensation truly evoked, to their alternatives? Considering where inspired self-assurance has brought us, to prefer humility, or at least egotism *tempered* by humility? To see something more useful, finally, more admirable in the reticence, generosity, and sympathy of a Maxwell Perkins (or an Andrew Turnbull) than in the miserable, hallucinated, prison house of ego who was the object of their sympathy?

5

From a French Notebook [1966–1967]

27 October 1966

. . . two straight, packed, utterly exhausting 8:30-to-7:30 days of *examens oraux,* desperately trying to grind untranslatable English sentences out of plain, dull, dark-eyed, well-meaning French college students, not one in five of whom really knew English, not one out of *ten* of whom showed a spark of originality. (But I could not be severe: every one was more bilingual than I. To the poor failed nun who came up after to ask for advice, all I could do was stutter away nonsense in all the wrong tenses.) They were simply beginners, feeding back stock phrases about Ze Puritaine Societee or 'Uckleberri Fine, ideas that seemed more freakishly alien in their mouths than *moules farcis* do in mine. Why ever have they chosen *American* Literature and Civilization to study, these pasty, overworked Languedociens? How foreign we all are, how many moons apart.

So that, of itself—interrogating a dozen or fifteen in a row each morning and afternoon, using three or four synonyms per word, trying to keep my mind on their wildly random accents and syntax, my eyes on their sad, nervous eyes—that took its toll. And then the constant, tiring, dispiriting embarrassment of being unable to keep up in French with my "colleagues," Gasc and Teissonier; and, worst of all, looking on at the barbaric, the Dark Ages horror of the 7:30 roll call of *passables,* hearing the sobs and sighs of all the pitiable *refusés* who had clustered in the cold dark corridors all day long, learning that another year was wasted. Unbearable. Wrong, even. Inhuman.

5 November

. . . the courtyard-apartments with their anonymous doors, black spiraling steep stone staircases, damp paving stones, mail-boxes, brass plates, *minuteries:* family life lived closed off utterly from the rest of the world, over-warm, entire unto itself; the high stone walls in front, the shutters.

On the one hand De Gaulle; as arrant a dictator as the free world knows, the austere, neo-religious captain of his great dedicated force of officials, the Party-State: the "Center," l'Etat, La Majorité, Le Gouvernement, the Gaullists—the party "qui se réclame de vous" (capital V?), the technocrats (a word of abuse, a word almost unknown in America, American as it sounds). Old, strong, silent, romantic, as full of vasty clichés as President Johnson, as evident a demagogue: but saved by his style, by the austerity of his presence and manner, the elegance of his phrasing. "Savoir bien parler est quelque chose qui approche de la tyrannie." *L'Express*, quoting (I think) Voltaire. And by the fact that false illusions—of France's power, for example—can become operational realities, as effective as a genuine hallucination. Something only the crafty romantic knows.

On the other hand, wild political parties that take themselves with frantic seriousness. For surely operating, large Communist and traditional-Socialist parties are as much an anachronism in "technocratic," post-ideological France as De Gaulle is. The vocal, impotent, angry Left, livid and frustrated, denouncing everything He or It (they are the same) does: the papers filled with the futile manifestos and protests of the Opposition, all the little oppositions—and never were oppositions more outside. Shall the Federation of the Left, if it manages to stay together, allow Communist candidates, and on what terms, and shall it only be to defeat Gaullism, and so on.

Meanwhile, *l'Etat* goes on, this massive, omnipotent centralized Parisian machine, spewing out thousands of concrete H.L.M. apartment houses in every city in France, slowly parcelling out highways and new University campuses, allotting so many pennies to this department, so many to that city, all of them so utterly, hopelessly dependent. An edict on musical education—for every school in France. How many civic operas or orchestras or regional theatres shall we permit this year? Hérault: Stop growing cheap wine-grapes, start growing tomatoes. Then we will build you six new seaside resorts. A new freshman year program (if not enough money for the teachers required) for *every university* in France!

To every local fête or celebration comes someone from the Paris Ministry that made it possible, to be thanked and praised and pleaded with for more. And, again futilely, the scrawled signs on bridges: "Occitaine Libre." (Or "Stop Importation de Vins." "Abstinez avec Poujade." "Pieds Noirs, Vous êtes tous bâtards." "F.E.N." "Paix en Viet Nam.") The omnipotent, omnicompetent state, reforming into an ugly, unknown, booming future, with Mongénéral at the top like the Sphinx, and the squabbling, barely-tolerated Opposition trying to absorb every variety of protest from a still-thinking, still free, still vaguely liberal people. The insulting affront to the thinking Free Frenchman of a totally, if quietly state-censored television— for all its cultural goodies. How madly un-American, un-British it all is.

And it all ties up. I'm sure it does. The Government, the Fouquet Reform, the Vallon Amendment, the scores of empty "luxury" co-op apartments, the extraordinary intellectual content of the daily press (philosophic reviews, the Nobel laureates, the *Académie*, linguistic debates, the national furor over university courses, admissions, examinations, methods). And the archaisms they will not let go of—open-air markets and fairs, inefficient shops and kitchens and homes and work-hours, ways of buying and selling, of charging and paying (everything cash: everything in person: everything before 12 or after 2:30). Wardrobe cupboards, a thousand daily "conveniences" unheard of.

Two most congenial afternoon drives last week, celebrating "Le Pont de Toussaint" in our own way. First, on a horrid, spirit-oppressing gray day, along the ugly road to Nîmes—the "main" red-line highway was one long gas station, a San Fernando Valley suburb. We hated it, wished we hadn't gone, said very little. But some sun came out at Nîmes, and we enjoyed all three of its three-star tourist stops with increasing relish. The Roman arena (handsome, masculine-carved, a perfect oval sweep in a wide open space; closed), the Maison Carée, with its "precincts" and steep, steep steps a perfect running-yard for Victoria—all in fine shape and proportion, even if the steps gave me the freezes, and I couldn't conjure up any "Roman" thoughts; and, best of all, the Public Gardens, by Le Nôtre out of ancient Rome—like the Forum in Rome, my favorite sort of wander-place, perfect for all three—water, fountains, swans, a stunning hillside terrace masterfully landscaped, a ruined temple to peek about in, Sunday strollers and bowlers: anyway, a nice afternoon at Nîmes.

We came back the alternate route via Sommières—and will never take the other again. Another planet. All past and beautiful, without one false or jarring note—a succession of diverse joys, so that we both kept exclaiming: châteaux ruined and whole, perfect old villages (arches, rooftops, alleyways, churches, squares); the fall-colored vineyards, yellow, red, orange over green, both near and far away; canyons even, crevasses, cliffs. A sun setting in the rear window, avenues of French highway trees arching their yellow-green leaves overhead: AND Victoria happy and good all the way! It was a fine golden bath for the soul, and I loved—we loved—every minute.

Then Tuesday, up the road past St. Martin de Londres, a most agreeable country highway, off a narrow twisty bit among thick foliage at the foot of the mountains to the Hérault River: a stop at the boarded-up St. Etienne church, of undetermined age, just up from a bridge so narrow the Cortina, all alone, just made it through and over the hump. Down, down, around and around, following the river through the garrigue, country very Western movie-wildernessy, except for the villages and vineyards. Our destination: St. Guilhem-le-Désert, the oldest village in our corner of France, its tile roofs and stone walls and TV antennas spilling beautifully down the cliffside from the monastery church. The church itself has been oversold, for all its age and sad story, considering what romanesque churches *can* be—especially with its cloister now reassembled in Upper Manhattan. But the village we loved, and will visit again—perhaps walk the whole length of its tiny lanes and tunnels, alive with cats and dogs and old ladies. We bought honey and grapes, and loved the whole day: again, Victoria held out in her private salon in back, trebling the day's pleasure. She too loved the steps and stones and kitties of St. G. (We also found a perfect picnic spot along the river: must not forget.)

Otherwise, the usual twice-daily drives to try to do trivial things in the burdensome, intimate, inefficient French fashion. Pouring rains and early frosts—real winter weather has settled in, ruining (among other things) the Foire des Ânes in the Arceaux, a gigantic drygoods and miscellaneous fair we were both dying to explore. (To be followed, apparently, by a rides-and-booths carnival: my least favorite kind.) I've been working harder at French, copying every word I don't understand in my *Mondes* and *Expresses*, and it begins to pay off—or would, if I kept it up. And writing letters, and nibbling at De Tocqueville, and beginning, just beginning, to feel I should get to work (and hence to feel more annoyed, slightly, at domestic chores): but all the while happy beyond measure not to be in Berkeley: each letter from there reconvinces.

11 November

. . . Aigues Mortes: One of my traditionally messy exits, stopping to check map every two blocks and feeling angry/embarrassed at Sheila's silence—or comment. Past the Pont-Juvénal football crowds to check out drearily unimpressive Château de Mogère, then across the grassy backlands to Palavas. Thence east along the sea, for one of our more frightening adventures— gale winds were blowing great road-hiding gusts of sand all the way along, piling up dunes in the middle of the road. At one deep "Congèrie de Sable" we had to be pushed across by the local police—like everyone else. Strange. Were we not so near home and help, I would have felt as helpless as I did driving through the Big Horn mountains in the dark of a foggy night, or up from New York in a snowstorm. The car rocked about the road like a boat in the pushy wind, as the swoops and sheets of fine sand swept like ghosts across the road: now the windows squeak painfully as you roll them up and down. But at Grau de Roi we turned inland and I left the winds, and soon came to the picture-book ramparts and tower of Aigues.

I drove the full circumference (a square circumference? perimeter, I suppose), in and out of the portals. A very solid, no-nonsense, city wall, the first I've ever seen entirely intact, with little angled-in window slits to shoot arrows from, and a walkway all along the top (to pour boiling oil?). The town was very average, worn-out ochre-brown French, but for a doddering church and some souvenir stores along the City Square, with its monument to St. Louis, who set sail from here for the Crusades back before the swamps took over. We went over the high-walled bridge to the Tour de Constance, a great vaulted prison-for-Protestants with walls twenty feet thick and more of those slit-windows cut at the end of strange triangular alleys. Awesome, very dark: I wonder what the prisoners *did* in here before they (we?) slaughtered them. In the name of God. (Our God.) I tried the spiral steps up to another tower, hoping for a view of the town, but it ended in mold and bats' nests. Home, then—Victoria good all the day—across the fields and villages, a handsome back-country drive to avoid the ugly road from Lunel to Castelnau. A packed afternoon of experiences—nothing grand or spectacular about A.M. (far more our little sandstorm); just very real, very strong, far more honestly evocative of its past than the more dazzling tourist monuments, where the dazzle keeps you from reading the human story. Carcassonne without the jazz.

Pic St. Loup: the most beautiful drive so far, thanks much to the manic fall colors of the roadside trees and the vineyards; but soured by perhaps a half hour of Victoria's whines. How she can kill the pure joy of something so fine—at least in the experiencing. The memory can simply cut her out, like a recording sound engineer removing static. I hope.

3 December

Yesterday was cluttered, and purposeless, and lost: today has been a joy.

We drove out early to take a giant, whimsical risk: Sunday lunch *out* with Victoria, at the last of the three local one-stars, the Hotel Central at Gignac. The meal was vast and fine and digestible, Victoria was as good, if not as gold, at least, say, as copper—she nibbled and sipped and wriggled and fed Teddy for *two hours*, then toddled about the room with a three-year-old boy, alternately affectionate and shy, or petted an ancient dog, or played peep-bo with the girl making out bills. We held our breaths through the hors d'oeuvres (pâté de grive) and fish (fresh salmon, for me écrevisses: however *do* they get them open?) and croquettes de volaille truffées; by then it was clear she was going to hold out, that the staff and the guests were on our side, and that the St. Saturnin rosé had soothed both her and us; it was downhill through the lovely roast pigeons and crêpes d'Aigoual (with a robust sort of stuffing), the ice cream and fruit and coffee. Then a longish, settling drive home through the country, with the usual picture-book cliffside town (Puébachon), *two* ruined (and two unruined) châteaux, two lovely towers, all to visit another time—as Victoria napped in the poop.

The country: I'm no good at giving it words. I just know it's winding its way deep into the cracks and crevices of my soul, that its colors and tones, its shapes and its easy old age have already become part of my landscape of memory. It's the sort of easy visual music, the unconscious "shaping" background I *wish* I had had all about me in my own green and arable years, in the seed-time of my soul—rather than a flat, new California suburb. It does shape the quieter reaches of the spirit; even now I feel it making up, correcting, easing out the ugliness. It's not English-lyrical, more masculine than feminine, more ochre-brown or gray-green than a wet luminous English green, sonnet-green. Worked and working vineyards, patches of odd shapes, never very big, tucked into every possible corner, dipping up and downhill—vineyards we've followed now from green through flame-yellow to clipped, chopped gnarled black stumps, as the horses plow the last season's rows and the clippings are burnt by the side of the road.

The garrigue, wild dark shrubs and trees growing out of the hard gray chalky rocks; hills, cliffs with God-made palisades and cloven ramparts of rock; up to Pic St. Loup's sharp point and the higher Cevennes beyond—today, a strong strong wind blew the sky so clear (leaves ran like squirrels, flew like butterflies across the road) we could see north to the snow, south to the sea, across the red-brown fields, still scattered with late yellow among the green.

It's not Grand Canyon spectacular, not Morocco-exotic, not Somerset-exquisite: it's hard, durable, worn smooth by age, the tones and edges blended and blurred: which is why its effect is most often unconscious. It flows in naturally, asking for no oohs and ahs, no roadside turnouts or camera shots. And it has its anarchic French ugliness, too—the omnipresent garbage dumps and abandoned, rust-rotten overturned cars; occasionally a village or town not so much charmingly as drably old, stained concrete instead of muted stone. And industrial horrors like Frontignan or the road to Nîmes. But it beats anything I've ever lived in the midst of by far: and again—how I wish it had been there, to flow in, all unconsciously, in the growing years. I've no great religious Myth of the Soil: but this is natural, human-scaled, easy to look at, to drive through, to think on. And sometimes—the perfect Cézannean compositions of worn-golden villages, walls and roofs all leaning one on another, the very invisible artist's image of communal shelter and accidental beauty—sometimes it is perfect. These *are* paintings, organically fallen into place over centuries, growing out of the local rock —a litter, a brood of houses and shops tumbling about the tired, proud old Mother Hen of a church. It's primeval sociology-turned-poetry. The buildings, their walls, the tiles of their roofs, the spindly church bell-tower seem as much and as naturally a part of the earth as the gnarled dark trees, the yellowy cliffs, the tiny patches of vines; or those creepy, *un*natural dark cypresses that loom up out of the high-walled cemeteries, like symbolic stakes out of dead men's hearts.

What ever happened to the new, people-conscious, economic eye of mine that "saw through" the walls and windows of Bristol and New York? What of these poor, out of date drudges in their hovels? I don't know: I just can't feel any suffering, and I don't *think* this is just purblind aestheticism. Oh, I know they're dying, these hamlets (were they ever thriving? Is not village-progress an *American* ideal only?), the children move away. Those that do make it into the 21st century will sprout ugly H.L.M.'s and toadstools of cars—*and* plumbing and conveniences and so on. But I don't see people in these —I am admiring a "composition," a unity of style and material and way of life, a sense of wholeness, shelter, and security that *made* the villages. So let them be near-ghost towns, let them fall quietly down: O.K. They are as handsome empty as full, they bear silent witness to a past the present can still use. And the future. If churches built to hold 200 now see only three or four black-shrouded old ladies in the corners—so be it. The last thing I want to do is restore and repeople these places: keep them liveable as long as people *want* to live in them; use the profitable nostalgia they evoke in summer visitors. But it's the story they tell, the past they bear that matters. They no more need people than all the marvelous ruined castles on the hilltops of Hérault. Just big graveyards, which some flowers still grow in, some vintners or old widows or pensioners inhabit, pumping their water, doing without phones, peeing out behind the shed. I despise the local-color mongering that wants to "preserve" ancient people as well as ancient buildings, that laments the end of wooden shoes and riverside laundering and Breton water sellers in lace headdresses. Purest touristy condescension, treating human beings like costumed poodle dogs, people sating their shallow boredom with a stupid, trivial lust for the superficially "different." Preserve us (and the Breton peasants) from that.

Let them name their own "differences," rather, however gross or invisible: the ritual of French widowhood, horses *or* tractors. Rotten road surfaces—but always rows of trees alongside. Z.U.P.s-full of concrete state apartment blocks to house the unhappy, to let them get out of these dank old smelly hovels; but also all the accidental country buildings, plain, ugly, unconsciously handsome, in their yellowing gray or graying yellow-brown. Television antennas on the tiles of St. Guilhem? Why not? There is the meanest, squirearchical inhumanism in the anti-modern nostalgia of a Betjemans, forever sneering at the tellymasts that mar country villages.

16 December

Gray outside, a worse gray inside. This asylum wallpaper of mine. To think that someone had to *design* something so ugly, actually elect these shapes and colors over other ones; and then that someone else chose to buy it.

I wonder how I shall assess this year when it's finished, seven months away. Sometimes it seems, France and all, to have grown as natural as my skin: it is simply where I am and what I am doing. Othertimes it seems so stupidly wrong: the sort of city one might find himself left in for a day between trains—

but *never* to live in, for a long and valuable year. All these streets after streets full of mud-colored, stained and crumbling buildings; the odd, purposeless daily circuits of Arceaux, through the Arch, Foch, Loge, around the Comédie, Sarrail and the Esplanade, around to Gambetta, around and around and around. I feel like a wind-up toy car on a tiny track, stopping and starting, popping up on sidewalks, in and out of shops, day after day.

So little "leisured," for all our leisure: so much jerking about. So little easeful, full, civilized, for all the history, the obvious age, the wining and dining: so much junior-scale clutter and full-time ineptness. The tall tiled house *is* the shell we live in, but it's not us or ours, and surely that wrongness works its way inside, day after unthinking day. That queer, petty-monumental red-tiled corridor, running imperially and directly from the cracking, warped wood and wrought iron door —to the toilet. The green walls of the living room; *this* horror, it will all do, but it *is* anti-human, as I have come, Californian, to define it. And the city is simply a Villa Aimée without walls.

. . . Our outings are balancing out. The overlong, strained drive with the Webers around the Bassin to Sète, via Agde, was a monumental mistake. My silent, ugly smugness while driving (bitterly rotating "It Wasn't *My* Idea" a hundred ways, while Sheila felt unhappy, uncomfortable, and tried wanly to interest Eden) didn't help: how we can *fondle* our selfish little bitternesses sometimes. Even the sea at Sète, clouded over and cold, seemed to have lost the Mediterranean magic. And when Weber made some crack about all French roads being equally dull, I felt like a wounded 44th generation Languedocien: if *only* I had forced us on to the ruins and Pic St. Loup, I kept grinding stupidly over and over. Nothing like making a little mistake seem like a catastrophe by over-thinking about it.

. . . But the luncheon chez Gasc was a gastronomic landmark. Good people, *ça va sans dire*, despite the guest of honor, a hatchet-faced, hatchet-voiced fool of a *fonctionnaire* down from the American Embassy to pick Fulbright candidates. But the dear Gascs are good enough to make up for anyone. And Victoria good, perhaps not quite so good as at Gignac, and more of a worry to Sheila (she didn't eat too well)—but good:

no more a real obstacle to pleasure than Miss Eckstein's voice. (The second-worst Franco-American accent we've heard.)

So the meal came through: carrot slices vinaigrette, mayonnaise-and-lemon-stuffed eggs Mimosa, sliced bamboo shoots (lovely), all this with a simple white wine *du pays*. Then a Périgord pâté with giant truffles, and with it a 1947 Sauterne, a jewel of a wine. Veal slices wrapped in bacon, peas cooked in the sauce (a red wine here, "private stock" from Grandpa's vines in Roussillon), cheeses (including a white cream "Pic St. Loup"), fruit, coffee, brandy. And, my head joyfully swimming, I had to dash away with Gasc and Foul Female to listen to four hours of her cruel, shrewish, stupid interviewing. Insanity. I scribbled hateful doodles about her and the French bureaucracy.

1 January 1967

. . . The drive Friday, gray but mellow Friday, through the red-brown wintering vine fields to our own ruined château was a first stage out of the pit, of our fiasco of a Christmas in Spain. Today we hoisted ourselves clear, with a long, five-hour drive to Les Baux, by way of Sommières and Nîmes, Beaucaire and Tarascon. Too long, really: and stung by a half-hour's (twenty minutes'?) genuine purgatorial panic at Les Baux when we lost each other—a horrible feeling. But, how beautiful it was, all of it really: how beautiful our part of France. That and the food, I thought this morning in the patisserie, piled with New Year's goodies: paysage, histoire, cuisine, et vin. The best of our France.

The red sticks jutting out of the gnarled black vine-stumps, casting their maroon glow over the powder-brown fields; the happily aristocratic profile of Castries, and the cosier elegance of Fontmagne around the bend, where we *wish* the châtelaine would ask us to dinner—the whole grand range of changing beauties on the Sommières road, in fact, every time: Sommières itself, Lawrence Durrell's town, from afar or from within, a perfect little city—"Ses esplanades, ses vieilles rues, ses remparts"; the grand, 180° panoramas over fields and hills and mountains; neat, droll, contented little villages en route like Restinclières, with their teen-age loungers on parade.

Or at Montlaur, again—the rolling ribbony ease of narrow, cosy French roads, the nearest I'll ever come to taking long country walks—and not a bad substitute. The fine ivy on the walls, the inside I *shall* explore, the rotting, lichen-yellow old tiles of the town, gradually fading to the color of the stone below. The "English" quality of driving under soft, unoppressive, mellowing, faintly luminous gray skies, the constant contentment that wells up from the little piles of anonymous, unconsciously unified villages, all of common stone and common tile, of a color with the earth, sculpted with mindless perfection about the singular steeple of Mother Church.

And the new parts of today, oh, so many things—that long, long avenue of plantanes east of Nîmes, the mirroring fine castles of Beaucaire and Tarascon (Tarascon's perfect pile—everyone's dream of a moated, rock-built, fortress-castle—we visited briefly). And then the mountain road up to Les Baux, like nothing I have ever seen. The vision, from across the valley, of this cliff-carved fortress town, growing ghost-like from the rock: more a super-romantic invention, some illustrator's fantasy, than a real, historical-geographical fact.

And Montmajour, taking Les Baux's overspill today; and the beauty of village and spire and exactly-etched tree branches and tree-rows all perfectly, painfully silhouetted against a sky turning from old blue to ochre to golden to pure burning orange, a pile of a town to the right blinking back the sun's sparkle in all its windows: well, it *was* too late, and too long, the panic at the parking lot was frightful; but a drive home like that is worth many more pains.

8 January

This is what Richardson called "writing to the moment." I am recollecting, not in tranquillity, but still in the tension of aftershock: my stomach nerves have not yet begun to unknot.

The winter, this last week, has taken a bitter, nordic turn, after that glorious New Year's Day—sub-freezing everywhere, even flurries of snow, dissolving in air. Today the flurries, beginning about noon, stopped dissolving, and settled on leaves and branches. I began to feel creeping out from my memory the old, sad Cambridge feeling of physical helplessness, of inner anger at the alien elements—I am balked enough anytime, but against snow I feel like a wagon driver confronting the Rockies. All I want to do is curl in a snug warm house and watch it melt, quickly.

But it was such a gentle, exotic fall—we decided (I gave in) to take our Sunday drive nonetheless, not to Arles, perhaps—but at least to Clermont l'Hérault, to look at the church and the ruins. Stopping first to take a snapshot in the garden, a joke for the record.

The fleecy specks continued pleasantly through the drive, ever so lightly, the hills and vineyards and villages all barely dusted with powdered sugar. The Clermont church was perfect, ancient, battered brown rock outside, clean intimate early Gothic within, with an admirable crèche and a stunning, surely original, rose window. The ruins were, for the moment, inaccessible, but fun to investigate. And, to close a lovely short day's drive, we stopped at a crossroads café in Gignac for coffee and liqueurs, and to let Victoria ingratiate herself with the throng.

Gignac—I just checked—is 30 kilometers from Montpellier: say 19 miles. Granted I did take the "long-cut" via Aniane, but still no more than 20. We were nearly two hours, and two more ghastly, nerve-cracking hours I hope not to spend this year. The snow flurries changed, suddenly, to a New England snowfall, thick, dark, smothering, miserably dangerous. It was bad enough, though smooth and fairly calm—I was taut, rather than knotted, and I *think* Sheila relaxed in my confidence—on the more or less empty, winding white road via Aniane, before we met the main highway to Montpellier.

But there we joined an endless, crawling convoy of red tail lights gleaming miserably through the slanting snow, all windshield wipers helpless, frozen with great chunks, hence all vision a dark blur dotted with red. Ten miles an hour, five, two, stop: worst of all, stop, braking with sickening care: moaning along in the lowest of lows, risking a run in second, Z-bend warnings looming like threats.

Once, sinking, I felt the car begin to spin toward the side, the bank, the ditch, at a frozen stretch where half a dozen cars were already stalled—toward, I saw at once, hours stuck in the snow, all night perhaps: phonecalls, walking off for help, tow-cars, taxis—Victoria no more helpless than I . . . All this, mere miles from home.

Once seriously, twice more momentarily, we glided out of control for seconds, and I read rules to myself about steering with the slide; fifty other times I imagined it about to happen. The kilometers, the tenths of miles, crept by at agonizing slow-ness. It was so dark, so white, so unknown, and yet so near: if only they could drive a *little* more quickly, a little more evenly. We strained to find landmarks that, in the past, had flown by in minutes: the walled-in farm; the dumps we mocked, and then the great curves in the road. A sign to Celle-neuve—11; then 7; then 3, 1.8 miles that dragged like counties. The Z.U.P., the underpass, Celleneuve itself no more comfort-ing than an isolated, abandoned mountain village: the insants-road home from there, where we run weekly with the laundry, was endless, a camel caravan in a sandstorm. The new apart-ments, the bar, *finally* Mas de Tesse; waiting through four changes of lights, the brakes sliding off to the right each time. The Château gates, Les Violettes, the big risk at our turnoff—leaving the pack—at the Liberation monument. And home. Hell with the garage. And the snow, like all snow, looked lovely, a poem. Nothing more horrible, dangerous, alien to man; nothing more lovely. Very Robinson Jeffers. Tropical shrubs looking like New Hampshire evergreens, rooftops and stone walls crested high, the streets soft white pads: the omi-nous silence broken only by the squawk of a distant ambu-lance. How many ambulances, tonight, how many tow-trucks, how many stranded, how many terror-stricken, how many killed. The snow.

Still, not wholly eased . . . One afternoon from our year abroad. Home to steaming Boeuf en Daube, and to read of Rea-gan's plans for Berkeley: even after that, it *still* may be better to be here than there.

16 February

A month more put away, a month closer to the end of this error. The illnesses and graynesses that have lingered on sul-lenly ever since Spain crested this last week with six days—so far—of drizzle and storm and gloom, along with six days—so far—of disgusting, deadening, all-enveloping ailments. We had identical symptoms, in a kind of counterpoint pattern, one puking and spewing one night, the other the next. Racking, phlegmy sore throats, shivering fits under mounds of blankets, horror at the thought of food, fatigue, ennui, imprisonment in a body, a house, a city you hate: all gray.

. . . I had some historico-poetico-philosophic thoughts to record about our visits to the droll little third-rate cathedrals in Lodève and Clermont, all these "handsome" towered village churches we so dote on: museums, now, for amoral dilletantes; nostalgia-factors for selfish escapists, condescending right-wing moralizers; rattly, candle-heated, crumbling shells for a shrunken and dated sect. How long? All this "past"—how much longer?

And even vaster, deeper ones, about Past-Present-Future, unreason and reason, America and the world, spun out of my happy encounter with Henry Adams.

And, I suppose, some note should be made of our joyful discovery of the mountains north of Ganges.

But there will be time.

. . . On seeing "historic monuments" in their present settings. Something no art historian ever talks about. The parking lot under the St. Trophime tympanum, the sailors and postcards in the Theatre at Arles. Hundreds of worse examples.

4 March

. . . We have had, one way and another, a virtual month of illness—something we had never known. We spent February selfish and isolated in our flaccid gray carcases, each sealed in his own drizzly wounds, his weaknesses physical, mental, and moral, cocooned in self-pity and a dull, sympathy-craving, sympathy-refusing defensiveness. The skies stayed gray (or wet), the car wouldn't start on the foulest day of all. . . .

28 March

R.S.: gag. His blockish, prissy-pedant's Great Books-level monologues, his absolute lack of sympathy or imagination; such a *small* head, so tightly packed with loads of learned lumber. Such a nothing human being, unhappily stripped to his naked nothingness by a scant two-days' visit. HOW I HATE SELFISH FOOLS. Those enunciated, endless "jokes," the ten-mile speech defending the Viet Nam war, down the splendid, unseen Gorges de l'Hérault. *So much* unseen, unheard, unno-ticed—all England, all France, all Europe, all life. Oh, I know, he isn't pure evil; but God: I could have screamed, sworn, snarled insults so many times, or let him stew in even worse silences than I did.

But even he, even he, could not destroy that happiest of Easter Sundays, damp mist or no: the spring green haze of new trees lacing the edges of the thick, uncanny green, paint-green, of the Hérault, down so far, snaking between mossy crags and cliffs; the perfection of Puébachon, with that one purple-flowering tree below (we forced him to take pictures of the things we loved); the vaults of St. Guilhem, Victoria at the candles and between the pews; and, above all, the matchless camaraderie of the lunch at Fonzes'—one huge, warm, happy family, waiters, hostess, the next two tables, the din of 300 diners, the scrambling kids—the dishwashers! Even our R. So fine, so joyful, so memorable—trading wines and clinking glasses, lending cigarettes and giving addresses, the staff from the *Tomate* of the night before. Arriving mentally numb from R.'s theories, and with my interior plumbing gone rotten, I still enjoyed it all.

29 March—tomorrow the Riviera, Lugano

Not that it matters, but I am sitting in my car in the big, bright, busy new Ford garage on the Montpellier-Sète high-way—shades of Chandlers Ford (I had to look up the name)—waiting for someone to find a missing part so they can finish putting together my new *galerie* (roof-top carrier). They've been at it two hours now, my pencil point is too stubby to go on editing Gide, I've walked around the building, gone to the bathroom twice: garages, even French garages, have limited long-range appeal. I wish it were done and we were on our way.

I haven't, obviously, the tranquillity here for cultural reflec-tions—though it's odd how little the noise bothers me. Less than the bland blank "modern" architecture all around me, in fact. I could *try* comparing Ford-Rte. de Séte with Ford-Chandlers Ford, but I won't. (Still, how *like* the *chefs:* how like their garçons.)

What I had in mind under "What is France" were two sorts of things—the one just a long long catalogue of sorts—porte-clefs, bright blue overalls, Johnny and Sylvie, de l'Académie Française fools, and so on: the other a sort of impressionistic "structural analysis" of France—France as a closed and completed system, a network from which nothing escapes, a society that makes sense only from inside, and which can, perforce, admit no outsider in. The second idea, in particular, has become for me a *ruling* idea, a dominant and satisfying concept by which, now, virtually everything French is explained: French food, stoves, French tax systems, child-raising, medical treatment, size of envelopes, toilets, traffic, the lot: especially medicine, education, and of course government, which is, ultimately, everything else. China makes sense, in every part, to someone brought up *entirely within* the windowless palace, to someone who has gone through the schools, taken the medicines, learned the songs, played the games. So must France. It is all, I am convinced, of a piece. (Perhaps the omnipresent, omnipotent web of l'État is only symbolic: an effect, a manifestation, and not the cause? Or does it all begin with Napoleon?)

I am not of it, hence I understand none of it: I can contribute nothing, I can take away nothing. No outsider can. By contrast, America—even England—is open, diverse, heterogeneous, different for every American, as freely offering as one is himself free to take. This is a gigantic (monstrous?), complex ballet-pattern which can neither be broken into nor out of.

Perhaps the best test for me, the best synthesis—not now, but closer to the end of the year—would be to tie together the two ways of defining France. First, make the list of objects—hundreds, even, *all* the phenomena that still seem to me, however trivial or transient, elementally "France": that seem, not on analysis, but intuitively, by taste, by whim, by accidental illumination. Then describe the web, the pattern, the vast closed logic and unity of it all—where does it come from, how does it connect, how survive—and why *here?* And finally try to give each item in the first its place in the pattern of the second: how do porte-clef's publicitaires fit into the omnicompetent Gaullist state? Or suppositories? Or nylon garter belts? Or Jacques Brel? That will be the scheme, the design, of my terminal essay on, my appreciation of, La Belle F——.

(Come on, morceau. I'm getting impatient. 11:10)

21 May

I've been too long away—too many sights, thoughts, evolutions of emotion to remember and record. Just now, I'm pleasantly tired after our happiest Sunday outing ever—a fine terrace lunch at a family restaurant in Gornies, under the orange blossoms and over the Vis; through the gorges to the stunning Cirque de Navacelles, with the village, the church and cascade and meadow at the bottom a dream image out of the pastoral-picturesque (and not a café, not an ice-cream stand, a postcard seller in sight); then back home through the meadows and mountains, goats scrambling among the pines, with vast, sweeping views to the sea and the pics under a warm blue sky: Montperoux's village carnival, for Victoria's turn on the merry-go-round; Gignac—and onto the Route de Lodève. A perfect day? A perfect day. They don't come often.

I've not recorded Carcassonne, or the Pyrenées—a mixed bag of a weekend if ever there was one, memorable for the English-green meadowland on the back-Capestang road from Béziers to Carcassonne—so handsome, following either the Aude or the Marseillette or the Canal du Midi so closely and so constantly we felt them like brothers (and not another car on the road); always treelined in an untrimmed, meandering, lovely way. *And* memorable for the other, even more splendid road—the skinny mountain road from Quillac to Mont-Louis: we had to find new words for our wonder with every turn. Again, following the Aude almost every mile of its course, through roads hewn into the overlooming rock, along the squeezing claustrophobic cliffs of a "gorge" or a "defile"; mountain spas, tiny villages; above all the glory of new green, spring green, light singing salad green scattered everywhere up and down the mountainsides among the dark evergreens: and the sun, so much of the way, doing wonderful painterly things to it all. Watching delayed autumn, prolonged winter vegetation as we mounted higher, sunk lower: a one day tour of the seasons.

It had all started inauspiciously, with foggy drizzles, bleak prospects, rotten guts. My Carcassonne lunch was another demi-fiasco from the ladies' point of view (thank God for today's success, to wipe out Sheila's growing resistance to the very idea of any more restaurant lunches). The Hotel de la Cité, all Gothicked up like a movie set (every square *inch:* morbidly interesting), was too too fancy for Sheila's comfort with Victoria; and Victoria merited her concern. Sheila's dinner was lousy—mine passable (a new kind of those shrimpy things—gampas?), which decided us for once and for all that we don't like the *écrevisse* family: they smell. Canéton aux olives, tasty. Strange oeufs en gelée, which Victoria ate out from under me. Factory ice cream. St. Emilion. As for Carc, we zipped in and out: I was so miffed at Sheila's not liking it, at my own exploding insides, at the whole unsuccess of *another* of my Too-Big plans, that I just jumped in the car (Sheila sullen and growling) and barrelled on out.

Before the lunch thing, we had found it fun: the far prospect (briefly) nothing short of stunning—all those towers, just like the postcards. And then the entry bridge, the double walls, the winding streets between souvenir shops. Fun: no more. No sense of the genuine, no breath of the really Medieval. A sort of very good, great-thing-for-the-kids, Viollet le Duc-Disneyland. All the crenellations so perfect you wondered if there was an original stone in the place. So, yeah, Carcassonne. I grant we didn't really look: but like Les Baux, I'm not sure I even want to. Give me Aigues-Mortes. Or even Les Matelles.

And then the Pyrenées. Nice mountainy mountains, white ranges all around—one especially handsome set Paulette showed us on our Saturday morning tour. But nothing so distant and commonplace as snowy peaks could ever come up to the color-spectacle of greens-on-cliffs of our drive up. (It ended, by the way, in a miserable gray drizzle, as it had begun: and I don't think I gave over expecting snow, ice, and blizzards on the road until we actually arrived at Saillagousse. I was really being, for me, terribly brave—and never dared tell Sheila how uncertain I was.) Pleasant were the Vitoux' (never so open, so humanly free, so much themselves: we had earlier wondered what we could find to talk about); the fun of scrambling through their half-built country house at Llo; the ambience of the downstairs regions of the hotel, if not the meals themselves, if certainly not the cramped, third-class room.

Back via Prades, avoiding Perpignan, after the second day's lunch, a day of promising sunshine and blue. The road, after the descent past happily-walled Mont-Louis, another funny old Medieval town further down, occasional picturebook villages in the hills—the road was dull and quick, or as quick as a hateful road-hogging red Mobil truck would let me make it. We were followed all the way from Béziers (neat new way through Béziers I discovered, me, all by myself) by a popsie in a convertible, whom I finally lost at the Lodève turnoff. Mysterious. An exhausting two days, perhaps in the balance—for all the lovely Aude valley road, the Vitoux *chez eux—too* exhausting. . . .

. . . a joyful Friday-off painting and sketching St. Jean de Cuculles for an absolutely mind-flushing, sunlit afternoon among the sheepbells and the wild thyme—a perfect escape, for both of us, with a new-discovered dream of a woodland road to start, between Montarnaud and Puébachon . . .

And the Anvers Philharmonic noisily retailing Brahms, Bartok, and Strauss; and our very own guided tour of the Château de Castries by M. le Duc, far better as story material than as an actual experience. Victoria fussed Sheila out of half the tour; the chateau rooms were sort of fun, but hardly beautiful—interesting primarily because lived in; and the Duke wasn't exactly ingratiating, as I suppose Dukes have a right not to be. I kicked myself for my club-footed French, and for not having boned up a bit on the Castries in advance; but how was I to know our guide would be a genuine Dook, bosom-buddy of De Gaulle and the Comte de Paris, honorary member of the Society of the Cincinnati (and presently angling for a *fauteuil* at the Academy, according to M. Temple)? I asked perhaps eight foolish questions and two intelligent ones, and he seemed glad to be quit of us. The gardens and the cour d'honneur were quite handsome, the day was perfect, and drinks after in a Castries café a nice idea, at least. Marie-José, in any event, was terribly impressed. And now Sheila has her story of David and the Dook.

To Quissac-St. Hippo with Victoria, last Sunday, Sheila begging out with fatigue: Sauve was a grand, cliff-walled, ancient city split by a river; the switch-backing up the hill toward Pompignan gave wide, wide views. Otherwise, just a chance to ink in obvious unfilled lines on my Michelin map.

31 May

A month, exactly, to go. No "events" to record—what's more, I'm tired of recording "events"—except a day in the sun at Carnon, chez Gasc, including great garlicky bowls of hundreds of tiny *tellines;* another day at Carnon—this one under gray, gray skies—and, finally, the marvelous old church at Mague-lone, so perfect in its jungle of greenery, at the end of that impassible, jeep-track road across the dunes. Fine old tomb-stone carvings of its bishops, a lineup of skulls, half-crumbled to dust, dug out of the sarcophagi: their graces, I suppose. Fine vaults, fine stone, deep darkness, black rooks in the tower, bar-barically simple and perfectly clear Christ and Co., carved over the door. Montpellier's one genuine tourist attraction. I'm pleased we saw it.

And my last lectures, damn their silly heads, on Hemingway and the French vs. American mind, respectively; a dull dinner party—of which there are more to come. End of "events."

I'm back to Gide, finally, willingly—how I love freedom from wretched academic obligations; and Proust, a kind of drugging cultural *devoir* I use to keep from doing Gide. Both I want to finish here anyway, both balance and complete, and fit the setting: two halves of my hourglass of obligation. Of Proust, I don't know. Still largely a "thing to do," to have done, rather than any creative enlightenment, any discovery. Such indulgence, such snobbery, such grandiose triflings: such *mannerism.* He isn't really "revealing hidden depths" or any such claim, through all his labyrinthine syntax. The psycholog-ical contortions become predictable, stylized, and Proustian, and the arabesques of grammar—sometimes even of diction, though there he can see newly—are there only for their own (i.e., his) sake, like the arabesques of Moslem decor. It's so much a matter of self-congratulation for having read, for hav-ing been able to read it all: and to swallow all the cheap bitchi-ness, the show-off snobbery (of author, narrator, *and* the mocked or idolized characters), to regard it as either grand or clever, without a breath of moral, modern protest, is to reveal oneself as the lowest, most hollow and sham of the lot.

Still, I shall try to finish it—now into IV of VII, *Sodome et Gommorhe*, my second go on this volume. Much of it is fun, some of it is fine, all of it is a fitting time-filling exercise for my final month in France.

Sheila packs, I plan—*étapes* at Salles-en-Beaujolais and Vézélay, our two days in Paris, Amiens and Touquet, our week in London: we have already seats for Olivier in *Love for Love* and the new *Three Sisters* at the National Theatre; perhaps three others, a concert, the smash hit Wesker (and Maxim's) in Paris—this weekend to the Raybaud's country-house in the Vaucluse; and, before two weeks are out, I insist, to the 15-franc two-star in old Avignon.

Our moods drift from low to neutral, my entrails suffer hellishly two days a week. Victoria has entered a period of frequent but erasable fits—over almost anything. The newspapers spill millions of words over the impending bit of Dark ages barbarism in the Near East—a hate-filled, racist Holy War, with nuclear weapons and superpower Big Brothers in places of scimitars and guillotines (though I expect they'll use those too). It's all so hopelessly inescapable and insane: they're both so glutted with "patriotism" and 7th century racist-nationalist pride they *want* the bloody war to begin! When was it—ten years ago or 300?—when two little countries could have a stupid little war without the whole world jumping in, bombs and bombers wagging, to take sides?

I'm not really thinking: I'm just sick of reading about it. And sicker of depending on these great stacks of newspapers for my truth.

Out of here, out, *out!* On to anywhere. Else.

From an American
Notebook [1967–1969]

For a start—and I cannot keep this from being a reflection of
me first, a portrait of the world second—let me say that I do
not hate Now. I say that because so many clearly do. If my
involvement with today is less than others', it is more a matter
of the limits of my belief than of revulsion. I find it very difficult to screw up my faith in the social fact, the mass, the historical to the point of active internal concern. My domain of impulsive imaginative assent—that which is "real" for me and not
fictional—is, short of a severe and momentary effort of will,
limited to the personal and the individual: and also, by and
large, the present and actual. There are many thinkers, I realize, on whose screen of active thought the metaphysical leaves
no trace; but surely there are far fewer as unmoved as I am by
the historical. Mass facts—wars, social changes, economic or
political crises—seem to me only artificial multiplications of individual facts. The individual facts—what this man thinks and
that man suffers—are real: the multiplication into history
strikes me as something contrived and presumptuous, like the
strange, self-assured games of the social scientists. Their very
discipline I despise (at first, instant response) as unreal. They
have adopted terms and methods valid in the realm of science,
natural science—and pretended to apply them to multiplications of people. Absurd. And yet—this absurdity, this gross

giant fiction controls the private lives of us all. These *are* the men of power: *They* believe in the mass. Anachronistic and impotent, I lag behind clutching my sole belief—in one man at a time.

Now to discuss all these things I don't believe in. (Remember my squirming discomfort last year at presuming to lecture on "American Civilization"—when I scarcely believe in American history: except as the abstract pattern that individual actions, seen together, happen to take.) But this is all visceral, spontaneous prejudice. "Intellectually," I suppose, I can risk the general.

So. So I don't hate Now. I can't hate the future—or fear it—because I can't (yet) imagine it. I'm also far too much an existentialist, my concerns frozen in what-is, to shiver or sweat over what may be. I think an awful lot of lies, of self-blinded ego-preening, mindless crap is spoken about all three faces of time. Almost all people who speak publicly speak falsely, and this bothers me. I hate the sham of most talk about "the world situation," from editorials about the hippies to the Pope's blatherings on Peace. Clearly one reason I say so little, think so little about public affairs is that there is so little truth to be spoken or known. I am always concerned with the nature and motive or this distortion or that, why the Peace Protesters lie their way and Johnson his: again—back to the only reality, the private human heart. So much hate, so much self-delusion, so much ego-defending, such elaborate structures of intricate inner warfare against others and ourselves masking as "thought." As a rhetorical analyst with a moralist's bias, I have my ground cut out.

But there we are back in the Ivory Tower, disdaining the ignoble strife, Godlike "seeing through" the mixed or sordid motives of everyone participating in the fray below, everyone else. I'm still avoiding the world.

What can I say, then, in something like truth, about such things as American politics and society, the war in Viet Nam, the student-intelligensia protest, the Negro rebellion, President Johnson, "poverty," capitalist power, the Americanization-by-technology of the world, the public's style and taste and pleasures, the power and morality of the mass communications media, the defense industry, mass education—and so on and on and on? Very little, without trying to say everything at once. Because nothing, no question, is independent—hence the absurdity (except as emotional release, which has its place; or public pressure; or, I suppose, as a personal act of faith by beings made unlike me) of every slogan of protest. To "understand," as I seem doomed to do, the complex human necessity for everything, however hateful, however petty, in my mock-Olympian way—is to render oneself almost unable to speak on any public issue. (Hence my professional bias for the biographical, my disbelief in the History of Ideas. Hence so many things.)

So when I am reminded of so-called political realities, I know what they mean—fragmentation bombs *are* being dropped, so many millions do starve, the labor unions will not permit x or y—but I do not feel them as realities, or find myself able to leap to, to embrace *any* answer.

But if there are social facts, then my first concern is that we know them correctly—or at least that I do. The air is one vast fireworks display, night and day, of interested distortions: the morning paper, the evening news, whole structures of necessary lies: of "press releases" from one interest group or another. The savor of *The New Republic*—for all its own droll self-delusions (Gene McCarthy?!)—is its dedication to blowing off the great layer of fluff, industrial-capitalist-advertising fluff from the daily news. A private war, of course—but it does make their version closer to the truth, say, than Gulf Oil's or Secretary Wirtz's or the *Chronicle's*. I instance this only as a taste of the crap-clearing, cant-clearing I can relish. Corporations, capitalist corporations are very large, very powerful, utterly amoral fictions—"Sociétés *anonymes*": hence *certain* distorters of the truth. So are governments—San Mateo County spits at San Francisco, France ritually insults Canada; labor unions—anything with a private interest.

And yet they are all very large facts, not soon (or desirably, perhaps) to be wished away. The world has *in point of fact* evolved to its present state of suprahuman institutional complexity: a great city of institutional towers and monuments and machines somehow set running by man; to some small degree still affected by man, though in great part now autonomous; and among which man, scarcely larger or more potent than he was in the naked jungle, wanders busily, distractedly, but rather helplessly for all that.

The suprahuman, ahuman institutional mountains are there, now, forever: they may transmute, combine, atomize and grow, but they'll never go away. We humans are now the *lesser*, the less important inhabitants in a world of foundations, computer-industries, diplomatic structures of fantastic and irreducible immensity, multiversities. The Invading Monster image is appropriate—although no one seems to know the Monsters are here. They look, after all, like human institutions: they have directors, stockholders, employees, bombardiers, voters, and so on—but really: how powerless. How utterly powerless. What on earth more impotent than a stockholder—except perhaps a director? How *little*, now, can be changed. How much is fixed. And what a dreadful delusion most protesters or reformers labor under. (I speak not, now, of the unchanging qualities of the human heart, but of the immovable inertia of institutions.)

So I sit and "understand": I understand why this Negro throws a bomb, why that one disrupts a meeting, why this other tries quietly to make it in the insurance company or college. I understand why the students sit-in, or smoke pot, or go naked—or join the Fijis, or the Peace Corps, or the priesthood. Why Crews and Parkinson and Burgess sign this and that petition, march, "speak out," write letters; and why California votes for Reagan—but draws the line at Shirley Temple. Why the French accept, even brag about France, De Gaulle, the lot. Tout comprendre—c'est . . . rien. It's why Shakespeare and Chekhov never ran for politics or wrote editorials.

30 December

Ah shit. Why pretend, why try? I can't even bear the decent cant of *Le Monde*, which at least *tries* to take the world seriously, morally, without excessive bias. *Nouvel Observateur* and *New Republic* are both, in their different ways, just partisan papers. The *Chronicle* has no opinion, nor does CBS News nor *Nouvelles Litteraires*—they just quote the press releases. You *can't* speak the "truth" about world affairs. And just now —one cocktail party, one pizza dinner down, after a week of gut-agonies and the egomaniac self-indulgences of Scott Fitz-

gerald—I say screw the world. Oh, I have ideas, notions, buried
somewhere back there, about mass education and democratic
tastes and warmaking power and political lies: but *so* far back.
Really, truly, all I care about is people. And mainly me.

If I could see a future to carve, but I can't. This new loss of
self-definition *is* a definite inner wound—I can't deny it. This is
why reading Fitzgerald has been such grief, why going into
Wheeler or thinking about courses—about anything—is so sor-
didly depressing. Yesterday was bleak, ghastly, bottom-of-
abyss. Why *write* about writers, *why* keep up this silly, need-
less game of "criticism"? But if not—what else?

Present and Future

Sense of an authentic revolution in world civilization that has
already taken place, but which is unseen, unacknowledged,
misinterpreted: because of the narrow, rigid, mean, and
thoughtless fixity of most people's minds; because of the pressure of investment in threatened, dated, *or* rising special interests; because of the archaic, humanist-renaissance 18th and 19th
Century European nature of our education, our language, and
hence the very inner structure of our minds, our ways of seeing
and responding.

What *sort* of revolution? One that renders the aforesaid
humanist-renaissance 18th and 19th Century European structure
of thought, response, and interpretation in great part irrelevant.
Not a new, bolt-from-the-blue Change: rather an extension of
the principles of this 2000 + year old tradition, but an extension
so far and so extreme that a change in quantity breaks through
into an absolute change in quality—as "Jeffersonian Democracy," pushed too far and too long, becomes laissez-faire capitalism, and *anti*-democratic. Moreover, these extreme exten-
sions—like energy-level shifts through which one element
becomes another—were, I think, by and large inevitable, their
establishment irreversible, their further extension (into what
new reality-states?) unstoppable. Still, had anyone in 400 B.C. or
1600 or 1850 been keen enough to read the implications, the
changes might at least have been channelled, used, correctly
interpreted. (See Henry Adams.) And surely the same is true
today. . . .

Much—perhaps most—of the change is epistemological, and this would have to be taken into account. Much depends on changing sources, reception, and speed of information and communication. These can work changes, mutations in man more absolute and radical than the move from ape to man. An 18th Century man's view of "history" (or geography, or psychology, or sex, or government, or God), to us so infantile, simplistic, clumsy, narrow, *wrong*—was not: it was all he had; for him, then, it was right. The oddity comes when we try to apply our vision to his life-records and materials, to psychoanalyze Dr. Johnson. Edinburgh *was* as epically far from London as he thought it; days were as long, hours as slow; the French as much jibbering alien moon-men, "America" as incredible a myth; science properly an affair of attic experiments. There were that few books, that few men that mattered; noblemen *were* superior beings, and God did make clear moral demands on men, to be punished or rewarded in eternity.

I am not being fictionally relativistic—I mean this: this *was all true*. UNTIL VERY RECENTLY, Negroes in America *were in fact* a subhuman species, just as until the 15th Century the world was flat—because people *knew* it to be so. I suppose I insist on all this just to guard myself from accepting any of the Assured Truths of 1968 as—anything more than that.

I see the *most* radical sources of reality-change in the universal dominion of the Egalitarian Idea (everything, identically, for everyone—health, longevity, "happiness," ease, higher and higher education, artistic talent, mobility; Spock on one-year olds, theorists on "disadvantaged" students, the California-college ideals, Medicare, and so on, all projected ahead into a mad, hedonistic-anarchic chaos); and in the mindless, unpredictably and infinitely expanding juggernaut of technology, utterly dominant over all human activity; to be far more so in the future; everywhere.

The latter seems so wholly out of man's conscious power to control—it is certainly impossible to turn back; it was from the start: Faust's bargain. The subdivisions and implications of these two, in necessary intersection, are immense: we shall now have both, always, with us. If I—and thousands, even millions more —continue to carve out a safe, serene, 18th and 19th Century-humanist-renaissance fantasy image (of Mozart—on record;

fine wines and food—frozen, flown in; of untouched landscape
—driven to on freeways; of Racine or Yeats—in paperback), it
is a necessary, satisfying, understandable delusion. But a delusion nonetheless. The juggernaut goes on, behind us, support-
ing it all, paying for it all, growing bigger and bigger. Consider
only the University structure that supports me, and *its* mindless, totally committed place in the mock-egalitarian technological downhill slide; consider my locus—San Francisco and its
future (BART, the new buildings, American cities generally,
the racial mix, the arts, the bay, the cost); California, and its
crucial symbolic role as the world's touchstone for the egalitar-
ian/technological mix to come. As the world rushes to follow
California, California speeds on blindly ahead. I might even
maintain my 18th Century dreamworld (with its 21st Century
comfort, efficiency, financing), an increasing anachronism, for
the rest of my life-span: after all, today's scene is filled with
wise, out-of-place, semi-contented old fossils . . .

The image of people like M., of a Sears' catalogue, is most
useful—it helps me see the thoughtless, mindless *adaptation* of
the autumn-leaf people to the winds of passing time, gives me a
vivid and near instance of the unconscious changes of a generation of America; in the idea of money, or time, or happiness, or
success, or style, or "home," or status-aspiration: of people reasonably free financially, but without any internal steering-
mechanism, at the absolute whim and mercy of the shifting
cultural winds.

Me too, of course. I am no wind-ignoring Olympian. But
then I haven't been adult and aware through a very long span
of time. I move from glo-sox to $7.00 Beatle-inspired haircuts,
but that is mere fashion. I grew up with television, after all; it
grew as I did. Most of the rest—suburbia, highways, bombs,
computers—has been simply an acceleration of phenomena
there all along.

But what I do see new, now, is a new kind of human awareness—granted that even this is partly a matter of my only just
growing up to it myself. After all, what would I have thought
if I had reached a comparable maturity in 1917, or 1933, or even
in McCarthyist 1952? Doubtless I would have thought myself
at just such an epochal turning. How is my revolution different
from theirs? Does everyone cut and hinge history at the mo-

ment of his own coming-of-age? To the frightened swimmer, every new wave looks tidal.

What is different: a radical inability to put up with most kinds of traditional crap. (But see Hemingway? No. Even Hemingway's crap. Even Sartre's. Hard old Camus seems mid-Victorian.) The end effect may be, politically or culturally, to lead one into still *vaster* fields of crap, the sublime, warfaring Utopianism or anarchy of the young resisters. It leads to, or is related to, the icy anodyne of the new nudity, of a sexual assertiveness than can only grow farther (from topless to decorated codpieces, then to bared genitals: more and more explicit filmed eroticism; commoner, younger, more obvious multisexuality—to what end? I've no idea. Like the other juggernaut. At what psychic price, cultural price? I've also no idea). It quashes political activism or participation,* demotes the standing of the business-world artifice (brand names, profits, advertising), leads to frenzied shifts in marginally exciting "styles," to a valueless cool hedonism in every domain. The Beatles, *Blow Up*, Marat-Sade à l'Anglaise. (Suddenly Beckett is dated, *l'Avventura*, *La Dolce Vita*—all so pushy, so serious, so uncool.)

I know. I'm describing myself still, my little world. But here I think, however much 46% of America may churchgo on Sundays, I do live in the wave of the coming, and feel the Cutting Edge. *Bonnie and Clyde*, wars on nightly television, riots staged *for* television, *Le Nouvel Observateur's* naked ads, saturated eight-lane freeways, the terribly, drily clever Alka-Seltzer commercials (or a score of others); all the radical, radical Berkeley thinking (of how to teach who and why, of the archaism of the very *Idea* of a University, of the Idea of Democracy, of the Idea of Personality, of the barbaric inanity of war, the absolute lie of compromising, game-playing governors and administrations).

Electronic companies buy up publishers, Xerox transforms the intellectual world, computer-people propose data-printing whole libraries—all this I only dimly see, surrounding myself still with lovely, solid cubes of the books McLuhan and Steiner regard as *passé*, books which I still read and savor slowly and closely like some pre-revolutionary, *ci-devant* dilletante. Tech-

* False: a new element.

nology spreads, television grows cheap, its seductive omnipotence draws to it billions in talent and pressure, till it refashions the daydreams and nightdreams, the aspirations and accents, the size of the world, the length of an hour, the machinery of thought, the sense of the self, the strategy, the group-identity, the nationality of every man: it brings the American Negro, slightly enfranchised, only lately acknowledged as human, to his feet, shouting, catapults him from his slight, cosy platform of "liberal improvement" into something very like an existential and inescapable state of total war.

So many easy-liberal ideas are false, Swiss-cheesed with holes, blurted out over and over again with no regard for the multiple implications of a hundred other domains. Is the world coming to realize this (because of immediate-naked "news" displays, masser and masser education), coming of age in the cant-clearing, coldly disgusted, selfishly sneering new stylish ways I describe—or is it only me, again, extrapolating out of egoism? Then how explain the Beatles, the Stones, the new films, the erotic fashions, the general bankruptcy of patriotic wartime rhetoric, as never before in any nation's history? The world does seem to be growing up, into something bloodless, icy, utterly unsentimental. (But then what of the newly doctrinaire "Left"?)

How do people see themselves, their lives, the world? With a frenzied, post-Freudian uncertainty (our fanatic urge to strip bare, to find a primacy, a surer "truth" in the unconscious, the sexual or sublimated, the instinctive and animal: a rejection of the priorities of the Age of Reason: Spock, new biographies, behaviorism everywhere, Paul Goodman and Norman O. Brown, new painting: but mostly ourselves, our sex lives and our worrying about them. Lives? I should think increasingly in hedonistic, ad-oriented, status-anxious terms, all readily explainable by historical sociologists: see M., or B.K., or undergraduates eluding the draft. At *each* intellectual/economic level, the same concern for "image," for style, for way of life —not for aim, product, stability, even family or fulfillment. Busy, busy leisure (filled in the chic ways of one's set), bright houses filled with new things. Antiqued.

Whipped, pummelled into manic numbness by the brash, glaring, blaring noise of the media—who sees or feels *Bonnie and Clyde,* of all the millions? And, at the other extreme (the extremes meet), cushioned in this numbness by tranquilizers, insipid fruits and vegetables, smooth roads and soft tires, Spockean childhoods, scholarshiped-manhoods, job security.

What is it like, such a life? (I should know: I lead it.) Old age no longer exists, manhood is eased into childhood by nested cocoons of school-security and certain jobs. Easier, softer, surer, smoother, deodorized: no crop failures, job hunts, racking diseases, childbirth anguish, wasting old age, inferior infant-status under tyrant parents and teachers, no Angry Gods, pregnancy fears, adolescent chaos.

To what end? Suave organ transplants, genetic control, nerve pills—or must there be an out, despite all the biological tinkering, for the mad, the centrifugal force? Into impotence, frigidity, sexual perversion—or the *need* for the flamboyant eroticism of today; into brutal bleeding violence, in Vietnam, in Detroit, in a movie house, on one's baby's back. Or one's own. De Sade—or Marat.

I don't relish the mass-picture of tomorrow, but then I don't that of today—or of yesterday. But I would like to see all three clearly—and then continue to shape my own private life in tasteful, sybaritic, productive, generous, self-realizing fashion, against or with (or ahead of) the current, as need be.

15 April 1968

. . . Intellectual's musings, spun especially by Gilman's two *New Republic* pieces on Negro writing—but also by Gide, RFK, the post-Martin Luther King riots, Reston's remarks on those, etc. *I'm not sure* if the revolution now in progress is in fact more radical, more total than those people were always seeing earlier in this century. I want to be very careful not to hear in mere noise the sound of a world turning, not to mistake the whirlwind *I* happen to be caught in now for the tornado of the age. But I do think this is something different. It has a tremendous lot to do with television (which is one reason I want to get back to it), the most powerful instrument of the century. It dominates politics, shapes a people's self-image, gives the country (and the world) a weird coherence, destroys the space of time—it has *suddenly* made war unbearable to the public at home (for the first time since man began); it forces

the election and rule of "personalities"; it is clearly reordering
the responding brain-cells of a population, as well as their
clothes, heroes, pace, morals, and so on. Ghetto (how quickly
we've institutionalized that metaphor) homes have TV even
when they haven't toilets, and they watch it for hours every
day. Surely television, with its hypnotic mass-omnipotence, its
instantaneity, its lowest-common-denominator streetfighting
reportage is the responsible unifying factor behind the American Negro's sudden explosive demand for his share of the great
national pie. His share, now—by breaking and looting, by
blackmail threats, by forcing of "guilty" white power-holders
of every sort, at all defiance of reason, desert, merit. They have
seen what they want; they have heard their demagogues; they
have seen that such blackmail works. It won't stop now: we're
in for—a century?—of unreasoned angry grabbing by the
Wretched of the Earth.

It's not easy to find oneself a comfortable moral seat for the
spectacle. I know what I *don't* like—the enormous, nationwide
sham of the King funeral rhetoric, not one man, black or
white, in a thousand speaking the truth. The bilge and blather
that came from white mouths! Stock, safe responses by the
cubic mile. More honesty in the open enmity of a Wallace,
selfish and subhuman though it be. The sham, to begin, of the
network televising of it all, of the two or three days of affected
mourning . . . Had I will and time, I'd write my own essay
now—on the televised sham-orgy of grief, guilt, and good intentions, on the *real* white response, the real black response, on
the overseas reaction, the city riots, the great blackmailing
game of hooligan-destruction, on Myrdal's trillions and the
Kerner Commission's ultimate indictment of—obviously—
white Americans' dislike of Negro Americans. (Or must I say
"black" now too?) . . .

Gilman's idea, become more and more mine: that the revolution, the coming reign of chaos, of darkness, of the wretched
of the earth, of the unordered psyche, of uncontrol, of unreason—is going to make me more and more irrelevant. Working
with Gide and Johnson and the rest forces my realization that I
am now, irrevocably, not of the New, but of the Old World—
the world of individualism, morality, clarity, style, integrity,
disciplined hedonism—of the imperial-aristocratic-capitalist

West, which fostered and paid for such luxuries. I cannot give it up: nor can I defend it, assert it, as the right and only way for everyone, as Gide could do. I can only try to sharpen and refine my own, aging moral way, and then see what light it can cast on the new and coming . . .

7 *June*

The television "coverage" lags dismally on and on; one man, because he is dead, because he was shot dead, because he was a Kennedy and running for President, is spread so thin, so far, forced to generate so many millions of words and images that he ceases to mean: because television exists, it alone must bear our ritual burden of official mourning (and it is now expert, ready at the crack of a gun, having had so much experience. It has formed and refined its own, *our* own new shapes and images of national mourning, to take the place of slow railway processions, black wreaths, Whitman's or Tennyson's odes: commentators at desks, in pairs, slowly, slowly filling hours with words, calling in their colleagues by tiny hearing aids to shove microphones, bristling fistfuls of them in anyone's face; the death scene over and over and over, the incumbent chaos of cries; headlights, biers, ambulances, hospital ante-rooms, bulletins from haggard press secretaries, planes leaving and arriving: and then the massive preparations for large-scale electronic-cum-medieval ritual. For a corpse.)

Because it exists, and because we must all pretend we *want* it to do this, it cancels all else and tries to make itself believe that the junior senator from New York warrants every hour of 200 million people's television-watching time—which is one hell of a national fiction. To have to talk, or write even, is hard enough; but to have to talk *so much* (so many words, sentiments degraded: is it any wonder one shrinks back into himself like a struck snail, into his private shell of silence?)—and to have to accompany it all with images. Give us his face, his living face to stare at—that lower lip, the disarming buck-teeth, the pulled-back smile, the down-drooping eyes, so keen and yet so tired, the constant return-to-questioner questions, the silences, the gentleness, the humble, self-uncertain, asymmetrical eyes . . . the timbre, the accent . . . the square shoulders on so lean, stick-thin, hard-muscled a body; the celebrated dropping swirl of thick brown hair . . .

Because that is the living man. That is what is gone. Not ideas, or projects, or a political force, but a human breathing thing, like me, like Sheila, like his own brother, my own brother. No motion has he now, no force; he neither hears nor sees. To die; to lie in mute obstruction and to rot . . .

Actually, of course, the death has receded from me. One lives these things, a nation lives these things, in stages, in great epic acts—from the election (voting, pushing the little marker after his name, like a million and a half other Californians), the slow-returning results (and "projections"): when, and how, one first heard; the 24 hours refusing even to allow entrance to the possibility of death or serious debility (while clearly, all along, doctors, associates, journalists knew); Pierre Salinger's breaking that stage so finally at 7 the next morning—yesterday morning. Talking *that* out, then another day of newspaper words, television pictures. Today, a day off, a lovely day, with Sheila in San Francisco—lunch, the shops at Ghirardelli Square and the Cannery, drinks, constant views of the bay and the Golden Gate under fresh clean skies . . . and now I cannot go to bed, I cannot sleep, the *Observer* made me morally ill, Gide has dissolved to dust, thoughts of school work (any work) repell me. Inside, I am sick.

He, it, has receded—tomorrow's stage, the televised funeral will arouse new aches, transform me again: as will dinner with the N.'s (surely McCarthyites), the work I *must* do for school, our anniversary on Monday. But at this point in time—11:30 Friday night—I am only internally sick, diseased with a moral ennui, the residue of it all: of this man's murder, dropped in the midst of the current moral-political confusion of my world.

H. thinks, talks of politics, aspiring Kennedyish activism; but H. reads the *Wall Street Journal*, writes to Charlie Ravenal, plays squash, consults for Avco. I am not H. (Still, thank God for someone to talk at, to think in front of; our conversations, as we both see, include no affection, "nothing personal," and hence *are* artificial, dual monologues. But how many can come as close . . . ?)

What really set off my sickness was reading a six-day old *Observer*. Weird. Not just Anthony Howard's vile, insulting piece on Kennedy (typical, for six days ago); but the Immigration nastiness, the manic, insular "analysis" of bloody France, Ascherson's and Tynan's mindless, browbeating leftism, Muggeridge's ever-insufferable smugness, the reviews of sickly, effete Bloomsbury (London's own 1950-S.F. beatniks), the whole horrid Englishness of it all. The world has changed *that much* in six days. (Wait till I get last month's *Mondes* and *Observateurs*. But then the French crackup still enlists my serious sympathy and curiosity; because, for some reason, France still does.)

What do I make of it all? Oh, God, I don't know. But I would like to be able to stop attacking others' lies or empty words or inadequate, partial answers, and risk a few true words of my own. But what can be said?

That egalitarianism is at most a religious notion, religion exported (with its full quotient of faith) to radical politics—Thomas Paine's, Marat's, today's radical left, perhaps communism. It is a shining transcendental idea, like the soul; it has no meaning of itself, it is not, actually, in any sense true. It does have force, power, both as a notion to fill and enflame men's minds, as a dream-nebula to measure fact against, and as a vague cross in the sky to stare at and march behind, shouting. It is one of the oldest dreams of man—*I* once believed it. I no longer do.

No—men are *not* equal: in fact, what matters in them is their uniqueness, their difference. The death of a Kennedy matters more than the deaths of 100,000 Vietnamese. The votes of 20,000 students *may be* less important than the opinion of a committee of five—or of a single man. Every man *does not* deserve everything.

This I believe. But, as I am a practical man, I realize that the combination of mass democracy and rising degrees of liberalism and technological wealth will invest more and more power, political power, in the opposite, the metaphysical, the egalitarian idea. There is no viable political assertion in the name of which today one can deny the masses as much political power as they can seize, be they California "property-owners" or Black Nationalists, French workers or Berkeley students.

Philosophically, they are wrong; politically, they are irresistable. There is no room for morality, private morality like mine, in the battle of power—see sage old Stokely Carmichael. That is politics.

Many things the majority (this majority, that majority) wants are wrong: to force Universities into tools of minority power, to dictate racist or counter-racist terms under threat of blackmail, to brutalize others in order to keep one's own garden tidy, to reject all gun laws, to *ignore* the impoverished outcasts of capitalism, and so on . . . the word "wrong," of course, I use as an idea: each of these things is large, open, complex: I simply mean to imply that egalitarian, so-called participating democracy has about it no assurance, or even likelihood, of justice.

But it can't be stopped: it's a 200-year old wave, and there's no holding it. That doesn't mean one must hop into uniform and join their army, with or against his own conscience, no matter. Nor leap to the side of the selfish, terrified Haves, pointing their rifle barrels out the peepholes of their mock-Mediterranean villas.

On the right, the possessors, the family-walled, the ascending, the materialist bourgeoisie, incapable of real sympathy, real selflessness, real sacrifice. Their name is selfish, and their name is legion. On the left, the have-nots (*relatively*: relatively. A Calcutta beggar, an African peasant, is not a Hunters' Point garbageman), OR the sanctified radicals. One half wants to take away the Haves' havings, to become themselves the selfish possessors (and they will, they will: see Fanon, on the hopeless cycle of successful revolutionary-turned-bourgeois); the other half, the Robespierres, Cohn-Bendits, and all, dislike this human state of things and preach, fight for, demand a better, with a Mohammedan bloody fervor. They are the dedicated, the puritan avengers, following that cross up in the sky; because they are virtuous, there shall be no more cakes and ale.

Between them, implacable hate. (Among them, as often as not.) Deadlock, forever, since both responses are as natural as rain or death. Eruptions, progresses and retreats from time to time, like the Western Front of 1915—a French General Strike, then a De Gaulle-bourgeoisie reassertion; the Czar,

1917, the resurgence of Russian materialism and selfishness; the very internal squabbles of Negro reformers; Holy-crusade riots that end in gleeful looting, then police repression, then public dramas of false moralizing, then Congressional stalemates that accurately represent the resistance of the Haves.

No, sign up with neither side, the right because they are selfish, the left because they are wrong (and will be, would be selfish if they could). But realize that both responses are natural, even (deep deep down) perhaps good. One is that of the mother, the *foyer*, man the builder: to build a home, protect that home, keep one's own children warm and safe and secure. As long as there are women, and women bear children they keep and rear, there will be a selfish bourgeoisie—whether it lives off Welfare checks or thievery or peonage, or off stock dividends. It could be no other way. The people who, even potentially, are unselfish and anti-possessive, are a handful—the comfortable intellectuals (Pascal and his *poèle*) (Me), the communal free spirits, the religious retreatants, the single and childless who happen to be dedicated. Communism (Russian, Chinese, Cuban) seems to be able to eradicate this spirit by rigid control of education, society, and economy; but, if the European example tells, only so long as the nation itself does not prosper. Once there are more than enough goods, then the possessive and selfish urge reasserts itself.

A poor country quite obviously could use something like Russian/Chinese/Cuban communism. There, the former Have/Have Not gap, the proportional difference, is so immense, so ludicrous, that to go on presuming the naturalness of bourgeois selfishness would be sinful folly. I only say that as soon as you can afford it, it will reassert itself. A great deal of American Negro protest is already an assertion, not of radical noble selfhood, but of "comparing" bourgeois selfishness: I have, but you have more; I want it.

Nor are we going to get rid of holy idealism, of course; nor should we. I can understand such militant unreason, such an existential ache at What Is seeing itself as practical political reformism, both psychologically and politically. Since politics is a balancing of powers, this militant unrealism does have real effect, as the monsters of Dickens' fiction can hurt the real people—so it cannot be ignored or dismissed, not even by a realist.

It reflects a natural, radical, even noble aspiration of finite man; it will never cease; and it can combine, organize (especially by rallying the potential selfishness of the have-nots: see Weiss' Marquis de Sade) into a force "to be conjured with," as they say—to be negotiated with, in fact, as at Columbia, the Sorbonne, Atlanta; it may even, on occasion, take over: ever so briefly.

I share neither, wholly; I try to understand both. As a timid, helpless hedonist, husband, and father, I am in part a selfish bourgeois; as a sympathetic, intelligent moralist aware of political realities, *part* of my spirit is marching with the marching mobs. So get you gone, Mario Savio, though with blessings on your head.

I am, as I almost told H., not really a "realist" at all, since that implies at least the possibility of political action, and (like the term "behaviorist" in political science) disclaims any order of values. I have sharp (often warring) values, and values such that I cannot act. What I am is a romantic cynic, like Fitzgerald (or Chekhov, or Shakespeare): I know that people, most people, are basically contemptible (morally)—even poor ones, even revolutionaries—dominated, if given the chance, by selfishness. I *couldn't* work for them, with them, directly: the lying manipulation involved would wreck me. I *know* I'm better and they're wrong. A cynic, then, as the world goes.

And yet I cry, I mourn the death of heroes, I believe in altruism, I love love, I relish pleasure, I treasure the past and weep for its passing; I can take comfort in the pattern of leaves on a footbridge, and ache at ugliness or cruelty or simply the thought of a week that won't come back. Tender; not, I think, sentimental, but certainly romantic.

So I stand between.

What do I think will happen? What do I think is happening? What *matters* on the current scene?

I don't know. I think we're in for at least twenty years (Christ: why only twenty?) of moral and political confusion equal to this one. Why should it stop, after all? The powers that be will *have* to be more or less like those existing today: hugely bureaucratic, more and more computerized and omnicompetent; morally bewildered, because representative (more or less) of morally bewildered people, property yielding to conscience only when forced; compromising (of course), lying (of course), directed by the old, the doctrinaire, the narrow. Tyranny can, in today's wide-open world, only be sporadic and exceptional. In every country, there will always be some who either are in fact poor (starving, jobless, unaided, unsheltered, gray thin animals that are born, work or waste, die) or poor by harsh comparison; or at least militantly envious. And there will always be younger generations without bureaucratic power, impatient of compromise, offended by politics—generations, given the new democracy, ever larger, noisier, and potentially more troublesome to these poor powers doing the best they can.

"End the war." Sure. "Get out of Vietnam." Yeah. A nasty war, as are all, overpublicized to a generation educated and at leisure enough to find the business of war morally offensive, when undertaken by our side. Once "over," the CBS cameras and Mary McCarthys gone, Sukarno-type bloodpurges, toppling chaoses of governments, Chinese embraces in the Lithuanian mode can all follow in order, and the young moralists will find some other Western offense to excoriate, whatever the cameras choose to point at—which is to say, wherever *we* are.

The races can go on hating, distrusting for decades, at least till intermarriage *is* the norm and races disappear. People are "racist," deep down, virtually all of them. Don't let's fake it. Which is why I can at least admire the published realism, presuming racism and proposing a politic that accepts it, of a Stokely Carmichael. If it is in fact unrealistic, that is its only ground of fault.

So: Stalemate. Worse and worse. Gradually, the "liberal" reforms forced out by good men (I do believe in them: and some know how to combine goodness with political maneuver) or by shows of militant force will effect belated, creaking changes in the West (in French education, U.S. tax structure, income distribution, the social relevance of universities, television, perhaps even the look of the land, though I doubt that: it's an anti-democratic luxury). Never fast enough, full enough for the angry visionaries, of course, who will then set fires and sit in and all the rest . . . but good men will understand, and go on working.

It's just a rotten shame the few we have get shot. (Why? American wealth, power-sense, impatience, crudity, trigger-finger.) And H.'s response is right: we who know we are good, who know *ourselves* to be of their sort, in their secret army, must stand up and take their places. His particular place may be in politics. Mine will be in . . . I don't know: telling the truth. It will get harder and harder to do, since there is so much of nature and even of justice on all these shrill, lying, half-blinded sides. Don't you go blind—either by staring at one man's sun too long, or by closing your eyes.

I'm sorry you're gone, both of you. I felt you as men, I knew what you were doing. My world is now smaller, underpopulated, reduced in spirit. In my way—which isn't yours, but is of it—I'll try to help keep the loss from being irreparable. Some people *are* worth millions of others. America without John Kennedy went gloomily downhill; 1968 without his brother is tasteless. Can the likes of H. and me make up for it? We think so. A matter of guts, that's all. And the path of the uncommitted critic (if I follow it) offers none of the satisfactions of either ardent alignment or productive action. Were they both alive, and asking my support, I couldn't give it. And yet I *do* support them. Still.

Requiescat. But not in peace. Like you, I love this messy world.

3 July

. . . Reading Eric Hoffer in the week of Berkeley's tiny taste of Trotskyist anarchy has pushed my critical position farther out on the limb, to a place still more tenuous, more lonely, more difficult to maintain than before. One must keep one's wits, one's sympathy, one's moral surety intact at each level, from the most immediate and local to the most Olympian, even though each stage in the ascent necessarily subsumes (and hence appears to contradict) the preceding. Now, to a cool, benign recognition of the desperate but necessary rule of warring interests—the only tenable human state, the only one that offers even a hope for something like justice. Beyond each battle—Mayor Johnson vs. Pete Camejo, De Gaulle vs. Cohn-

Bendit, Eric Hoffer vs. the Intelligentsia or the Faithful, Capitalist Democracy vs. Communism—beyond each battle, both of whose infinitely complex sides one must try to understand (and to one of which he will be temperamentally, temporarily drawn), beyond each there is a higher plateau of resolution, wherein both are comprehended. A sort of Olympian (gradus ad Olympum) intellectual dialectic.

All this I shall try to get down in words before the long holiday (Independence Day!) is over: it marks a new stage in my own social-political thought so pronounced that I cannot but feel it breaking out, taking shape, changing *me* as it works itself out even beneath the level of thought. Crucial was the recognition (thanks both to Hoffer and the Young Socialists) of my breaking loose from the liberal intelligentsia with whom I had so long half-identified myself—for want of anyone else. I now see, and dimly begin to see the reasons for, their own doctrinaire dependence on a single, limiting view—in which anti-Americanism comes more easily than anti-Communism, all Negroes are suffering and all riots justified, all police brutal and all wars evil. To cut the cord that ties me to this group is painful, since it will entail almost absolute intellectual aloneness. But is that not what Gide preaches? Is it not what I admire most in him? (Yes, I know, so does Eric Hoffer. Grant it him: no one *else* I've read had sufficient independence, right or left, to make me see the liberal-intellectual for the timid, party-lining, one-eyed Groupthinker he is—and I have been. Beyond this, though, Hoffer's independence reveals a frightened, narrow, selfish man. Gide's independence was a goad, a driving moral imperative to ever-increasing *openness*, to constant and radical *self*-examination, not simply to clever, insulting, "objective" analyses of the still-dependent opposition.) . . .

20 September

. . . Generally, a painfully bewildering, sick-making summer. The rasp of events, radical and reactionary, on my nerves is proving almost too grating, and I am already closing in the fences, pulling in the limits I so proudly advanced just a few months ago. It's so ugly: and I see no useful, functional place in it—the world of events, of *événéments*, of "hard news"—for a man, like me, trying to keep his moral balance. It is clearly the time for taking the historian's, not the journalist's perspective: and look where I'm going.

"Events" are like stinging little pellets against a hypersensitive skin: each day's can send you into jittery little fits, chain reactions of spasmodic responses—whether you be a journalist (who simply must sit there and, willingly, be shot at, day after day, never distinguishing the material from the immaterial) or one who feeds on them. Some people, most people thrive on this daily flagellation of nerves and reason. I don't. So right now I'm trying to hollow out a fictitious private retreat, a hole in time, where I can shelter myself in a world I understand and (somewhat) admire, and do useful work. . . .

8 October

I admit it: the threatening, arrogant, militantly partisan know-nothing demands of the Berkeley radicals—specifically, today, the "Afro-Americans" against Subject A (and the Bible, the Middle Ages, the Renaissance, anything not black-race-promotional, celebrational)—I admit it gets to me. It gets to me because it is growing and thriving within the University, with the tacit, timid, intimidated support of the frightened and insecure administration. Because the University—which I cling to and trust as a last haven of reason, of honest and careful thought, seems to be—as President Hitch, in fact, implied—killing itself: selling out, for fear of reprisals, for fear of insult, for fear of riot, for fear of looking illiberal or being labeled racist, selling out to the shrill partisan know-nothings, the anti-reason faction, and thus *earning* the distrust, and hatred of right, middle, and me.

My conscience is stung, and feels gloomily guilty about doing nothing, saying nothing, remaining silent. I will grant all the injustices of American anti-Negro racism: but also lay claim to a private battle, aside from that war, on behalf of truth —which is *not* being told, OR DEFENDED. No one seems to dare, for fear—for fear of all those hate-staring, new-emancipated, nothing-to-lose black militants.

I *hate* to see such gross leftist-radical, frozen-minded lying in triumph everywhere in the intellectual world, without a really brave, outspoken, unafraid Orwellian critic to rebut it: and, since I claim the role, or would like to, I feel this *is* my call, my chance, to prove my fitness. A letter to the *Daily Cal*, later interviews, an article on Black Power lies and administrative spinelessness.

But I won't. And I'll feel sick because I haven't. How will I justify my silence, my ostrich-refusal even to read the student handouts, *Daily Cal* editorials, the lot?

1. That my last and only venture into a rational response to the demands of "Black Pride" ended so nastily, and I don't want any more of *that*. I clearly can no more keep out of political implications, given my moral-literary commitments, than Orwell or Wilson or Gide: but there is no point in inviting irresponsible rebuttal when I can cope neither physically nor emotionally . . . nor can my family. Words *are* weapons, and one can be fairly shot back at for them.

2. That my values—reason, culture, the past, the word, the truth, moral discrimination—are likely to prevail, if only because (at the University) they have so much entrenched power on their side. The opposition, though noisy, physical, intimidating, and well-publicized, is still more ineffectual than not. Vast MLA projects go on, the library buys Renaissance tomes, the Art Museum Puvis de Chavannes, courses are taught at highest standards despite CPE nonsense: these latest barbarians are only a handful of freshmen with a ditto machine. You ignored them at Montpellier: why not here?

(Clearly, a cheap answer, a rapidly-melting ground of assurance.) Do I *want* to rest my trust in reason on MLA grants and Lewis Feuer's Institute? Can I curl up with my books and values inside the cushioned armor of a despicable (or somewhat despicable) academic corporate fund-getting machine, one vast cushy indefensible *position acquise?*

No. No, ethically. Hence I must stand on my own. Hence, logically, I should answer back. But I don't want to: I don't want to and I do. I'm afraid of idiotic violence and partisan abuse: I know that the idea of debate with such Holy Bigots is out of the question. But damn it, SOMEBODY should answer them, and not let the University go on and on, smirking, wincing, yielding before these abusive and mindless partisan ultimata.

3. The expense of spirit in a waste of shame. It comes to that. And yet the heroic role would be to assume the unfilled

place of telling, and demanding, the truth amidst all this warfaring mythology, this bloody cant, this devaluation of all language and meaning to propagandist shrieks. ("Racist" = anyone who resists our "Afro-American" demands, whatever they
be. Establishment. Liberals. Media. Confrontations. Be-Ins. Es-
calate. Co-opt. Counter-insurgency. Tokenism. Hawks. Fascists.
Pigs.) The lowest point language has reached in my thinking
lifetime—and I sit by and do nothing.

But were I to answer, I should be committed to keep answering, to fight and fight and fight—to what end? Is there a cool, a
safe, a non-frustrating way to assume the Orwellian role? I
hope so, because I can't live with myself much longer if I don't
. . . to go on, safely and yet in good conscience, ignoring the
rain of sleazy, black-myth lies that seems so to be corrupting
the University. I feel myself, daily, at Berkeley, freezing into
angry, spiteful, 18th Century Rationalist reaction: I call it a
personal claim on, a private assertion of Western Culture, with
a kind of Proustian languor, locked outside in anachronism:
but I only partly believe that. I do think they're wrong, that
my classical-elitist standards are right: I do care more for the
rich than the poor, and despise the take-over rise of mobocracy
(black or white) as much as any Carlyle. (Or Fitzgerald, or
Faulkner, or Yeats, or Shakespeare. Etc. My Crowd.)

But there's no point, I suppose, in saying all that out loud. I'd
best "assert" it by the individual, non-political acts of my life:
my reviews, my standards for written and spoken prose, my
courses . . .

So let the ranters rant, the demanders demand; and try not to
feel compelled to answer every one of them *now*. You are, by
now, incorrigibly elitist: you are not one for Dialogues with
the People. Admit it, let it be, do *your* thing, which is criticism
on rational-literary-moralist Western standards. Let the noise
roll on, and don't jump up just because the shots seem to be
coming closer to home. Your values will clearly be expressed
every day, in the very style of your life and work. Please: don't
feel morally compelled *yet* to play the Aron role, just because no
one else seems to be doing it: you haven't the political guts or
savvy. Do what you do best—TV and periodical reviewing,
large personal-moral honest assessments of figures you admire
(or don't). The TV half-hours of wider scope. Teach-

ing. Situations you can control, guarded against anarchic and
irrational exchanges and "confrontations." Know your place,
and accept it. If one day you earn the larger, more public role,
fine. Today can do without you, uniquely honest though you
may egotistically feel.

Quiet, conscience: down. Let me get back to work. Please.
Pretend you're not at Berkeley.

Saturday, 26 October
(From an unsent letter)

. . . the Cassandra role grows arid and selfish, the Olympian
sneer tiresome, the self-preserving artist's retreat-from-it-all a
bit questionable . . .

I want the University to keep rolling gigantically on,
theoretically apolitical (like me), vast and bracing in its intellectual liberty, demanding only the highest and surest activity
and quality of mind and rewarding it with lifelong shelter, sus-
tenance, and stimulation. So, selfishly, and as a religiously-dedi-
cated intellectual, a Western man of the mind, I *hate* any inter-
ferences or disruptions; politically-heated junior faculty who
league with *engagés* (*enragés?*) students to insinuate propa-
ganda-series into our programs in the guise of "courses"; politi-
cally-fixated governors and regents, either angling for easy
votes or genuinely terrified by radicals, especially non-White
All American ones, who presume to assume control of this institution (whose only real value and validity is its freedom
from control); an administration so thousand-eyed and fearful
of *all* opinion that it must speak as softly and crookedly as any
campaigning politician to these abuses; and finally, the animal
terrorist tactics of students whose minds *have* been given up to
their "Cause," who think now (respond, rather) only in Good
Guy/Bad Guy terms, doctrinaire neo-manicheism, and breathe
only slogans. "End' U' Č Ra'-cǐ-sm̃, End' U' Č Ra'-cǐ-sm̃," happily chanted, mindlessly over and over, like "We Wanna
Touchdown," albeit with considerably less clarity about what
it is that is wanted . . .

Still, my ideal, my dream University is clearly a self-indulgent fiction. The University has always been political: once
covertly, today overtly. The NSF fund-flap proves that, as
does that Maharaja-styled arsenal of intellect we call "The

Hill." (To say nothing of Livermore, Los Alamos, H.S.'s world generally.) No medieval *communitas* there! (but then, medieval Universities were just branches of the Church, as terrified of heresy as any Reagan or Rafferty. Academic Freedom is a very new—and perhaps very fragile—idea . . .)

So the student accusation, that our status-quo-preserving silence, the ostrich-pose of the humanist-individualist professoriate, worrying only about freedom for thought and quality of mind *is in fact* wanton social and political irresponsibility: that by our willful, "apolitical" uninvolvement we are in fact giving aid and active support to the immoral, anti-human juggernaut of corporate power that rules America (and the University)— that accusation I may soon be forced to listen to, though I have not yet brought myself to the Holy War Against Corporate Power position held by most of my liberal colleagues. And now that so many regard a college degree—even an advanced degree—as the minimal passport to positions of authority, we (the Parnassian, apolitical *universitaires*) do clearly shape, judge, determine, force the structure of American power by our admission, grading, and graduation policies.

I know, I know: we are no longer, perhaps we never were, mere island-harbors of free intellectual inquiry: in a technological world, we are the very channel, perhaps the very source of social structures and political power, and I ignore this at my peril . . .

We move into a day of frenzied activism, of the politicization of all things: already Broadway hits are anarcho-leftist propaganda pieces, cheered by the liberal intelligensia just as they were in the 30's; already black students are "demanding" nothing but "relevant" courses—i.e., contemporary, race-oriented, political. We are indeed in for a repetition of the 30's, that great gray doctrinaire humorless desert: necessary, I suppose—out of the warfare, the dogma, the polarization came a kind of energy-level leap to a new plateau of egalitarian opportunity, which is what we call democracy. Now corporate hegemony has frozen and hardened over America again, at a higher, thicker level, a more pervasive if less obvious level than in 1880 or 1920, and clearly another warfaring decade of insults and threats and manifestoes and lists of signatures, of blacklists and backlash, of party lines and denunciations, of bonfires and barricades, of "violence in the streets" and "police brutality" is upon us.

90% of me, oh, say 75%, wants to retire for the decade to a mental cloister, preserving old values like some Dark Ages monk for the day when a rational, humane sun may shine again. . . . The other fraction is both seduced by the swirl of Today, aching to join the mad pageant (hence the TV—the Beatles, Mailer, Antonioni): and terrified of Emerson's imperative— that if a man is *not* involved in the problems of his own day, he may as well never have lived . . .

I know; I personalize everything hysterically; but that's my nature, the response of the literary man, the novelist *manqué:* I can't talk about politics for ten minutes without reducing it all back to *me.* . . .

. . . I do, ultimately, care more about language and truth than about power and justice: about quality than equality; about beauty than suffering. Sorry, but that's the way I am. I'd really love to, Mr. President, but you'll have to find another Secretary of State. The sullen, sulking-in-his-tent posture of the benchwarming critic, who frankly despises the game everyone else is playing, while he wishes he didn't—it's no great fun. But I see no other place.

. . . We'll just have to get used to riots, murders, burnings, "confrontations," numb ourselves to terrorist tactics—or the terrorists will have their way, and precipitate an armed state of constant readiness for panic, with all the destruction and all the repression that would imply . . . Ahead, a long tunnel of TV-splashed horrors in the darkness: some real pitched and bloody battles; much mess, waste, hatred, and lying. All Europe knew such a time in 1914–18, 1939–45, much of the time in between, and survived the wiser. Sartre always thought America soulless and shallow, because she had never known the nightmare horrors of old Europe. Maybe our time has come. I'm certainly not going to encourage it, or try specifically to retard it; to hail it on or lament it: just to expect it and try to survive it . . .

15 November

Sheila is right, of course. I have been growing increasingly conservative, politically and culturally, these last few months— no doubt about it: defining a willfully rear-guard position for myself, and leaping spontaneously to identify myself with any other ex-liberal intellectual (Kauffmann and Gilman and Brustein, Mailer and Howe) I find retreating, at last, taking a cold backward step from the revolutionary avalanche. The flames are coming closer, so I no longer merely keep silent, ignore them: I *publicly* announce my enmity, opposition, scorn, disgust.

I have lost all sense of sympathy with and understanding of the *enragés*, be they rule-despising, New World questing, liberated youth, or ghetto-oppressed and racism-depressed Negroes: so Sheila claims, and she is right. I have even played with the thought of admitting to myself that I have no social conscience; that the suffering and starvation and oppression of billions does not really touch me; that my own tastes, responses, training were so formed by a class-structured, hierarchical, elitist society (the luxury of literature, the education of a gentleman, the anti-democratic English tradition, things like wine and opera and Scott Fitzgerald, Racine and Cap d'Antibes)— that I simply cannot be of service to a real democracy, that in my heart I despise egalitarianism, that my *real* admiration is reserved for an aristocracy of intellect, taste, style, tradition, language . . .

Simplistically, for the moment, let me say that I conceive of two absolutely opposed, necessarily warring camps. (The political and liberal folly is to pretend they can be reconciled.) Either is valid: a mix of the two is not.

One: the traditional. As old as recorded history. Based on reason, order, excellence, discipline, achievement. Language properly used, the arts respected as highly as religion once was. The system that lies behind all the traditional University disciplines, and the University itself. The pattern of culture France (after Greece) thinks it invented and still owns, and which American intellectuals foolishly pretend to have inherited. Clearly unconcerned with or uninvolved with the amelioration of radical social injustice or inequality, since it is itself a whole galaxy of *positions acquises*, elitist and hierarchical by definition. Quality rather than quantity, truth and beauty rather than Christian egalitarian sharing. Source of most "acknowledged" art, the history that has been recorded: the ½% of populations that literature, history, all reflective and recorded activity have concerned themselves with in the Western adventure. Probably depends on repression, exploitation, Samuel Johnson's Great System of Subordination, corrupt or anti-democratic governments . . . and yet the source of art, honor, much real human generosity and unselfishness. But it *is* all of a piece, and it may well be evil to grow rapturous over the Sistine Chapel ceiling without some sense of the social system that allowed it. This tradition has formed me, and my responses: but that doesn't mean it isn't wrong, and would not be an unfit education for those to come.

Two: the Egalitarian-human. As old as slave revolts, but in particular as old as 1789: recall the dread portents of Arnold, Carlyle, Newman; the backing off stage of Edmund Burke. Respects *persons* and their individual welfare, not tradition: would, at an extreme, see all art and literature burned if it would feed the world's hungry. Desperately, anxiously aware of gross human suffering: impatient of order, design, received rituals, genteel compromises, restraints. The very ½% audience of most art (opera; Dior; Château Margaux) proves to these people its cruel irrelevance. The comforts of American affluence are humanity's greatest blot, considering India or Biafra. Language as *action*—propaganda, blackmail, inspiration, inflammation—rather than as logic or truth, whose patient, aristocracy-serving day is past. The logically ultimate extension of 1789: once all are equally free and worthy—where end before all are levelled? At the expense of all the traditionalists hold dear and live for? So be it. As long as men are starving, suffering, being bombed or abused—what else have we time for but, what loss is not justified by Revolution? Fires, if need be, terrorism, strikes, civil wars, pornography and vandalism: a very small price.

I regard it as, honestly seen, so clearly, cleanly drawn a battle that I consider the Red Guards' rejection of all art, the most "wanton" instances of vandalism, torture, or terrorism right for authentic parties of the second part. Only Fanon, I think, of those I have read, proclaims so radical a posture of tradition-defiance.

Many, many people try to have both, and it is clearly a human response. Few can cast off the tradition that has made them, few can today utterly reject the radical appeal of egalitarianism.

So they picket and buy fine clothes, love Mozart and Mao, and my questioning heart cannot bear the contradiction.

We *are* at war, though most pretend we are not. It looks as if the radicals will win in time, the torch-bearing levellers, but I'm not sure. The female/maternal urge toward home and security for one's own; the lust for creature comforts; a lingering nostalgia for the past—these may never go away.

So let me only say that a State of War, the War to End all Wars, exists, though often unnoticed. And that what I shall do in it, from my now entrenched position on the Traditional/Rational/Quality side, is to try and use my intellectual tools at least to understand the other, the growing, the noisier and more "contemporary" party. Not to join it; heavens no: impossible. But to understand it better.

Products of, members of the quality-oriented, hierarchical system actively worrying about and working for social reform and amelioration: it is what *all* educated liberals in their comfortable family homes do—see their tax returns: so much for the Opera Association, so much for the Cleaver Defense Fund. The final Democratic Party-compromise: an endless ache of moral concerns; a constant business about good works of one sort or another to ease the ache (checks to Negro Scholarship Funds or Aid for Biafra, stamping envelopes for McCarthy or Save the Bay, picketing or protest signing, clucking with mild outrage over the small percentage of black people in General Motors or City Hall or Stanford); but all this on top of an ever-understood, never-stated unwillingness or inability to budge from the position of comfort and security one has earned himself, thanks to the structures and values of the Traditional, hierarchical system. And therefore, when all is said and done, when whatever honor is due it is paid to the will-to-reform, the sympathy with suffering, the basic (sentimental?) benevolence, they are right back in the position of the Rich Young Man of the Gospel (the radical's ideal textbook).

> Jesus said unto him, If thou wilt be perfect, go and sell what thou hast, and give to the poor, and thou shalt have treasure in heaven; and come and follow me.

But when the young man heard that saying, he went away sorrowful: for he had great possessions.

Then said Jesus unto his disciples, Verily I say unto you, that a rich man shall with difficulty enter into the Kingdom of Heaven.

"He went away sorrowful, for he had many possessions": my text for today—S., Mailer, Paul Jacobs, the lot. For all the millions of dollars and hours spent, for all the ache and anguish that may well be there, it remains an 18th Century kind of condescending charity, the bowing down of a Lady Bountiful, a *Dame Patronesse:* Of course I'll do all I can to help you, you poor dear things; as long as it doesn't hurt me. Which leads me to believe that Snow's latest dire prediction (world famine, an unbelievable increase in the destitution of the third world, *unless* the imperialist world begins at once to tax itself to the limit in order to help)—that insofar as it is economically and scientifically accurate, it *will* be realized. Because people who *have* are not, willfully, going to undergo pain and loss and deprivation, give up their second (or first) cars, or leisure, or bank accounts, or children's schooling in order to feed starving Chinese. They simply aren't: it would, frankly, be unnatural; unhuman. On a national scale, the same thing: at best, certain responses of fear or economic necessity (i.e., sell to Negroes, hire Negroes) will be added to the trickle of *de haut en bas* benevolence—but more than that, no. It's impossible.

My image of the liberal: a man in a high, comfortable old chair who is trying to bend over and do something, help people on the floor—*without getting out of the chair.* (You could I suppose carry this further and have the chair on their backs, or built by their efforts, but that's getting too acrobatic to be a useful image: moreover, allegorically, I don't like that line. It's one thing to say my professorial chair is one of the products of a 2500-year old tradition of reason and hierarchical evaluations and anti-democratic principles; it's quite another, a leap into polemic, to say it's an oppressor's chair today, borne on the backs of the suffering poor.) He went away sorrowful, for he had many possessions.

And I don't like this elitist conspiracy, this pretense. It is the human way, to be selfish *and* unselfish at once, to be defensive of one's *biens*, one's household and status and family and prospects (benevolent, war-hating liberals—T.P.—who speculate in stocks and property, who bitch about taxes!)—*and* to worry about, to want to help the less fortunate.

Because it clearly does look as if the "less fortunate"—the great mob of them, outside America particularly—are never going to be "helped" by our voluntary charity, by the scraps from the master's table. A system born of, built up through 2500, 3000 years of Subordination, hierarchy, power for the few and subservience for the many—with all its lovely side-products like art and logic and civility and social institutions—probably cannot be reformed into a system for all, despite all the efforts men of good will have been making, inch by hard-yielded inch, since 1789. That goes for Universities as well as Corporate Capitalism: voting power, civil rights in that formal, minimal guise, is only the slightest of gestures.

What stance is admissible, then? Well, this one, the one I've been describing, of course: logically it is not, perhaps; but men are not logical. It comes closest to satisfying the contradictory human impulses of the ninety and nine in one guise or another. There are very few real tyrants of ego, very few Jesus Christs. As Fanon pointed out, once the dispossessed start possessing (whether by revolutionary takeover or the fruits of capitalistic largesse), they become as defiantly defensive of their "property" as any suburban Republican with a Buick station wagon. So a lot of this will probably go on and on and on.

But the starving and suffering, the outcast and ignored are going to become more and more visible—also more and more aware of their state; and, short of a great moral ice age descending on the comfortable states of the West, a mass hardening of hearts, something is going to have to give. And since I frankly cannot see even the best of Western benevolists following Christ's injunction, the only alternative is revolution. Defiance. The violent, "pointless" demands of the frustrated, excluded (from "life's feast," as the Pope so icily puts it), the *enragés*—spit, insults, bombs, torches, broken windows, chopped trees, burnt cars (*the* symbol of it all), universities occupied and struck down, museums vandalized, the safe suburbs harassed, middle-class children tormented: terrorist tactics of every sort. For in this ultimate "confrontation," anything goes. Not to submit to arbitration—of course not!

Enough of compromise. Intransigence from this moment on, endless harassment and disruption of a system that *cannot* be reformed. Always to demand more than can possibly be given, so as never to need yield one's posture of defiant refusal. Mockery and insult to those who, bending down from their comfortable seats, would like to help.

Of course, yes, for many of these there are ways "up": they could quietly, doggedly vote and study and work and be civil and play the elaborate game called Civilization—having of course to work harder at it, suffer (and harden? Ralph Ellison) more than the rest of us, since the rest of us basically dislike and distrust them: they could (and many will, most if they could) climb slowly up to the boardroom or faculty club or opera house. Inch their way up, join the system, climb up one day on a high chair of their own, as the Goldwaters and Buckleys and Whitney Youngs keep telling them. Then the high chairs will have more brown people and yellow people than they do now (just as the accents and origins and manners of their occupants are far more mixed today than they were 100, 200, 2000 years ago). And there may even be more chairs.

But there will still be billions swarming, suffering, scrambling, starving, dying in anonymity, in the prison of absolute poverty down on the floor. And those of the dispossessed who climb do so only by ignoring all these others. For as the system now operates—short of some whole new world order, like Lenin's internationalist dream—there must always be a majority of poor.

So those who, by origins or radical sympathy, do keep their eyes fixed on the suffering mass, see more vividly the Vietnamese or Indian or Biafran or slum-child than all the other structures, achievements, and values of civilization (which I, by nature and training, so treasure)—these cannot be expected to want, selfishly, nothing more than incorporation into, elevation to the system above—EVEN THOUGH they could make it if they wanted to (I speak of the intelligent radical, who clearly has the capacity for such ascent). Oh they may backslide, very humanly, long for the comforts or joys the structured society creates now and then: but basically their hearts are with the dispossessed, the forgotten, the oppressed: and they adamantly *refuse* to be incorporated into the system that allows and sustains this order of things. Voting, reasoning, logic, arbitration, civil discourse, these, they have long since learned, are not going to crack the system and relieve the poor, are not going to spread the wealth evenly enough.

So the terrorism, the vandalism, the fire and obscenity, the thousand and one ways of insulting, rejecting, harassing the system. To no end, you claim? On behalf of no new and better, demonstrably viable, demonstrably *fairer* system? No: we tried that once, and look at communism. Destroyed all the best of the old hierarchical civilization—individualism, freedom of thought, creativity, complexity, the style and art of aristocracy —but put nothing in its place but new suffering, new selfishness. No: just revolt, protest, *existential* protest. In one who is truly engaged in the lot of the suffering world—whose imagination is in fact haunted beyond all else by the picture of starving or burning children, men and women ground into the dirt by powers larger and more distant than gods (that is, America, Russia, all of us)—in such a one I understand, respect such pure, absolute, and existential protest. This given, the questions then *do* become tactical, political, rather than moral: how *best* to harass, to annoy, to mess up, to terrify the system, its chairholders and stockholders, its *actionnaires* and supporters.

Odd, though: you see, then, the old existential criteria, so at odds with traditional values, *do* come into play—and I'm not too happy about that. "Authenticity," sincerity, purity—that sort of thing. I say this because I still want to give myself room to scorn and despise the selfish, self-serving, mouthy radicals who use protest and sloganeering, vandalism and sitting-in as little more than private therapy for private ills. I don't want to fall into Eric Hoffer's, Lewis Feuer's error of branding all protestors with the same brush: nor turn so psychoanalytic as nastily, unsympathetically to ferret out some private, embarrassing, deflating affliction or aberration at the heart of any altruistic radical's dedication. OK, OK: they probably *are* all "abnormal"; but since normalcy is clearly defined as selfishness, thank God for the sick. (Parallel argument to the "Wound and the Bow" theory of artists, Gide on Dostoevsky or Nietzsche. It *is* the "unnatural," the aberrant, the $1/10^6$ imagination that sees and suffers for the sufferings of many others. It is, for example, not mine. But it is not only to be tolerated, it is to be honored: it is the salt of the earth. Without it, the human race would deserve very little praise indeed.)

—BUT: in many cases, the Hoffers and Buckleys are right. And though the Sartrean criteria are fluid and vague and impossible to apply, I must allow myself the right to distinguish— very carefully—between the radical whose dominant impulse is one of *sympathy*—that rare, fine man who can mourn with them that mourn, however many, distant, or alien they be (he may burn, even kill, destroy and torture for all that: see Brecht's *Masnähme:* but be careful); and the "radical" whose impulses are a turbid mixture of private confusion, guilt, envy, and hatred. Here I speak of the middle-class radical, he who is himself not starving or oppressed, the Jewish-student sort; confusion, envy, and hatred are more understandable among, say, black American teenagers. No, I mean those whose asserted concern is for *other* people's sufferings, the Moses Hall sitters in, the SDS. A Negro American has a certain born *right* to protest out of private hate: a white American needs better motives than that.*

> . . . And we pass through all this tumult, great and small, seated before the inexorable shadows of a television set—certainly the greatest psychic disturber ever created by man. Only it is capable of producing unrest, fear, and unbridled envy, and at the same time, of numbing us to the human reality of that which disturbs us.
>
> Richard N. Goodwin, "Reflections,"
> *The New Yorker*, January 4, 1969

> . . . They had had their minds jabbed and poked and twitched and probed and finally galvanized into surrealistic modes of response by commercials cutting into dramatic narratives, and parents flipping from network to network—they were forced willy-nilly to build their idea of the space-time continuum

---

* A certain unfairness here, I now realize (May '69), a certain irrelevant puritanism with regard to the right or motive to revolt. The very prospect of having to grow into the existing order, however well-off or well-descended one may be (as many defenders of student rebellions are now pointing out)—let alone the prospect of enforced military service or imprisonment—may well be morally sufficient internal justifications for a great variety of revolutionary acts.

(and therefore the nervous system) on the jumps and cracks and leaps and breaks which every phenomenon from the media seemed to contain within it.

Norman Mailer, *Armies of the Night*

Two reflections on television.

. . . during the struggle for liberation . . . All the Mediterranean values—the triumph of the human individual, of clarity, and of beauty—become lifeless, colorless knickknacks. All those speeches seem like collections of dead words; those values which seemed to uplift the soul are revealed as worthless, simply because they have nothing to do with the concrete conflict in which the people is engaged.

Individualism is the first to disappear. . . .

Frantz Fanon, *The Wretched of the Earth*

. . . in the present phase of interracial existence in America moral and intellectual "truths" have not the same reality for Negroes and whites . . .

. . . We can no longer talk to Negroes, or Negroes to us, in the traditional humanistic ways. The old Mediterranean values —the belief in the sanctity of the individual soul, the importance of logical clarity, brotherhood, reason as arbiter, political order, community—are dead as *useful* frames of reference or pertinent guides to procedure; they are even making some of us sick with a sense of lacerating irony.

Richard Gilman in *The New Republic*
March 9 and April 13, 1968

Two further reflections. They have dominated my year.

22 January 69

Two and a quarter hours, enough, no doubt, to finish typing out the marginal notes from Simone de Beauvoir's book that I am to compose into a review for the *New Republic,* so I can get back to Gide, after, of course, reviewing *Mourning Becomes Electra,* seeing two plays, and sitting through three meetings. (Writing for display: excuse it: I shall get down to the rock directly.)

But I am sick, too sick for Simone de Beauvoir this morning, sick within and without. A strike, two strikes are due at the University today, and my intestines are clearly worried about what that will mean to me—not that my ragged, raw intestines need any excuse of late for aching: picket lines, blocked exits, ugly jeers, even the scratched cars and firebombs of S.F. State. But am I really (inside, unaware) worried about that? I don't know: so physically helpless, I am a man of *no* physical resources, hence of no physical courage. For me, it would be pointless, insane—if it meant anything at all—I can't even let myself get caught in a crowd. But I still think the ache is more in anticipation of a state of psychological tension, hostility, unreason: I know very well these exist, these flame up, at our troubled campuses: I can, at home, comfortably, securely breathing reason's clear air, observe them, study them, understand them: but there, on the spot, in the red air of anger and will-to-violence, I am as lost, as devalued, as helpless and wretchedly ill-at-ease as a tiny child. None of the resources that provide my strength are then of any use, and I am sick, sick with impotence and alien dismay.

Still I shall go—this very minute T.B. called to see if I wanted to "pass" his Ph.D. candidate by telephone to avoid having to meet on campus "under the present circumstances." I did not—no heroism there, just a refusal to believe that things have got that bad—so we shall meet. I presume. But that's not going to help my intestines any.

Still, I'm not here to talk about my intestines, *or* today's strike, but to try to get a hold on something larger. Or at least to get a hold on myself. Strikes and firebombings—and far worse—are taking place at campuses everywhere—it would be foolish, just on the basis of statistical probability, to expect my University—which after all began it all—to remain visibly tranquil, to keep a calm academic uncluttered path *for me* between the miraculously parted seas of discontent. Moreover, who could be safer? No classes all quarter, no real need to be there; a closed campus would give me all the more excuse to spend my time here on Gide. . . .

23 January

And today Wheeler Auditorium is a great obscene black hole, hideously ugly and profoundly demoralizing: because any fine, large, human, useful thing burnt to black ash is ugly and demoralizing; but especially because someone did it—purposefully—because it is so near; because it is in some way mine. It isn't fear or anger one feels, but discouragement, disheartening —a sense of the heart going out of one—depression, a feeling sustained by the thick damp smell of smoke that suffuses the poor great building (its own heart a black hole, man-made by hate), that will linger for weeks, that is still in front of me now in the books I've brought home. And it is to this hate-burned building I shall go back each week to work.

No reflections beyond these much too personal ones. The flames that exhilarate and set free the hating black revolutionary leave for me only sodden ashes, acrid smells, a memory and symbol of *my* world—lectures, theatre, mind and art, Sears, Jayne and *The Tempest*, senate meetings and my own 46B lectures on England in the Blitz—burned to a black, nightmarish hole, a stage-setting for a pageant of hell. *Ecœuré.* Sick at heart.

28 January

Oh, to hell with politics and the social conscience: I am a *fool* to let myself get trapped into thinking I have, should have, *can* have something to say about such things, just because the world immediately around me is suddenly abuzz with the noises of revolutionaries and counterrevolutionaries. Because all the English Department think MLA (which is, of course, a kind of politics, a massed fiction-for-power), did I ever once feel a moral compunction to join them? If suddenly a religious revival swept the campus, would I feel privately pressed to start formulating my opinions on God and his angels? I don't care if *all the world* is thinking and responding "politically": I insist on asserting (and with plenty of support) that it remains only *one*, possible, contingent, non-absolute, non-compulsory mode of vision, way of seeing, imagining, thinking, responding.

A time will seem more or less political, depending I suppose on how many people start worrying about power—there are clearly times (late 18th Century, 1848, 1930's, now) when suddenly mobs, millions of average people start concerning themselves about how things are run, for one reason or another. This happens to be a very political time, and I am feeling the pressure—faculty petitions, books and TV, every reporter, museum director, and Junior Leaguer suddenly studying "racism"—to be more political myself; I wonder, in the midst of all

this frenzy, if I may not otherwise run the risk of "getting off
the world," becoming irrelevant, losing touch—which is, let us
admit, a serious error for a 31-year-old intellectual to make.
Now this isn't entirely simple. BUT. I *must* keep my head
clear, my independence of judgment and direction unqualified.
Numbers here mean, for my purposes, nothing. "Most people"
still call themselves Christians in this country, for heaven's
sake. The sharper difficulty with politicization, however, is
that most *thinking* people seem, at least, to have yielded to it,
to have freely joined in the fight: not just "mostpeople." I can't
dismiss the American Revolution as easily as I can, say, Glea-
son's claims for Rock music.

But I've got to cut, and keep to, my own line. I am as susceptible to the petty temptations of petty political place as a cour-
tier, as some effete sonneteer invited to Elizabeth's service
. . . I keep indulging the inane delusion that "I" can do something about the Afro-American students, just because I am
asked to, just because I wrote a very private and apolitical
book. *I have no place* in such counsels, I can be of *no service
whatever* in political activities, I falsify myself ludicrously in
the very act of pretending to a place. *Me,* in the "Committee of
200," *me,* giving quotations to the *Daily Cal,* or offering my
services to the Dean! It is absurd. Oh, for heaven's sake, indulge your various daydreams—but NOT the ones of Presi-
dential Assistant and Benign Conciliator: it is worse than senseless.

Feel free, right, and justified, beginning today, in taking no
part in anything that may be called political. Oh, observe it,
study it—that's part of your job: but only up to the actual
limit of your curiosity, which you must admit is pretty low.
The nation may be in *flames,* I tell you, or a fascist fortress, and
you *still* need feel no obligation to involve yourself in questions
or actions of power. Admit yourself—to whoever asks—con-
stitutionally apolitical; and be quit of it. As you have said so
often, you no more believe in, your imagination and passion
and curiosity are no more *engaged* by what goes by the name
of politics (*or* economics, or sociology: questions of masses, of
money, of power) than by religion or science: less. It is so, and
so be it.

I know, no less surely, what I *do* care about, where my useful talents lie, what I can do of value. And it has nothing to do with politics, science, or religion, and never shall. I know—I know: these (at least science and social science) are going to dominate, shape, control the world: they rule the century, they will fix the landscape and read the mind, they are where power is, what the media care about—but *I DON'T CARE.* I care about the individual human spirit (emotions, ideas, ideals, passions, pains, *that* domain) and about language at its best; about individual morality and individual pleasure (sensual, aesthetic, intellectual); about lies and truth. Humanist, individualist, existentialist, moralist (beautiful job-description), critic, . . . I don't know what to call what I am. But damn it, it's time to recognize it, for once and all, and stop wavering—as I did last week—in little shivers of affected guilt for not being something else, just because other people are, or because 1969 seems to favor other sorts.

I shall be out-of-step, *contre-courant* for the rest of my life: so what the hell? Who of value is not? Don't forget that most of the new American millions who think or call themselves intellectuals today clearly *aren't:* there isn't a real independent thinker in a hundred thousand. They're simply the petty professoriate, and because they teach "History" or "Literature" doesn't mean they're any less clerks, any less the little power-conscious, union-joining, ladder-climbing junior executives of the Academic Corporation. RESISTEZ. You may *think* you've found a home in the University, but don't fool yourself: the University, as organized and operating, the Department, the "profession" really *hate* the independent thinker: they work through politics, power, mass, money, and compromise. All that is in you of value is in opposition not only to suburbia and corporate capitalism and political machines—but also—and here's where we've been too long deceiving ourselves—to the University as well (whose corporate title, remember, is: The Regents of the University of California. You are working for *them*). It hasn't been a "community of independent thinkers," primarily devoted to the search for, fight for, preservation of truth—for centuries, if ever it was. It is political, immensely so, it is a source and seat of power, and all the strikes and protests and demands and insurrections it is suffering are absolutely appropriate—as appropriate as they were against a 19th Century monarchy or corporation. But they only make it all the more clear that I am, at best, ill at ease, at worst unwelcome there.

5 March

Sick, for some reason, morose, earthbound, unfired, uninspired ever since I finished Chapter II. I can't isolate a reason—perhaps it has something to do with a particular period of Gide's life coinciding with a particular period of mine—a time when one feels talented, ready, past the fire of youth—but useless, unwanted, and irrelevant.

I come near, very near, deciding flatly to avoid the political altogether, insofar as that is possible. By which I mean neither reading about nor watching (let alone participating in, talking about) each day's activities in the various power plays that surround us, to which the newspapers, magazines, television news, and much too much of conversation have grown hypnotically, myopically devoted. In this there is both reason and temper: the reason that tells me that I am useless in such ugly warfare over power, petty day-by-day squabbles over bits and pieces of symbolic power; that my spirit is only rent and lacerated, rubbed raw by the least kind of involvement (except the occasional and necessary sanity-restoring conversation, once a month perhaps) in all this messy, ugly *quotidien*. And temper: I am developing a hard, bloody edge of resistance—I can feel it behind my eyes—against all the little daily lies and false quarrels that rise from the smoke of rhetoric and then get sanctified by the press: police "brutality" or "overreaction" or the supposed irresistible "provocation" of a policeman's very presence: the notion that one cannot "work" or "think" with police about—as if one could when they were not; the whole ugly stew of self-serving, self-blinded, dehumanizing lies and quarter-truths and partisan-anger slogans masking as truths that supposed intellectuals pour out about the police, about the destruction, about "ethnic studies" and "participation" and "relevant education." The *language*. "Implement," "confrontation," "relevance," "participation," so easily and uncritically mixed with "pigs" and "burn it down" and "kill" . . .

I do not want to mingle myself, to involve myself in any activity—however "essential," however "crucial"—that necessarily accepts, gives itself to, *deals at all* with such gross and brutal dehumanizing rhetoric and unreason. This is not willed blindness or ostrichism. I am well aware that the rhetoric and the strategies or eruptions of ugly anti-order are, in some respect, both the product of and the faintest reflection of the brutality and dehumanizing state in which millions of people live. I know that. And it is because I know that, to these people —most of the world's people, I suspect—a few broken windows or cut faces or abuses of syntax or "lies" or burnt buildings mean damn little, that I must absent myself.

I am not a democrat, my concerns are not theirs, they never will be. I can recognize but not feel the justice—insofar as democratic equality equals justice—of their cause and even of their methods. But I cannot help them, because I am not a democrat. Nor can I fight them, because I have no reason to expect them to share my values. So I *must* be silent, withdraw as far as possible from the fray, and try very hard to ignore, not to read, talk, or even think about the Political and Current. I am on occasion driven by a small itch to try to think the "police" idea, or the "school integration" idea, or even the "students' role in universities" idea through to some state of complex rationality—but I give up. When obliged, I shall act only as a prod toward reason, as an agent toward a larger vision in those who force the issue upon me: or else simply be silent. Do not, above all do not express yourself on questions a) in which your soul is uninvolved (busing, the police . . .) and b) to which you know there are no answers.

By which—back to the Gidean malaise—I am only condemning myself to a greater silence and isolation than before. Rest apolitical around J.L.? Or even Sheila? Or the KQED liberals, the student radicals? Yes.

The University, as an institution, is clearly becoming less and less an acceptable and genial haven for me, the more it responds to democratic, political pressures, the more it becomes a *serving* rather than a preserving force. This was, I suppose, only to be expected of a state, a "people's" university, as soon as the *facts* of American democracy began to approach our professions of it. It is becoming, as all public institutions are being asked to become (kindergartens, museums, opera boards, BART), a *social service* agency, another mechanism for equalizing wealth and power.

BUT I AM NOT INTERESTED IN EQUALIZING WEALTH AND POWER. I am, to some degree, willing to entertain the notion that it may be useful or good or necessary to do so. But I am not sure, because I am not interested, because my heart is not *in* the question, I feel no compulsion to make myself more sure. I *insist* that no one is morally compelled to interest himself in or dedicate himself to any *particular* problem. That I must serve, make and give as much of myself as I can, I do regard as an imperative. But that anyone can dictate *how*, I flatly deny. It will not, cannot be by "working for" racial equality or Power to the People or any form of political strategy. *That* I can assure you.

So the University—eventually most State Universities?—will drift toward social welfare and democratizing reform; I will accept its patronage as long as I can ignore that fact, that change of definition in my own work . . .

How then serve, if I must serve? Being apolitical does not only mean that I cannot and don't want to join the marching and arguing rebels; it also means that I have no desire to freeze myself into some self-righteous reactionary "Stop-The-World" illusion, mouthing on about Lost Values and The Family and Rational Discourse and the Evil of television. One simply cannot hate today or resist tomorrow and live, except in some kind of twisted, self-imprisoned, sick icy egoism. (One doesn't have to cheer it on, either. Just face it, live with it, we'll get on, go on, we'll manage. If reason, reading, and religion are to go, so they'll go. Our children will develop the resources they need to cope. No generation's life is going to be like the one before's—you don't like freeway jams or public housing blocks? Would you prefer horse-and-buggy immobility and the doom of slums? Adapt, buddy. Hold on to yourself, your own inner solidity, and live in the world that is.)

So I look for a way to work and serve, in *this* world, as it is and as it is becoming, given the thing I am. And I hang on to the notion that one can, in fact, say all that needs to be said, speak clearly, usefully, morally, currently, relevantly by means of the free and autonomous work of art: and hence—even more publicly and pedagogically—by means of the proper *criticism* of that work. By continuing to assess, to evaluate plays and books and buildings and the uses of language—without

ever, necessarily, referring to today's particular bonfire or bal-
lot or battle, without ever even, necessarily, devoting myself
to the apparently newer works of art—I can continue to say all
I have to say, all I can usefully say, about the world I live in.
By ignoring the Living Theatre and meticulously assessing
Three Sisters or *Much Ado*, I am making a statement: I am
manifesting the values I hold and represent. They happen to be
Western European, rational-aesthetic, humane but not politically egalitarian, hedonist-classical within the limits of that humanism, and yet open to the romantic and extra-rational: So be
it. If you want Oriental mysticism or African barbarism, go
ahead, *you* defend or support or represent that. If they're
what's coming, let them. I'm not trying to stop oceans. Just to
express what *I* value in the best way I can.

OK? Now can I get back to work, back to the early days of
the *N.R.F.*, and ignore the Richmond school crisis, the Third
World College, and the thin missile system?

Next time you feel rotten don't write anything new: just
reread this. You always end up saying the same thing.

6

Looking Back

This final piece, the earliest in the collection, was first published as an anonymous letter in The Harvard Crimson *for January 26, 1962. It was written in reply to another essay in similar vein, the gist of which can probably be intuited from my "Grader's Reply." The two pieces have since been reprinted by the* Crimson *in tandem during final exam periods.*

I include it as a nostalgic gesture to a time, eight long years ago, when my image of University life was somewhat more innocent than it is now.

The Grader Replies [1962]

Gentlemen:

I have, I must confess, serious doubts about the efficacy—or even the integrity—of the "classic" exam-period editorial, "Beating the System," you reprinted on Monday; I almost suspect this so-called "Donald Carswell '50" of being rather one of Us—The Bad Guys—than one of You. If your readers have been following Mr. Carswell's advice for the last eleven years, then your readers have been going down the tubes. It is time to disillusion.

He is right, of course, about the third alternative, and a very sensible one it is—working out some system of fooling the grader; although I think I should prefer the word "impressing." We admit to being impressionable, but *not* hypercredulous simps. His first two tactics for system-beating, his Vague Generalities and Artful Equivocations, seem to presume the latter, and are only going to convince *Crimson*-reading graders (there are a few, and we tell our friends) that the time has come to tighten the screws just a bit more.

Think, Mr. Carswell (wherever you are), think, all of you: imagine the situation of your grader. (Unless, of course, he is of the Wheatstone Bridge-double differential-$CH_3C_6H_2(NO_2)_3$-set. These people are mere cogs, automata; they simply feel to make sure you've punched the right holes. As they cannot think, they cannot be impressed; they are clods. The only way

to bear *their* system is to cheat.) In the humanities and social
sciences, it is well to remember, there is a man (occasionally a
woman), a human type filling out your picture postcards. What
does he want to read? How, in a word, can he be snowed?

Not, let me insist and insist again, by Vague Generalities. We
abhor V.G.'s, we skim right past them, we start wondering
what kind of a C to give from the first V.G. we encounter; and
as they pile up, we decide: C—. (Harvard being Harvard, one
does not give D's. Consider C— a failure.) Why? Not because
they are a sign the student doesn't know the material, or hasn't
thought carefully, or any of that folly. They simply make tedious reading. "Locke is a transitional figure." "The whole thing
boils down to human rights." Now I ask you. I have 92 blue-
books to read this week, and all I ask, really, is that you keep
me awake. Talk to me. Is that so much?

Artful Equivocations are even worse; lynx-eyed sly little ras-
cals that we are, we see right through them. (Up to Exam #40.
Then our lynx-eyelids droop, and grading habits relax. Try to
get on the bottom of the pile.) Again, it is not that A.E.'s are
vicious or ludicrous as such: but in quantity they become sheer
madness. Or induce it. "The 20th Century has never recovered
from the effects of Marx and Freud" (V.G.); "but whether
this is a good thing or a bad is difficult to say" (A.E.). Now,
one such might be droll enough. But by the dozen? This, the
quantitative aspect of grading—we are, after all, getting five
dollars a head for you dolts and therefore pile up as many of
you apiece as we can get—this is what too many of you seem
to forget. "Coleridge may be said to be both a classic *and* a
romantic, but then, so may Dryden, depending on your point
of view. In some respects, this statement is unquestionably
true; but in others. . . ." On through the night.

I hope my implication is clear. The A's go to people who
wake us up, who talk to us, who are sparkling and different and
bright. (The B's go to Radcliffe girls who memorize the text
and quote it verbatim, in perfectly looped letters with circles
over the i's.) *Not*, I remind you, necessarily to people who
have locked themselves in Lamont for a week and seminared
and outlined and underlined and typed their notes and argued
out all of Leibniz's fallacies with their mothers. They often get

A's too, but, as Mr. Carswell sagely observed, this takes too long. There are other ways.

His third suggestion, the Overpowering Assumption, I think is the best: but not for the reasons he suggests—that the assumption is so cosmic it may sometimes be accepted. It is rarely "accepted"; we aren't here to accept or reject, we're here to be amused. The more dazzling, personal, unorthodox, paradoxic your assumptions (paradoxes are *not* equivocations), the more interesting an essay is likely to be. (If you have a chance to confer with the assistant in advance, of course—and we like to be called "assistants," not "graders"—you may be able to ferret out one or two cosmic assumptions of his own; seeing them in your blue book, he can only applaud your uncommon perception. For example, while most graders are politically unconcerned, not *all* are agnostic. This is an older generation, recall. Some may be tired of seeing St. Augustine flattened by a phrase, or reading about the "Xian myth.")

Carswell's further discussion of the O.A. is quite to the point —he himself realizes its superiority to any E., however A. His illustration includes one of the key "Wake Up the Grader" phrases—"It is absurd." What force! What gall! What fun! "Ridiculous," "hopeless," "nonsense," on the one hand; "doubtless," "obvious," "unquestionable" on the other, will have the same effect. A hint of nostalgic, anti-academic languor at this stage as well may well match the grader's own mood: "It seems more than obvious to one entangled in the petty quibbles of contemporary Medievalists—at times, indeed, approaching the ludicrous—that, smile as we may at its follies, or denounce its barbarities, the truly monumental achievements of the Middle Ages have become too vast for us to cope with, or even understand: we are too small, and too afraid." Let me offer this as an ideal opening sentence to *any* question even tangentially nudging on the Middle Ages. And now, you see, having dazzled me, won me by your personal, involved, independently-minded assertion, your only job is to *keep* me awake. When I sleep I give C's.

How? By FACTS. *Any* kind, but *do* get them in. *They* are what we look for, as we skim our lynx-eyes over every other page—a name, a place, an allusion, an object, a brand of deodorant, the titles of six poems in a row, even an occasional date. This, son, makes for interesting (if effortless) reading: and that is what gets A's. Underline them, capitalize them, inset them in outline form: be *sure* we don't miss them. Why do you think all exams insist at the top, "Illustrate"; "Be Specific"; etc.? They *mean* it. The illustrations needn't, of course, be singularly relevant; but they must be there. If Vague Generalities are anathema, sparkling chips of concrete scattered through your bluebook will have you up for sainthood. Or at least Dean's List. Name at least the titles of every other book Hume ever wrote; don't say just "Medieval cathedrals"—name nine; think of a few specific *examples* of "contemporary decadence," like Natalie Wood. If you can't come up with titles, try a few sharp metaphors of your own; they have at least the solid clink of pseudo-facts.

That's the secret, really. Don't write out "TIME!!" in inch-high scrawls—it only brings out the sadist in us. Don't ('Cliffies) write offers to come over and read aloud to us your illegible remarks—we can (officially) read anything, and we may be married. Write on both sides of the page—single-bluebook finals look like less work to grade, and win points. This chic shaded calligraphic script so many are affecting lately *is* handsome, and is probably worth a good five extra points if you can hack it.

But above all, keep us entertained, keep us awake. Be bold, be personal, be witty, be chock-full-of-facts. I'm *sure* you can do it without studying if you try. We did.

Best wishes,

A GRADER

This book was set on the linotype in
Janson. The display type is Perpetua.
Composed, printed and bound at H. Wolff
Book Manufacturing Co., New York.
Designed by Jacqueline Schuman.

PS 3562
I 785
I 5

UNIVERSITY OF RHODE ISLAND

3 1222 00753 1539

NO LONGER THE PROPERTY
OF THE
UNIVERSITY OF R.I. LIBRARY